SOME MODERN FRENCH WRITERS

SOME MODERN FRENCH WRITERS

A STUDY IN BERGSONISM

By

G. TURQUET-MILNES

Essay Index Reprint Series

BOOKS FOR LIBRARIES PRESS

FREEPORT, NEW YORK

First Published 1921
Reprinted 1968

LIBRARY OF CONGRESS CATALOG CARD NUMBER:

68-24858

PRINTED IN THE UNITED STATES OF AMERICA

CONTENTS

PREFACE

THOSE critics who study the destiny of philosophical ideas for the ironical pleasure of seeing them work in exactly the opposite direction from that which their founders intended have not failed to remark that the two great movements of French thought since the 16th century — Calvinism and Cartesianism — developed states of mind utterly different from those Calvin and Descartes wished to create. Descartes would have been horrified to hear himself called the father of the French Revolution, and Calvin equally so at being called one of the founders of free thought.

It would seem, then, that in addition to the impetus given by a powerful writer, there is another and more powerful movement to which the first must conform, if it is to succeed. The fact is, that when we cut up society into slices, two important groups are soon discovered — the political and the literary, and the former always ends by absorbing the latter, except in the very rare case of a genius who is both legislative and poetical: Mahomet, for example. The social aspirations of a people always manage to get themselves adopted in the end, and that for obvious reasons. *Vox populi, Vox Dei.* The only doctrines which have a chance of surviving are those which in the course of time blend not only with the tendencies of the moment, but with the general spirit of a nation, nay, of mankind.

A study of history shows us humanity's progress

as one long, long journey towards an increasingly complete, ever-higher freedom. In truth no spectacle is better calculated to rejoice the heart of the idealist, since humanity, in spite of stumbles and backslidings, succeeds little by little in freeing itself from its material and materialistic fetters, and in ushering in a reign of more justice, more happiness, more liberty.

In France, just before the outbreak of the war, we were looking on at a philosophic and literary movement which, in the width of responsive undulations it has produced in the world at large, may well be compared with the movement determined by Descartes. Greatly as we may esteem certain modern philosophers, it is no insult to them to say that it is M. Bergson who has the widest world-reputation. Japan studies him with the same ardor as Sweden or America. Every year sees the roll of his disciples swelling in England. Attention to him and to his famous doctrine of *la réalité qui se fait* becomes more and more pronounced all over the world.

What fate does the future hold in store for him? Only our grandchildren can answer that question. Still, it is permissible to foretell the future, or even, in the pragmatist's way, to make it.

If we questioned Bergson himself on this point, he would tell us that his doctrine, like every product of the human brain, is a progressive thing, by no means perfect nor complete nor absolute. I am only a man; therefore you must not ask me for more than I can give. I have merely tried to get into close touch with that nature which always eludes us. For the riches of nature are inexhaustible — things do not begin, nor do they end, nor are they as we see them, nor as we should wish them to be.

We are placed in front of an admirable and beneficent fluid in which anything may happen, especially the unexpected; and philosophical systems can never be more than the mind's points of view, more or less correct, but really incomplete, in comparison with Reality, the Reality which we shall know some day. So that it would be a great mistake to ask of science the divine light to guide us through the reefs and shoals of existence, for the very good reason that life is not made for our intellect, but our intellect for life. Nature, too, is ever present to teach us modesty and patience. But it will take us a long time to correct ourselves of this habit of constructing and deducing *ad infinitum* — if we ever do. And we should therefore not be astonished to find that many have sought a supreme rule in Bergsonian philosophy, and that they have seen in Bergson first and foremost a director of consciences and even a new prophet. And yet, up to the present, M. Bergson's works are not concerned with ethical questions. It may even be said that the religious idea appears only late in Bergsonian philosophy.

To tell the truth, after the publication of his first book, *Essai sur les données immédiates de la Conscience* (1887), philosophers also had wondered what consequences were to be deduced from a doctrine which aimed at destroying all metaphysical constructions, and at being guided only by experience. It is enough to remember an article by M. Jean Weber: *Une nouvelle théorie de l'acte et ses conséquences,* which appeared in the *Revue de Métaphysique et de Morale* in September, 1894. It seems that at that date, Bergson's budding doctrine appeared to some as an excellent excuse for all the actions of human nature, licit or illicit, and Bergson himself as a new Seneca to new Neroes!

And M. J. Segond in a note in his book on *l'Intuition bergsonienne* (p. 144) tells us that M. Ravaisson, towards the same date, asked M. Bergson if he were to be classed among the adepts of such a brutal naturalism.

The attitude of the Bergson of those days was far from being clearly defined; it seemed Janus-faced. And at the same time, this philosopher who only wanted to be a philosopher found himself hailed as the enemy of science and the slanderer of intellect.

What is the truth of the matter? M. Bergson's other books, *Matter and Memory, Creative Evolution*, soon dispersed the doubts in the public mind. Little by little, in spite of misunderstandings, Bergson appeared as the apostle of conscience, freedom, action and creation. But so many had been that before him, in a different way, it is true, yet groping along the same path, that we are forced to try and explain the immense success of Bergson in France to-day.

Bergson is a part of a vast movement of contemporary French thought. He is not the creator of the movement, but he has profited by it: the great social, literary and philosophic wave has carried him on to fame. He would be the first to acknowledge it, ever ready as he is to take into account the society in which a human being moves, and his natural surroundings.*

---

*That is the explanation of his love of metaphor with which some critics have reproached him. According to Bergson these brilliant pictures are given to us by Nature herself; through them we enter into a more complete union with Reality. That is also the reason why men of letters study him, because he is so literary himself and so intensely preoccupied with life. Take for example that passage in *Time and Free Will*: "How do you become aware of

Bergson's influence drew additional strength from
the enormous impetus in contemporary science and
metaphysics, from the idea underlying all the great
work of the Nineteenth Century that life is an
absolutely original movement, and that truth is
more or less biological, always in the making. Mr.
Chesterton has a good page in his *Victorian Age
in Literature* where he says that the struggle
between the old spiritual theory and the new
material theory ended in a deadlock. I should be
more inclined to say that the movement ended in a
tangent, in escape from the materialist as well as
from the spiritual circle. Life is not due to a
synthesis of material elements, nor, for the matter
of that, is it a kind of entelechy conceived as an
external principle to matter. Moreover, Darwin
had taught that the universe had not been created
once for all, Hegel that the Idea was the living
energy of an intelligence always on the march: the
former saw life as still unfolding itself, the latter
saw history as a thing of flux and mobility, since
the Absolute is the Becoming. The same poetical
thought petrified into a theory could be found, more
or less disguised, in such works as Newman's *Essay
on the Development of Christian Doctrine*;* it is
like a seed floating in the air and takes root in every
country and in all parts of every country.

Adaptiveness might be the formula for such
doctrine: the struggle for truth is the life of truth.

Therefore, when Bergson came with his announce-

a deep passion once it has taken hold of you, if not by perceiving
that the same objects no longer impress you in the same manner?"
Every great novelist proves the truth of Bergson's words when he
tries to show his hero or heroine in the grip of a deep passion.

*There is one of the *Cahiers de la Quinzaine, Catholicisme et
Critique*, by M. Paul Desjardins, which is full of the Bergsonian
doctrine when read between the lines.

ment that reality is the flux and that things are views of the flux, he found an audience in an extraordinary state of receptivity, because it was already convinced that in the world, as in each of us, there is a vitality which grows and evolves from within.

A philosophy which does not wish to use logical exposition, but which appeals to our primordial intuitions and above all to the æsthetic instinct, had every chance of success in the France of 1890. Of course, many influences were working in the same direction as that of Bergson. Many brooks swelled the waters of the Bergsonian river, before it joined the great contemporary flood which bears us on past the illusions of finalism and mechanism into the kingdom of the unfettered and intuitive Spirit.

Thus it would be very rash to tie down the literary movement of the last years of the Nineteenth Century and of the opening ones of the Twentieth to the single name of Bergson. He did not endow it with those dreamy, subtle, suggestive, essentially musical qualities which we admire in it. Symbolist poetry, the art of Barrès and of Maeterlinck came before the triumph of the Bergsonian philosophy, and certainly before its influence. *Natura non facit saltum*. If by Bergsonism we understand the feeling of the unity and brotherhood in life, or even the doctrine of the intuitive method, then Bergsonism was in existence before Bergson. After the Parnassian school which aimed at reproducing the plastic beauty of antiquity, after the Realistic school which sought either to paint society in its various sections, or simply to show human nature at its ugliest, a new literary group formed which had respect for the soul and above all a love of spiritual and mortal life, and which was to be joined by a second group whose cult was action.

So that, leaving on one side the pornographic publications, produced mainly for foreign consumption, and the purely worldly novel, the connection between Bergsonism and contemporary French literature is merely a link of harmony. Flaubert, in one of his letters to Georges Sand, says: "Have you ever noticed the current of similar ideas there is sometimes in the air? I have just been reading a novel, *Les Forces Perdues,* by my friend Du Camp. In many ways it is very like what I am now writing myself.''*

In any case, if Bergsonism owes its success to a long-felt spiritual need, it must also be admitted that it has singularly helped to bring about the triumph of this tendency. It is a wonderful leaven pervading an enormous mass of literature and changing it into a nourishing substance.

The history of literature from 1890 to 1918 is largely the history of a vast reaction on the part of young writers against the mechanist philosophy. Now Bergson, by affirming that the reigning intellectualism of his youth misread life with its countless aspects, and nature with her infinite fecundity; that our concepts were but schematic designs of a fluid and complex reality; that there was such a thing as Psychological Time, and that we were free precisely on account of this Psychological Time; that life is the ultimate reality; that we live in a universe in which *tout n'est pas donné,* in which something new happens at every moment, in which there is freedom at the heart of things,—rendered invaluable assistance to the young generation which was seeking to break the chains which weighed so heavily upon it.

*Correspondence III, p. 481. *Oeuvres Complètes de Flaubert.* *Paris.* Louis Conrad, MCMX.

Once again, we must not exaggerate nor attribute
to Bergson more than his due. Philosophy rules
one kingdom and literature another. It would be
very easy for a critic to show that Zola's works
were being printed in their thousands, while Bergson's were making their way very slowly. To
believe that "to any given poetical tendency there
corresponds at the same time a philosophical
tendency," to quote M. T. de Visan,* is to fall victim
to a formula. Consider for a moment the Victorian
Age of English literature. At a moment when
Darwin and Huxley triumphed in so many minds,
there were also writing Carlyle, Ruskin, Newman,
Tennyson, Browning, all anti-intellectualists with
something of the Bergsonian spirit and before
Bergson's time.† There are too many currents and
under-currents in modern society to allow of arrival
at absolute truth on this point. The writer, who
saw in the pragmatism of William James, or the
humanism of Professor Schiller, a proof of Anglo-
Saxon mysticism, would be immediately contradicted by another writer, who would show that these
philosophical movements are the outcome of Anglo-
Saxon common sense.

However that may be, Bergson found himself in
harmony with certain theories of a certain school
towards 1890. But when the "lycéens" of 1890-1905
began to write they naturally tried to express what
they had been taught by their favorite philosopher

---

*Tancrède de Visan. *L'attitude du lyrisme contemporain*, p. 432.
Paris. Mercure de France.

†I have often wondered whether Bergson may not have been
profoundly, albeit unconsciously, influenced by these writers, through
his upbringing, which was partly English. In any case one could
make a complete study of Browning, giving his work Bergson's
philosophy for substratum. The resemblances are striking even for
the most casual reader. See also on this subject *Bergson and the
Modern Spirit*, by G. R. Dodson, pp. 290-1.

—Bergson — or by their professor's favorite philosopher — again Bergson.

But here once more it would be easy to find among these young men the two types which Flaubert painted for the generation of 1848 in his *Education Sentimentale*: the Frédéric Moreau type, sentimental, dreamy, and consequently with some leanings towards a certain kind of Bergsonism; and the Deslauriers type, hardworking, energetic, *arriviste*, and with leanings toward politics.

Just as, according to Bergson, there are two modes of apprehending reality, intellect and intuition, so there are two different types of minds, the realist and the nominalist, the intellectual and the mystic, the prosaic and the idealist. The most we can succeed in showing is the recrudescence of mysticism,* and the renewal of poetry in our own day. If to that we add the numerous works which have appeared on the reduplication of personality, on psychic phenomena, or spiritism, or occultism, or the idea spread abroad by poets and philosophers that our psychological depths are rich in unexplored treasure, or Comte's two favorite ideas that the living are governed by the dead, and that reason must not be separated from instinct, we see that Bergson's philosophy had everything to gain from such contemporary states of mind.

---

*We must always bear in mind that, strange as it may appear to some of his followers, Bergson's doctrine is a protest against mysticism. "If by mysticism be meant (as it almost always is nowadays) a reaction against positive science, the doctrine which I defend is in the end only a protest against mysticism." (*Introd. to the Philosophy of Bergson.* A. D. Lindsay, p. 19.) For M. Bergson there are other sciences than mathematics; in the biological sciences, for instance, there are inquiries which have their own standard and which give us certain and positive knowledge. In reality Bergson is at one with Descartes, whose *Cogito ergo sum* is not a syllogism, but a thing known of itself. Mind sees itself as a first reality, by an intuition which precedes all deduction and every syllogism.

One is almost tempted to apply to Bergson Carlyle's words on Diderot: "Grant doubtless that a certain perennial spirit true for all times and all countries, can and must look through the thinking of certain men, be it in what dialect soever. . . . . Let us remember that the highly gifted, high-striving Diderot was born in the point of Time and of Space when of all uses he could turn himself to, of all dialects speak in, this of Polemical Philosophism, and no other, seemed the most promising and fittest. Let us remember, too, that no earnest man, in any time, ever spoke what was wholly meaningless." We might adapt Carlyle by saying, not that a perpetual spirit was created for Bergson, but that a tendency, an impulse, brought him to the height of the evolution of French Thought, of that thought which is always eminently sociable and humane, always "suspicious of the inelasticity of things."*

In this sense Bergson has been the conscience of his pupils in the lycée, of his disciples at the Collège de France, of his admirers in the world, and through them of an important part of contemporary France, and of a time. Through him have been clarified certain ideas which are still half obscure in his contemporaries; above all, his method has imposed itself more and more — a method essentially suited to the French genius, made up of common sense, humanity, kindness and sympathy.

The man, who has so rightly emphasized the social function of laughter, has never ceased to be amused by those men who regard life as a pre-arranged programme, and it may be said that the Bergsonian doctrine is above all the doctrine of a mind which is always open to life, and which refuses to be imprisoned in any system. *Omnis determinatio*

*Bergson: *Le Rire*.

negatio, said Spinoza. That might be Bergson's motto, even as it is that of the best minds of his time.

The aim of the following pages is to show that c rtain temperaments at the close of the 19th Century have felt with Bergson the need of reaction against the mechanism of a purely conceptualist philosophy, and that others have clearly been influenced by Bergsonian philosophy and have propagated it in their writings.*

Bergson will be the first to rejoice in his harmony with some of the best literature of his day: he will see therein proof that he has not missed his way. Books like those of Maurice Barrès and Claudel, of two great travelers amid spiritual and material scenery, are well calculated to explain a doctrine which has been wittily called "the doctrine of the cinema."† *Omnis comparatio claudicat,* and this comparison is really misleading. For the cinema at its best is nothing but a Punch and Judy show in which life is split up into a certain number of tragic or comic scenes, linked together in a fictitious unity, and teaching a somewhat histrionic morality. But in Bergson's philosophy time flows on unceasingly, like an endless and ever new melody which cannot be divided or subdivided, but would vanish away at the first attempt to number its component notes. History might be made to give us the best illustration of Bergsonian time, for History never repeats itself, nor can its phenomena be predicted, yet it is always intelligible, nay, full of pregnant lessons, when in

---

*M. Bergson, in his "notice" on M. Félix Ravaisson-Mollien, showed very clearly that the tendency of philosophers and scholars who deepen the nature of life is to "reintegrate thought in the heart of nature," and as examples he cites Auguste Comte and Claude Bernard.

†M. Gaston Rageot. *Revue de Paris,* February, 1918.

the hands of genius. No one could have foreseen that the Napoleonic empire would arise after Robespierre's fall; and if Waterloo was indeed won on the playing fields of Eton, other Waterloos have been lost on those same fields. The truth of the matter is that neither History nor Time is a panorama on rollers wrapping and unwrapping their matter one on to the other.

Society is not the creation of pure reason, it was not created by any "social contract." It is the creation of Time, and this appears as a complex indivisible whole in which every citizen is the continuation of his forefathers.* We are limited, but reality is making itself, world without end.

If the philosophy of duration has become the philosophy of free will, if Bergson in a celebrated speech has chastised the German barbarism, which is due to Prussian administration and military mechanism, it is because every philosophical system can be sustained only by a frankly spiritual idea, and that is the greatest homage the universe can render to metaphysics!

In this way the moral questions Bergson wished to banish from his books necessarily re-enter.† Mr. Balfour, writing of Bergson, says: "This free consciousness pursues no final end, it follows no predetermined design. . . . . It is ignorant not only of its course but of its goal; and for the sufficient reason, that, in M. Bergson's view, these things are not only unknown, but unknowable. . . . .

---

*It is pleasant to quote M. Barrès in this connection. Speaking of himself and his companions, he says: "Tout l'univers pour nous, je le vois maintenant, était *désossé en quelque sorte*, sans charpente, privé de ce qui fait la stabilité dans ses changements." (*Stanislas de Guaita*, p. 135. *Amori et Dolori Sacrum*.)

†"Humanity will not, and cannot acquiesce in a Godless world," p. 118. *Pragmatism and Idealism*, by Caldwell William, London, A. & C. Black, 1913.

Creation, freedom, will, — these, doubtless, are great things; but we cannot lastingly admire them unless we know their drift."

But perhaps Mr. Balfour had forgotten these words of Bergson's: "I see in the whole evolution of life on our planet an effort of this essentially creative force to arrive by traversing matter, at something which is only realized in man, and which, moreover, even in man is realized only imperfectly."* These words, not to mention the letter to Father de Tonquedec, show clearly that for Bergson, *after all*, life must have an aim, but at the same time must be always in the making. For otherwise what would become of free-will? Morality enfolds us on every side, or if we will have none of it, Love, or if that be lacking, Life itself would teach. Bergson's disciples, as we shall see, have fully realized this.

What happens to-day? The radiance of those countries which have fought for right and freedom is the outcome of the fact that they are the living symbol of the immutable, universal, and necessary conscience of the human race, the sign of those moral forces which will in the end prove of more effect than physical forces in putting an end to strifes which are the shame of humanity.

East Wittering. 1916-1918.

*Life and Consciousness. The Hibbert Journal, October, 1911, p. 38. Bergson adds, p. 40, "I doubt that the evolution of life will ever be explained by a mere combination of mechanical forces. Obviously there is a vital impulse: what I was just calling an impulse towards a higher and higher efficiency, something which ever seeks to transcend itself, to extract from itself *more* than there is — in a word, to create."

THE TREND OF CONTEMPORARY FRENCH THOUGHT

IF there is a law which seems to rule literature as also human thought, it is the law of reaction, or, as it might be called, the law of contradiction. I mean that law which none of us can escape, and which instinctively forces us to examine, criticize, and generally combat an opinion laid before us, and admitted by a certain group of men. In France, particularly, we see this law working in all the efforts of human thought, as we look back upon the centuries of the Christian era. So long as man's mind is preoccupied mainly by religious problems, we see countless heresies standing in the path of orthodox faith. When the Gallic mind first longed to represent the spectacle of life, there sprang up at once the *fabliaux,* all that caustic, *gaulois,* and not infrequently obscene, literature which makes mock of the *chansons de geste.*

Later, after the emancipation of the Renaissance, the Seventeenth Century busies itself with finding an answer to the Sixteenth: Pascal fights Montaigne. In the Seventeenth Century itself the so-called classical school with Molière, Boileau and Racine is opposed to the romanticism of 1630, Théophile de Viau, St. Amand as well as Corneille. The Eighteenth Century—from the point of view of ideas alone—is one long struggle against the so-called religious despotism of the Seventeenth. Yet even in the Eighteenth Century we have Rousseau forming a link with the tradition of Pascal and offering opposition to Voltaire. Then Romanticism, born of Rousseau and Bernardin de Saint Pierre, is in its turn attacked by the positivist school. Finally in our own time we see the great positivist school of 1850 harassed by pragmatism, and we look on at an extraordinary religious revival. It is remarkable that as we advance in time the reactionary movements lose in breadth. The Renaissance, for example, is an immense opposition to the Middle Ages taken as a whole. The Encyclopædic School is another no less formidable to Seventeenth-Century thought. But after 1750 it may be said that the movements of flux and reflux are much less marked. They are gentle swings of the pendulum. In Rousseau's day and in Chateaubriand's, Voltairean thought has its partisans, just as today. Thence springs a great feeling of uneasiness in a society divided against itself, and which has by turns thirst for, and horror of, reality, or what it believes to be reality. Those are the two great needs of humanity ever clamoring for satisfaction and it sometimes happens, as with Balzac and Flaubert, that a realist and a romanticist are to be found in the same man — constantly tripping up one another. For the various philosophies and various schools are the product of conflicting temperaments, as well as of different environment. There are moments as well as humors in which positivism and naturalism seem to be the last word of human thought. At other moments it may be that idealism, in all its meanings, appears as the open sesame of metaphysics and truth.

The most important thing to do, then, is to try and sketch the two main doctrines that are shared by French minds of today. The first, which is that of the French positivists, "savants," and "agnostics," is preached by very different thinkers — by Comte in the first place, then by Taine and Renan, to take only a few great names in literature. This school, which is called sometimes the naturalistic school, has for its foundation the ideas that the world is a purely mechanical problem, that science is merely an affair of analysis or mathematics, that man is a walking theorem, or a product pure and simple of his own sensations.

These views have received earnest support from such men as Dr. Charcot who at the Salpêtrière hospital undertook to reproduce most of the miracles of the Gospel: or from Zola and his school whose *Roman expérimental* was supposed to be an exposition of the ideas of Claude Bernard. It is easy to understand that such views had an immense success with the French mind, which is above all a critical investigating mind, with a passion for arranging the universe and for building it up into a symmetrical Versailles Palace or French garden. To the Frenchman, living as he does under a bright sky against which everything stands out clearly defined, the universe seems to be something easily understood and known. Nothing is true save that which Reason discovers.

But from time to time Inspiration bursts into flame, and then the icy splendors of Logic melt before the fiery light of Instinct, that inscrutable, invincible force of nature which rules the world from its very beginning.* The French mind, delighting in accurate, clear-cut form and order, hating the extravagant and the shapeless, does not trust such a terrifying revolutionary Power; it believes that sci-

*Bergson, *An Introduction to Metaphysics:* authorized translation by T. E. Hulme.

entific knowledge is a science "pre-formed and even pre-formulated in Nature as Aristotle believed." Bergson makes fun of this tendency and his illustration is too neat not to be quoted. "Great discoveries then serve only to illuminate point by point the already drawn line of this logic, immanent in things, just as on the night of a fête we light up one by one the rows of gas jets which already outline the shape of our building."*

Descartes had affirmed universal mechanism, but he was always careful to keep man's free will. Following him, taking him as their authority, the greater number of French scholars and philosophers saw nothing but a system of laws in the universe. With the Nineteenth Century came the biologists who declared that the phenomena of thought, like the phenomena of life, speech, circulation, respiration, digestion, were all alike physico-chemical phenomena, which are at once very complicated and very simple. With marvellous ingenuity and depth of knowledge, they showed how heredity can explain the problems of natural selection and variability, the formation of the different living species, and the adaptability which links every living being to its surroundings. So that if, as they hold, every living being is composed of cells which are practically similar in the whole animal and vegetable scale, the problem of the origin of life is that of the primary origin of the living cell. Primeval mud must be the ancestor of the whole fauna and flora of this planet, and life must have emerged automatically from inorganic matter. We see also that man is an affair of machinery; his thought is only a trans-

---

*Bergson, *An Introduction to Metaphysics:* authorized translation by T. E. Hulme.

formed sensation; given the brain, thought is also given; suppress the brain, thought also is suppressed — and thus thinking appears not only as the natural function of the brain, but as the ephemeral effect of an explosive force. In fine, man is an automaton created by thousands of causes, at the knowledge of which we may some day arrive.* There is neither instinct nor intelligence, but merely a cerebral function or phosphorescence which is better developed in man than in, say, an ant: man's reason being only a mental peculiarity advantageous to the survival of the species, and therefore safeguarded by heredity.

Taine is, in France, the great representative writer who best personified this mode of thought. The conception, of course, existed long before his day, but his was the gift of clothing his phrases with a magic style, and the mysterious power of his art gave him an extraordinary influence over two generations of Frenchmen.

Yet, at the moment when this materialistic philosophy seemed to triumph, a large number of minds were reacting against it. Most of them called to their help all those thinkers who had declared that pure reason was unable to furnish a serious foundation of morality. It is only fair to add here that Kant by his recognition of man as a moral being had thereby placed him above nature. Moreover his doctrine of the Categorical Imperative worked wonders in minds impassioned for justice and making facts the slaves of Right. And, as this was the great

*It seems a far cry to the time when a man will have the courage to say that the brain does not trace all the details of consciousness and that consciousness itself is not a function of the brain. Bergson, *L'âme et le corps,* p. 17. *Le matérialisme actuel,* Paris, Ernest Flammarion.

moment of German influence in the world, coinciding with a renaissance of Protestantism in France, Kant's star shone forth with added lustre, and the German Romantics, Novalis, Schlegel, Schelling, as well as Jacobi and Herder, told us at every turn that logical intelligence was as nothing compared with spontaneous sentiment. Schopenhauer himself tried to prove later on that the *Will to live* dominated intelligence, and Hartmann that the subconscious in nature played by far the most important part. In any case, this more or less German metaphysic (for its inspiration can be traced to Rousseau) would not have met with the success it did if science herself had not come to its help. For the mind is never content with a single hypothesis, and quickly wearies of one generalization, especially if that generalization aim at imposing a purely determinist theory. The battles waged by scholar upon scholar soon convinced the thinking public that all scientific theories might be after all only hypotheses.

M. Henri Poincaré in France echoed Lord Kelvin in England, when he declared that science was a matter of practical results and could never unveil the mystery enfolding us on every side. "I have always felt," said Lord Kelvin, "that the hypothesis of natural selection does not contain the true theory of evolution, if evolution there has been in biology. . . . I feel profoundly convinced that the argument of design has been greatly too much lost sight of in recent zoological speculations. Overpoweringly strong proofs of intelligent and benevolent design lie around us."

Again, as M. Gaston Bonnier has shown, even Darwin finds and obeys this idea of design; the flowers make themselves beautiful in order to please the bees; they spread their perfume abroad to attract

these visitors. The doctrine of the "happy accident" is itself a doctrine of finalism.*

William James proved abundantly that Darwinism, rightly understood, cast the most serious doubts
on the "final adequacy of the mechanistic philosophy from which it seemed to spring."† Indeed the
ideas of philosophers upon science, with their subversive tendencies, would never have been so popular if scientific men had not themselves revolution-
ised man's idea of science. *Nous avons changé tout
cela:* for it is not only the Sybil who writes on leaves
scattered by the wind. Messrs. Duhem, Le Roy,
Milhaud, Bernard Brunhes, Henri Poincaré, have
tried to prove in various articles and books that
science had for real object not so much to discover
and to know as to conquer and harness nature to
her car. "The mind is built up of practical interests": a discovery is above all a useful truth.
Claude Bernard in his famous *Introduction à la
Médécine Expérimentale* had rightly dwelt on the
fact that the human mind, far from submitting itself
to nature, picked out from among the phenomena
under observation the particular one or ones which
were to lead to a desired conclusion, and raised a
class of facts into a law by a utilitarian and deliberate choice. Nature seen and understood — sometimes misunderstood — by Mind: such is science. It
is only the man of genius who, as William James
puts it, "sticks in his bill at the right moment, and
brings it out with the right element." If so, it is
clear that the spontaneous activity of a free mind
is at work in the creations of science. William
James's *Principles of Psychology* appeared in 1891:
granting that the book was not widely read in

*See *La Revue Hebdomadaire*, 1 Juillet 1911. Gaston Bonnier,
Pour et contre le Darwinisme.
†See *W. James*, by Howard V. Knox. Constable & Co., 1914.

France, we can nevertheless surmise from the relations between Renouvier and his disciples and William James, that the ideas, original as they are, were yet in the air at that moment.

M. Duhem, in a very important article in the *Revue des Questions Scientifiques de Bruxelles* (July, 1894), may be said to have belled the cat for French readers. M. Milhaud in his book *le Rationnel* (Paris, 1898) showed clearly and intelligibly that there is not a single scientific reasoning in which the mind has not the initiative. "The mind is at every stage a theatre of simultaneous possibilities, and knows it too. The old Latin dictum, *nihil naturae imperandum nisi parendo,* must be properly understood. The mind submits to nature but to a nature chosen by itself." All theories are merely symbols, and symbols are like pictures of an eternal nature — endowed with momentary truth. Science is simply the angle of vision from which certain savants contemplate the universe. Such men as Le Roy, Bernard Brunhes, Duhem or Milhaud were repulsed by the idea of the Universe seen as a kind of Farmer's Almanac. These men hold that arithmetic cannot be the riddle of the Sphinx. Before their day we were taught that all sensations were illusions of the mind, except those of motion. But why make this exception? There is no reason for privileging motions. They may be illusions, too. There is no splendid and imperial isolation for one set of sensations. To admit one is to admit them all, quality as well as quantity. No one would want to add, say, flavors as you add temperatures, or claim that any cabbage contains forty per cent mustiness or any carrot thirty-five per cent redness and twenty-five per cent acidity. There are certainly some things which are irreducible to quantity.

"Quand nous faisons une théorie générale," said Claude Bernard, "la seule chose dont nous soyons certains, est que toutes ces théories sont fausses, absolument parlant. . . . Les systèmes tendent à asservir l'esprit humain. . . . La philosophie et la science ne doivent point être systématiques."

Mechanics, physics and chemistry have their own laws and dwell apart. They are and must be independent of one another. Life is too big a thing to be betrayed into a chemistry book, a kind of new *summum scientiae,* and wrapped in the gown of a don. Such was the conclusion at which Pasteur and Claude Bernard had arrived.

Science, then, — I speak of science in France, — is nowadays not so arrogant as she used to be. M. le Dantec, for instance, though an out-and-out materialist, shows a certain impatience and a pleasing fastidiousness over the lowly pretenses of some of his colleagues. Science for him is not a fairy godmother who brings us the sugar plums of more happiness, more justice — the golden age, in fact. No, science must content herself with the part of a kind of Cinderella, busied with retorts and crucibles and lancets and knives and herbariums and larders; she must be satisfied with verifying certain facts. *Ne sutor ultra crepidam.*

M. Emile Boutroux, the great French philosopher who is so well known in England and America, had succeeded before the advent of Bergson in introducing into our notion of science a far more subtle notion of science, or, to use his own words, in replacing "la science faite" by "la science qui se fait." His wonderfully clear style, with all its sincerity and fervor, has perhaps contributed more than anything else to showing that the only science that exists is science in the making, and that science in such a case is not a discovery but an invention.

He is a true "Pascalist"; his cheek flushes when he speaks of the great French thinker; and to my mind, when he realized that science is born of human thought and can preserve its truth only by remaining closely allied with our spiritual activity, it was after long reflection over Pascal's words: "If our view be arrested there, let our imagination pass beyond: it will sooner exhaust the power of conception than nature that of supplying material for conception. The whole visible world is only an imperceptible atom in the ample bosom of nature." "Is science really destined to absorb the whole man and to reduce him to the dust of atoms? That hypothesis arises from a misunderstanding which Descartes denounced long ago. It supposes a confusion between science already formed or made and science which is in the making, or rather, a confusion between science considered as a thing in itself and science as it actually exists. If science were a thing in itself, ready made from all eternity, — if man had nothing to do but to discover it as a treasure buried in the ground is discovered, — then it would be true that man does not really exist except in a scientific form — that is to say, so far as he is a man, he does not exist at all. But that so-called science in itself is nothing but a creation of reason imagined by metaphysicians of the Absolute, or by university professors inclined by profession to dogmatism. The only science which exists is the science which is being formed, the science which is becoming science — and that is not really a discovery, it is rather an invention. If there is one result which is plain, from the deep study which, in our day especially, has been made of the origin of science, it is this:

the essential and continuous part which the original activity of the mind has played and plays, both in the formation and elaboration of scientific concepts and in establishing the relations of phenomena to those concepts. I would be glad to apply to all science the theory which I have seen my master, M. Michel Bréal, sustain in regard to language. Against those who assume to explain the phenomena of language by purely mechanical laws immanent in language itself, to wit: by simple invariable connections of elementary linguistic phenomena, Michel Bréal sustains the proposition that the mind, for its own ends and by its own activity, with its capacity for trying, for groping its way, for choice, for adaptation, for æsthetic arrangement, for improving, is the true creator and modifier of language. *Mens agitat molem.*"*

But M. Emile Boutroux is not the only shrewd and frank French philosopher whose speculations are cheered by a bracing love of freedom. There were and are scores of writers whose task has been to free us from the fetters of self as of science, and to help us realize that the immense river of Life, compassed about and circumscribed by laws, oozes through all our dams and locks.

Renouvier and Secrétan and their disciples understood that the problems of conscience and free will were such that it was well worth a man's while to devote his whole life to their consideration. After them came Bergson, hand in hand with William James, the latter being perhaps the most widely read of all of them in France! They are surrounded by a brilliant group of philosophers

*Emile Boutroux, *Science and Culture.* Princeton University Press, 1914. Pp. 22, 23.

and scientists, such as Maurice Blondel, Edouard Le Roy, Joseph Wilbois, Gaston Milhaud, Marc Sangnier, to name only a few.

A philosopher, however, is unlike an apothecary in that if he gives us a pill, it is we who gild it. And such philosophers as those we have named would not be supported by the public were it not that a large body of men of letters leads us to their dispensary. Among these literary men are names such as Brunetière, Bourget, Barrès, E. M. de Vogüé, Faguet, so well known that it is needless to dwell here upon their characteristics. Different each from the other they all are, but all agree on one point — on trying not to broaden, but to deepen, the French mind. Nor should one forget the Taine of his later years, who desired a religious burial because he had realized the importance of ethics and religion.

Towards 1850, or perhaps later, between 1850 and 1880, science was the supreme idol before which all the other idols were sacrificed. Yet a certain number of writers refused to bend the knee before the idol, and it is their books which at the present moment are the favorite reading of thousands of Frenchmen; writings of men like Bergson or Boutroux or Blondel or Le Roy, who appeal to professional philosophers, down to M. Barrès, the successor of Paul Déroulède at the head of the nationalist movement, and immortal author of *Colette Baudoche*.

All of these writers — and their agreement is worthy of remark — all without exception, whether Catholic or Protestant, repentant positivists or spiritualists, all begin by declaring that if we have certain physical needs, we have moral needs which are no less exacting, and that we must have a moral nourishment which will make us live by making us desire to live.   They all declare that our intelligence can only pick reality to pieces, can only give us schematic patterns of things.   Anatole France, in *Le Jardin d'Epicure,* has a happy image where he compares metaphysical systems with the platinum threads in astronomical telescopes.   "Les fils sont utiles à l'observation des astres, mais ils sont de l'homme et non du ciel.   Il est bon qu'il y ait des fils de platine dans les lunettes, mais il ne faut pas oublier que c'est l'opticien qui les a mis."

Reason is poor, but — which is worse — it is demoralizing.   The rationalistic doctrine is a doctrine of despair and death.   "Naturalistic philosophy," says Secrétan, "does not agree with the moral faith which is the mainstay of our existence.   Every moral doctrine rests upon duty and presupposes liberty."[*] "Les formules ne sont pas vraies, elles sont commodes," says M. H. Poincaré."[†]

What thesis has scientific philosophy other than determinism?   If all things are obedient to regular mechanical laws, the sacrifice of a mother for her child, or that of the scientist who gives his life for a discovery which shall benefit humanity, are movements every whit as necessary as the movement of the earth round the sun; they are the outcome of some primary movement — probably that of a monkey in past ages defending a member of his tribe against the enemy.

But if I accept this doctrine, if I may not believe in my freedom, I likewise am not at liberty to take seriously the dictates of my conscience.   Kant proclaimed this in no uncertain fashion.   "I ought" implies "I can."   If my liberty is only a phantom

---

[*]Secrétan, *Le principe de la morale.*
[†]*La Science et l'hypothèse,* 1907.

there is no question of *ought,* for in that case I *can* neither obey nor disobey duty.*

Renouvier devoted the whole of a long and admirably industrious life to restating Kant's philosophy, while affirming the independence of human reason and reintegrating liberty in the world. Of course he has been laughed at by the naturalistic school. But, as Stevenson says, "It is men who hold what seems to us a dangerous lie, who can extend our restricted field of knowledge and rouse our drowsy consciences."

It is Renouvier who gave its impulse to pragmatism, which measures the truth of every idea by the consequences contained therein. For him philosophy is the handmaiden of ethics.

With his name should be associated not only that of his brilliant disciple Lequier, whose book *la Feuille de Charmille* should be read by every would-be believer in human liberty, but also that of a potent personality in the world of metaphysics, Félix Ravaisson, whose *Rapport sur la Philosophie en France au XIX^c siècle,* written on the occasion of the French Exhibition of 1867, will always remain a model of dialectics and resourceful strategy in defense of ethics and spirituality. Félix Ravaisson, for the twenty years following 1863, was President of the *"Concours d'Agrégation de Philosophie"*; his influence on French teachers of philosophy was therefore considerable. To him as to his master, Maine de Biran, is due that intellectual irritation at the stupidity of a purely mechanistic philosophy, as well as that charm of style, that poetical view of the world, that hellenic capacity for understanding things and that wonderful power of hovering on the

*See André Cresson, *Le Malaise de la pensée philosophique,* or F. Pillon, *Philosophie de Secrétan.*

boundary line which divides poetry from prose,
which are the main characteristics of the work of
such men as Léon Ollé-Laprune, Maurice Blondel,
Dunan or Le Roy. Nor may we omit to mention the
names of such brilliant thinkers as Pillon, Victor
Brochard, Victor Egger, Lionel Dauriac, Octave
Hamelin, Penjon, Victor Delbos or Brunschvicg —
to choose only a few — who, each in his separate
style and for the most part holding aloof from any
religious creed, have harassed the self-complacency
of smug materialism. And this same note of revolt
against false gods is to be heard in almost any number of *la Critique Philosophique* (1868-1889) (continued as *l'Année Philosophique* from 1889 with M.
Pillon as editor) and in *La Revue de Métaphysique
et de Morale* (1890 in progress).

There the reader may discover inexhaustible
treasures of ideas and systems, and the most con-
vincing proof, if proof were needed, of man's tireless energy in the pursuit of ideals.

According to Renouvier and his followers, to assert a law is but to assert an hypothesis. *"Hypotheses non fingo,"* said wise Sir Isaac Newton. By
all means let us have hypotheses, but let us treat
them only as inferences and hints and suggestions
of reality.

Experience allows us to state a certain number of
cases where one phenomenon follows precisely upon
another. The idea occurs to us that these phenomena may be connected; our experiments show us
that they appeared together, say, hundreds of times.
What right have we to conclude that they are, or
will be, the same always and in all the solar systems
of the universe?

To establish such a law, we ought to exhaust all
possibilities in time and space. Thus when we af-

firm the truth of a law, we are not content with hazarding a conjecture; we boldly declare that we believe the world owes immediate and irrevocable obedience to our hypothesis.

The genesis of our ideas, or rather of our certitude, according to Renouvier, is rather alarming for browbeating people. It is our will which sets to itself a certain goal, and when the goal is attained, our mind dwells thereafter in happy certitude. Thus I should say we pin our faith to determinism, because the spiritualistic doctrine, for some personal motive, irritates us; and we believe the laws of nature to be absolutely binding for ever and everywhere, because, from a personal motive, we have faith in determinism.

Our every-day expressions, if we paid more heed to them, would show us such processes of our mind. We "*give* a grudging assent"; we "*surrender* to evidence"; we "*submit* to reason" — all of which phrases clearly manifest the part our will plays in our very act of believing.

Science and philosophy tell us that our sensations are part of ourselves: the same might be said of our beliefs. Doubtless we are not conscious of such a phenomenon. To know that there is a subjective element in our creed might discourage many of us. And yet when we remember how many more men have been killed by bigotry than by skepticism, we may congratulate ourselves upon having learned, if not to respect and love our neighbor, at least to refrain from sending him to the stake. Besides, we are natural believers. Therefore, Renouvier and Secrétan are not so audacious as might first appear. All they really want to say can be summed up in these words of Secrétan: "Il n'y a pas de preuve de l'existence de Dieu: Dieu n'est pas l'objet d'une science, mais d'une foi."*

We are on the way to pragmatism. In order to believe, a man must first become a skeptic. The Pyrrhonist's alley leads to the temple. The best argument in favor of Renouvier's theory may be drawn from the attitude of such different philosophers as Malebranche and Renan. Both believe absolutely that "Dieu n'agit pas dans le monde par des volontés particulières," that is, by miracles; yet Malebranche was a fervent Catholic, and Renan a pronounced skeptic! Our philosophical theories lead us only whither we allow them to lead us: the mind is the heart's servant.

The force of Renouvier's argument (which is also Secrétan's) in favor of our liberty is apparent. The determinist denies our free will only because he believes in principles which appeal to him.

"Temperaments with their cravings and refusals do determine men in their philosophies and always will," says William James.† And as Pascal profoundly remarks, "The will is one of the chief factors of belief; not that it creates belief, but because things are true or false according to the aspect in which we look at them. The will which prefers one aspect to another turns away the mind from considering the qualities of all that it does not like to see." That is the best formula for what happens in spiritual matters; a reasoning is only likely to persuade us if we give it our attention, if we adopt it as our own. But Renouvier goes much further than Pascal. "Whoever wants to believe will believe," he assures

*Cf. Secrétan, *La Civilisation et la croyance*. Cf. also Renouvier, *La Nouvelle Monadologie, ou Deuxième Essai de Critique générale*.
†*Pragmatism*, p. 35.

us in his *Deuxième Essai de Critique Générale;* and Secrétan uses almost the same language. Believe what your conscience tells you is true. You can do so. Desire your belief, for you can believe at will. Will is an inexhaustible spring of action; you have only to turn the tap. Such, according to Renouvier, is the foundation of man's liberty, which is the same thing as sincerity. "To thine own self be true" is not only the guiding principle of our actions, but also that of our most intimate convictions. The things of which we are certain are those which we judge suitable to our high moral destiny, and this very approbation is an act of liberty. In this way there is a very intimate connection between certitude and faith, between faith and will.*

"Liberty cannot be demonstrated," writes Secrétan; "neither can determinism be proved. Moral life develops in belief in liberty, science develops in belief in the determinist hypothesis. The interests of morality plead for liberty, the interests of theoretical science plead for necessity." At its last analysis "determinism affirms a faith, the partisan of free will expresses another. The two clash, but neither has the right to claim that he has changed his faith into knowledge and that he has proved its truth."

Let us go further. We perceive the world through senses which deform reality. The result is that however intelligible, however coherent, a system may appear to us, it proves only one thing, namely, that it appears true to our mind, but very probably it is in no wise the image of truth. We can admit that the inhabitant of Sirius or Neptune or Mars has

---

*Anyone wishing to remonstrate may profitably turn to an article which appeared in the (*London*) *Times* of February 17, 1917, *The Modern Distrust of Religion.*

quite a different conception of things, just as the ant, the bee, or the dog around us has a view very unlike ours. As M. Henri Poincaré once put it: "Concevez l'esprit humain sous la forme d'une punaise infiniment plate et qui se meut sur une sphère parfaite, alors le plus court chemin d'un point à l'autre sera pour cet esprit, non pas la ligne droite, dont il n'a pas l'idée, mais l'arc de cercle. Et toutes les propositions qui dérivent de la ligne droite considéréc comme le plus court chemin d'un point à un autre n'auront désormais qu'une valeur humaine, qu'une valeur relative."*

Thus experiment is powerless to establish irrefutably the truth of a law. When we formulate a law we translate the nature of our mind rather than that of the universe. And thus not only observation and experiment are unable to prove rigorously the existence of laws, but they can only apply to states of consciousness, pure and simple phenomena. How can anyone believe that in a summary he holds all truth, past, present and future, as one holds a quivering bird in one's hand?

And the conclusion of these remarks might be taken from those words of Nietzsche: "It is high time to replace the Kantian question, 'How are synthetic judgments *a priori* possible?' by another question, 'Why is belief in such judgments necessary?' In effect, it is high time that we should understand that such judgments must be believed to be true, for the sake of the preservation of creatures like ourselves. Though they still might naturally be *false* judgments! Or, more plainly spoken, and roughly and readily — synthetic judgments *a priori* should not 'be possible' at all; we have no right to them;

*Cf. Andrè Beaunier, "*Visages d'hier et d'aujourd'hui,*" Paris, 1911. p. 165.

in our mouths they are nothing but false judgments. Only, of course, the belief in their truth is necessary, as plausible belief and ocular evidence belonging to the perspective view of life. . . ."*

This amounts to saying that a philosophy should have as its principal aim not knowledge, but service: its end is to make men wish to live. And it is in this way that the philosophy of Renouvier and Secrétan has cleared the way for the pragmatism of William James and Professor Schiller and their disciples, as well as for M. Bergson's philosophy of intuition, and that it has given an added impetus to Brunetière's traditionalism and to M. Barrès's nationalism. Indeed, it could hardly be otherwise, since this philosophy sang the praises of will, of that "dumb conviction that the truth must be in one direction rather than another." In spite of the many considerable differences between Bergson and William James, both agree in declaring that life is prior to intellect, and that true reality cannot be apprehended save in the living experience itself. On the one hand Bergson affirms that intuition, by an effort of which we place ourselves from the first in the flow of reality, attains the absolute: on the other the pragmatists declare that we have only one edition of the universe, unfinished, growing in all sorts of places, especially in the places where thinking beings are at work.†

Both these theorists — starting from widely different points of view — are alike in their aim at plunging us into life "in order to feel our force and also to succeed in intensifying it."‡

The doctrine of Bergson is every bit as courage-

---

*Beyond Good and Evil, translated by Helen Zimmern, p. 18.
†Pragmatism, p. 259.
‡"Life and Consciousness," Bergson. Hibbert Journal, Oct., 1911.

ous as that of William James. This in spite of Mr. Kallen's saying: "For the pragmatist truth is what we live by, not what we rest in: with a sly dig at the Bergsonians who 'rest in the absolute.' " M. Bergson has rightly protested against such an interpretation of his teaching. We should not forget that William James said of Bergson, "Reading his books is what has made me *bold*." Far more important than theories is a man's attitude. Doubtless Mr. Kallen is right when he says, "For James experience is all, each piece of it hanging to the other by its edges, and the whole, self-containing, hanging on nothing"; whilst for Bergson life transcends experience, and his philosophy with its famous *élan vital* implies pure metaphysical substrata.

But the man in the street is not going to try to fathom mystical utterances. He is perfectly impious in his skepticism of theory; and his sound common sense asks only: what is truth, according to these philosophers?

Now for Bergson and for James the true idea is the idea *which pays*. No doubt M. Bergson will not express himself in such a brutal way. His philosophy has mellowed into metaphysics. The pure air of French culture has sweetened the tough and hard nature of pragmatism. But his philosophy, which looks on matter as the enemy, which takes account of "values," and is content with no doctrine which ignores them, is a philosophy of earnest belief in sincerity, in freedom, in unselfish greatness.

We hear on one side James shouting from his pulpit: "The possession of true thoughts means everywhere the possession of invaluable instruments of action;"[*] and on the other Bergson whispers in our

Pragmatism, p. 202.

ear, "The Universe is the battle-ground between freedom and necessity."

For both of them true philosophy is philanthropy which does not squander its golden words in self-laudation, but invests them in the human heart. The gist of such doctrine is to force us into becoming what we are capable of becoming.

To act is to know, — a deep saying. Hence the necessity for training our will; hence also the necessity for training our hearts. "I therefore for one cannot see my way to accepting the agnostic rules for truth seeking," James writes, and his will to believe has already worked wonders. There is no such insurmountable barrier as determinism. It is a poor mind that does not see the means to fly over it. Naturalism says, "Tell me what your surroundings are and I will tell you who you are." But true realism replies, "Tell me what you are and I will tell you what your surroundings will be."*

On the whole, art and literature have created our

---

*The Philosophy of William James, by Thomas Flournoy, professor in the faculty of Sciences at the University of Geneva (authorized translation by Edwin B. Holt and William James, Jr.), is a very important work for those who wish to understand James's philosophy and to differentiate it from that of Secrétan, Renouvier and Bergson. Pp. 191-196 are full of recollections: the philosophic tone is laid aside. They include a letter from James to Flournoy concerning Renouvier and Secrétan. "I entirely agree," he writes, "that Renouvier's system fails to satisfy, but it seems to me the classical and constant expression of one of the great attitudes, that of insisting on logically intelligible formulas. If one goes beyond, one must abandon the hope of formulas altogether, which is what all pious sentimentalists do; and with them, M. Secrétan, since he fails to give any articulate substitute for the criticism he finds so unsatisfactory. Most philosophers give formulas, and inadmissible ones, as when Secrétan makes a mémoire sans oubli = duratio tota simul = eternity!" (p. 125; see also Flournoy's interesting remarks). Clearly William James early tired of formulas and the hollow rationalistic method and threw himself whole-heartedly into radical empiricism, because he had given up all hope of understanding the world in a logical way. (See The Will to Believe, New York, 1903, p. 29.)

milieu. We come back to Whistler's reply to the lady who remarked that a certain sunset reminded her of one of his pictures: "Ah! Madam, Nature is looking up!" In the glorious manifestations of a free art, as they are shown by the masterpieces of a Michelangelo, or a Beethoven, we see, according to Bergson, the final reality of the universe. John Stuart Mill's father was a pragmatist, or a Bergsonian *avant la lettre.* "He was fond of putting into my hands books which exhibited men of energy and resource in unusual circumstances struggling against difficulties and overcoming them."*

Bergson, be it said to his credit, has had an intuition of the indomitable nature whence we spring. His "vital impetus" is but a device for telling us that mankind has a privileged part in the world and that we must judge our forefathers from a more divine position than that of the mollusk. The ancients had placed perfection in the normal development of our whole being, and Bergson and James are classicists in that sense that they put us in an heroic heart about life.

The reader sees now how such preaching reacted against the pessimism and maudlin sentimentality of a part of French literature. The Romanticists had been tootling too long on their trumpets; the day of judgment had not come except for them, and now was the time to sound the healthy drum of action.

II

A writer very different from Bergson and James, Joseph de Maistre, had said a long time before them: "Man ought to act as if he were able to do every-

*John Stuart Mill. *Autobiography*, p. 5. **Longmans Green & Co.,** 1908.

thing, and submit as if he could do nothing." The
name of this very interesting thinker brings us naturally to the doctrine of M. Brunetière, for M. Brunetière has done little else than repeat and perfect
the ideas of Joseph de Maistre; but he has halted at
many stages on the road to religion. No scholar has
worked harder at finding truth; and a very tempest
of passion fills his pilgrim mantle as he wanders
about. He has been called a man of formulæ, and
certainly no man was more tossed by the storms of
his country; nor has any man listened with more
attentive ear to the countless thronging echoes of
the present times. At one moment, Comte was his
god, at another, Darwin his idol. But his so-called
failures only steeled his great heart; they were the
harbingers of his final triumph. His *Discours de
Combat* are not only an exposition of the view that
science is incapable of offering an explanation or
even an acceptable interpretation of the universe,
but also a proof of the real courage of this purveyor
of thought for young *"normaliens."* For a long
time he believed in science, and then experience, the
very fact that human nature demands a moral code,
taught him that all he had written so far was not the
real thing. Instead of pursuing the same course as
many men, when their prior actions prove too strong
and enslave them, Brunetière started afresh, when
well over forty, and dwelt, as his wont was, on the
truth he had discovered. Those who knew him tell
us that his moral suffering was great; nor was that
all, — his religious attitude hindered his university
career, and he was never appointed professor at the
Collège de France, as he had had every right to expect. I cannot read his *Discours de Combat* without imagining Brunetière, like a Greek hero, drawing his wounds, while he cries in a lusty voice: "On

ne se débarrasse pas du besoin de croire. Il est
ancré dans le coeur de l'homme.'' And his fighting
eloquence, ever wielding lance and shield, challenges
contest. ''Il y a de vieilles idées dont la vie de l'hu-
manité ne saurait pas plus se passer que de pain.''
Who said that the wise skeptic is a bad citizen? Such
is Brunetière's opinion. And truly if those old-fash-
ioned ideas, as Renan used to call them, morality,
love of family, love of fatherland, self-sacrifice, all
the generous possibilities, waver for a moment, the
whole social structure totters, and the skeptic himself is hurled into bottomless confusion. Brunetière
is the intellectual nephew of Bossuet, and in his eyes
the speaker's art is truly a sacred thing. But there
again his spirit of adventure (I should like to underline that, for Brunetière appears to many readers
as a kind of scarecrow, old before he was through
his teens), his spirit of adventure, then, made him
realize that the most up-to-date things are common-
places, the daily bread of the mind's life, the substance and fabric of our moral existence. Job's
complaint is ever fresh and new; he struck the deepest note and the most familiar; yet all our fine æs-
thetes of yesterday, with their sickly, puling rigma-
role and hysterical sadness, are now and for ever
forgotten. Real culture can be told not by the number of books which have been read, nor by any wonderful and multicolored sensations, nor by kinemat-
ographic emotions, nor by far-fetched sentimentality,
but by depth of feeling and sincerity. Brunetière's
speeches are like those old Dutch pictures which are
so extraordinarily bracing in their solidity and sto-
lidity. It was a grand thing to busy yourself with
pots and pans like those old Flemish women, with
your face turned towards real life.

From this point of view Brunetière's work sym-

bolizes a whole phase in the history of modern contemporary thought.   If he fights so desperately
against individualism, it is because the individualist
is an obstacle to social life.   The egotist leads one
merely to a *cul de sac*.   M. Brunetière is his antago-
nist, and the apostle of the two religions — the cult
of the dead and worship of the fatherland.   "La tradition," he says, "pour nous ce n'est pas ce qui est
mort, c'est au contraire ce qui vit; c'est ce qui survit
du passé dans le présent, c'est ce qui dépasse l'heure
actuelle; et de nous tous, tant que nous sommes, ce
ne sera pour ceux qui viendront après nous, que ce
qui vivra plus que nous."   And he goes on to show
how this survival of the past unites with the future.
"Non seulement la religion n'a rien d'incompatible
avec le progrès, mais au contraire le vrai progrès,
le progrès durable n'est possible qu'en accordance
avec la tradition, et par le moyen de la tradition."

The curious thing is that this hatred of individualism led Brunetière to his traditionalism, while another great writer, M. Maurice Barrès, has become a
traditionalist on account of his individualism.

M. Barrès firmly believes that our personality attains its full development only when it is in conformity with the tradition of our race, and that our
life expands and gains in breadth when it draws its
strength from the soil of our own country.   It is
through excess of individualism that Barrès cher-
ishes the belief that the best part of our dead lives
again in us, and he has developed this idea with
great subtlety and poetic power in most of his books.

It is really most interesting to see two minds so
widely different arrive at the same conclusion.
Barrès's influence, I should think, has been the
greater of the two.   His works, because they are
works of fiction, appeal to a larger public.   They are

not only true to the human tragi-comedy, but through all the pages there blows the wind of a high way of feeling which places *Colette Baudoche* on a level with the great masterpieces of French literature.

By the side of Barrès and Brunetière, I should like to place a younger man, an essayist like Barrès, a genuine investigator in the realm of thoughts like Brunetière. M. André Beaunier's novels, *l'Homme qui a perdu son moi* (1911) and *la Révolte* (1914), have been widely read in France, and his literary criticisms in the *Figaro* and in *Revue des Deux Mondes* manifest a caustic humor and a silvery sensitiveness which at times remind the reader of Charles Lamb. Beaunier's recollections of his childhood* remind the reader of *Old China,* for with him as with Lamb the desire of depicting himself is his real motive for writing.

M. Beaunier belongs, I should say, to that extraordinary generation of 1880 (or is it 1895?) intoxicated with all ideas and above all with symbolism, and of course in love with the German subjective idealism, as well as with Dante and the primitive Italian painters. His friends might have feared, at a certain moment of his life, that his ever changing and protean mind would never enjoy the cosy inglenook of firm belief; and the philistine often wondered whether so irrepressible an epigrammatist were not laughing at his reader and even at himself. His book *Trois Amies de Chateaubriand* scandalized all those simple folk who take themselves — and Chateaubriand — too seriously. Truly a *chef* wonderfully well versed in the delicate art of tickling the jaded Parisian appetite with the cool malignity

*See André Beaunier, *des Idées et des Hommes. Deuxième Série.* Paris, 1915.

of highly seasoned criticism: plenty of cayenne among the bays of laurel for the subjects of his studies; and yet behold this humorist, the least narrow-minded, dogmatic or intolerant of men, become now a stern moralist, what his enemies would call a formalist, a limited man! Is this yet another of the jester's tricks? Far from it. He has become a great believer, and the fact that he may express his faith in a skeptic tone of voice, or in peculiar turns of phrase, only proves the strength of this faith.

There is an entertaining scene, pregnant with meaning, in his book *La Révolte,* which leaves us in no doubt as to M. Beaunier's state of mind: I mean the conversation between the young heroine and the professor of philosophy. M. Darbenne-Mincenot is evidently what M. Beaunier was himself once upon a time, the philosopher convinced that everything undulates and flows, the tired Pyrrhonist who, realizing the abyss between man and his performance, refuses to act and spends his life between sleeping and yawning in the easy chair of skepticism. The vivid portrayal of this modern professor of philosophy is a good indication of the light in which M. Beaunier looks at him today. He snaps his fingers in the face of such *cui-bono* philosophy. In the hundreds of books in M. Darbenne-Mincenot's library, life is nothing but a spiritualized, deformed and abstract person sprung fully armed from the minds of thinkers, a scheme pure and simple built upon preconceived ideas, devoid of justness and proportion. Would to God that it were only a *chimæra bombinans in vacuo!*

M. Beaunier, by admitting the relativity of things, has been led to realize that human strength and wisdom lie not in extreme dogmatism, in believing true some empty dream or doubtful operation of the mind, but in avoiding extremes. "Man is neither angel nor brute, and the unfortunate thing is that he who would act the angel, acts the brute." And M. Beaunier, from the day when he understood that literature meant for him the picture of life freed from all the shackles of life (shall we say under the influence of Bergson?), when he understood that a novel must above all be full of true humor, wrote his two masterpieces, *l'Homme qui a perdu son moi,* and *la Révolte.* It may be that the atmosphere therein is cold or even cruel, too intellectually exciting; but, then, M. Beaunier has little pity for mankind led astray by knaves or fools.

Beside M. Beaunier should be placed the brilliant dramatist, François de Curel, who shows us very clearly what is the soul of the contemporary movement. His best known play, *la Nouvelle Idole,* was first performed in 1899; but at that time the French public, accustomed as it was to live in full blooded and complacent paganism, delighting in the verbal orgies of the *Théâtre libre* or the coarse cynicism of Boulevard theatres, was hardly ready to appreciate this new venture. In 1914 and 1915 the play was revived and, thanks to the shadows cast by war, met with the success it deserved. The whole point of the play is its question: has a savant the right to sacrifice to science human lives already condemned by fate? François de Curel, an aristocrat in irony and independence of mind, saw the tendency of the time to worship science, the New Idol, and challenged it. He represents a real wave of French feeling such as is rarely perceived by the outsider who has not lived many years in the depths of a French province — such feeling as Montaigne has so admirably portrayed when speaking of the stoicism of his poor neighbors. "Quand il s'agit de ne pas crever comme un chien, mais de finir noblement, c'est encore auprès des humbles qui adorent Dieu et des coeurs ardents qui vivent avec ton héröisme que les philosophes ont à chercher des leçons de logique.''*

We now come naturally to Jules Lemaître and Emile Faguet. Although Faguet and Lemaître belong to another generation than Curel or Beaunier — since Faguet was born in 1847 and Lemaître in 1853 — the history of their so-called evolution throws light upon the frame of mind of Curel or Beaunier. The student of French literature sees the same idea taking hold of the mind of so many different men between 1890 and 1910, here remaining a sentiment, there tending to become a fixed idea, almost a law, that he is bound to believe in that doctrine of compensation so dear to Emerson's heart. It was at the moment when anarchy was at its high-water mark in France, under the name of intellectualism, that all these men rose up and declared that they would not be so misgoverned any longer.

The more I read Jules Lemaître — and about him — the more convinced I am that his conversion was a case of patriotism pure and simple. Every grain of his wit went to counterbalance every grain of his adversaries' folly, solely and simply because he loved his Orléanais. Anatole France in his *Vie littéraire* quotes a beautiful page of Jules Lemaître which goes far to explain the author of *Opinions à répandre* or the fact of his becoming *President de la Patrie française.*

''Quand j'entends déclamer sur l'amour de la patrie, je reste froid, je renfonce mon amour en moi-même avec jalousie pour le dérober aux banalités de la rhétorique qui en feraient je ne sais quoi de faux, de vide et de convenu. Mais quand j'embrasse de

La Nouvelle Idole, last scene.

quelque courbe de la rive, la Loire étalée et bleue comme un lac, avec ses prairies, ses peupliers, ses ilots blonds, ses touffes d'osiers bleuâtres, son ciel léger, la douceur épandue dans l'air, et non loin dans ce pays aimé de nos anciens rois, quelque château ciselé comme un bijou qui me rappelle la vieille France, ce qu'elle a été dans la monde, alors je me sens pris d'une infinie tendresse pour cette terre maternelle où j'ai partout des racines si délicates et si fortes.''*

If the masterpieces of sculpture and painting are a fine education (and nobody denies it), why should not beautiful nature — majestic old oaks, a stately river, the play of shadows on rock and cave, graceful hills stretching their delicate limbs against an opal sunset, stars seen at night through the branches of a group of cypresses, birches white and moving gently in the breeze like a band of nymphs — why should not this most classical landscape exert an enduring influence upon a sensitive mind? Lemaître was born to be a gentleman farmer. He is a part of the soil of France. Every real French gentleman is.

Emile Faguet on the other hand is a *citadin,* the child of cities, and his world is the world of ideas. Just as in the soul of the artist there exists something more delicate, more sensitive, than in the average man which enables him to understand and feel beauty in its deepest sense, so M. Faguet's mind has an exquisite finesse, a subtle and spiritual scale, that enables him to weigh, reject or accept the gold or dross of ideas. Hence the creation of his books, above all of his three volumes on the moralists and political writers of the Nineteenth Century.

''It is to the eternal honor of man,'' he once wrote, ''that a hundred thousand facts shall never prevail

Vie Littéraire, 3eme série, p. 154.

over one idea.'' Still, lover of ideas does not mean
an ideologist. No man was ever fonder of facts than
Faguet. If he took no active part in public affairs,
he mixed freely with men and even with *boulevar-
diers* — that is what gives him a certain sense of
reality and an unfailing sense of humor. The book
he called *Political Questions* might just as well be
named *Social Maladies,* and should be the vade mecum of our present-day statesmen. ''Science, to
whom all men turned to find happiness, has created
a rough, violent, terribly agitated and panting
world.'' M. Faguet wrote those words before the
great war; and in their light one would fain inquire:
What manner of German did science make?

This world which is so tired, so drunken with unsatisfied desires, this feverish, restless plutocracy
powerless to find happiness, cannot exist indefinitely
without a moral and intellectual ideal.

It was in order to feel under him the solid ground
of fact that Faguet devoted all his talent in the latter part of his life to social problems. He stands
in that respect for an epitome of all those men of
letters who wish to see clearly the problem not of
destiny, but of their own destiny. As he said so well,
''L'avenir national est une chose autrement impor-
tante que l'avenir littéraire.'' That is why he wrote
his *Culte de l'Incompétence,* and his *l'Horreur des
Responsabilités,* and so many articles in so many
papers.

III

Now M. Faguet is, more than anyone else, a representative of all those men of letters who, however
original they may be, are the product rather than
the creators of a movement. Side by side with philosophers such as Renouvier, and great authors such

as Barrès, who are capable in themselves of originating a movement and being its fountain heads,
there are all those talented writers who, while they
undergo the influence of ideas which are in the air
at the moment, at the same time give them a fresh
impulse. This reactionary revival which we are now
considering was begun as early as 1885 and by *quite
young writers.*

Critics in general make a great mistake when they
pay attention only to the middle-aged — to those
men who have already made their way and won their
reputations. It is young men who create new movements. They are like children who spread abroad
the beauty they carry within themselves and are
rebellious towards any influence which goes against
their grain. Most of us have noticed the imitativeness of the child, but few have stopped to admire his
act of self-defense, his instinctive combativeness,
nay, his self-reliance and desire to innovate, his art
of *improvisation,* of creative play. A child has a
magnetic nature in subtle relation with the forces of
the earth: like the morning sun, he shows us the
right way by his profound and resistless sincerity.
The real business of the critic is to know what the
young men are about. In the present case he must
consult the Parisian reviews of 1895 to 1900 in order
to realize what were the ideas which swayed the
young writers of that time. Before the appearance
of the *Mercure de France,* which is the most important repertory, and which is to-day more vigorous
than ever, there were the *Revue Contemporaine, la
Vogue, la Revue Indépendante,* and above all the
Revue Wagnérienne.

The *Revue Wagnérienne* which was founded in
1885 by Edouard Dujardin and on the staff of which
J. K. Huysmans met Catulle Mendès, Téodor de

Wyzewa, L. de Fourcaud, etc., is a very good indication of German influence in France. Téodor
de Wyzewa, together with Catulle Mendès, was the
great apostle of Wagner.

His book, *Nos Maîtres,* in which he has repub-
lished articles which had appeared between 1885 and
1895 in the *Revue Wagnérienne, la Vogue, la Revue
Indépendante, la Revue bleue, le Figaro, le Mercure
de France,* is valuable for the Wagnerian enthusiasm
which it breathes. This extraordinarily brilliant
young Pole worships Wagner as the prophet of a
new order of things. But of course the high priest
of all these young men seeking to renew the inspiration of the arts is Baudelaire, who, as far back as
1861 in his famous study of Richard Wagner and
Tannhäuser, had proclaimed that this music was the
expression of all that is most hidden in the heart of
man.

Together with this influence of Wagner must be
taken that of Villiers de l'Isle Adam, an influence
so important that it merits a chapter to itself. He
reinforced the influence of Germany by the very fact
that he expressed Hegelian and Wagnerian ideas in
intelligible French.

Finally, it would be neglecting the expression of
the time that will perhaps live longest if we neglected the painters; such men as Puvis de Cha-
vannes, Gustave Moreau, Besnard, Whistler, Cazin,
Maurice Denis, all of whom aim at expressing the
human soul rather than externals and who appeal
to our feelings rather than to our eyes. The pleasures of the eye are for them an end, but not the supreme end: they seek rather to awaken by means
of these pleasures the profound emotion created in
us by fine music and sublime poetry. Indeed, every-
things holds together; the world of art, the world of

ideas, and the world of life act and react one
upon another; and were it not for the miraculous
action of genius, or of faith interrupting the chain
of cause and effect, upsetting our little schemes, we
should be tempted to believe in a universal determinism.   Art itself, which is pure intuition, entire
spontaneity, utterly free from self-consciousness,
every now and then submits to the influence of
environment.

Proudhon, in his book, *du Principe de l'art et de
sa Destination sociale,* when studying the work of
Courbet, declares: "This critical, analytical, synthetic, humanitarian painter is an expression of his
time.   His work coincides with Comte's *Philosophie
positive,* with Vacherot's *Métaphysique positive,* and
with my own *le Droit humain ou Justice immanente;*
the right to work and the rights of the workman,
proclaiming the end of capitalism and the sovereignty of labor; the phrenology of Gall and Spurz-
heim; the physiognomy of Lavater."   Proudhon was
right when he spoke in this way of Courbet, who
was a great artist but a shallow mind.   But it was
precisely against the excesses of this realistic school
of painting that Gustave Moreau rebelled.   "Je ne
crois ni à ce que je touche, ni à ce que je vois: je ne
crois qu'à ce que je ne vois pas, et à ce que je sens."
It might even be said of this mystic painter with his
passion for the invisible, his curiosity about the most
elusive expressions of the human soul, ever seeking
an emotion by means of philosophic speculation, that
he forestalls the philosophy of Bergson.   It would
of course be highly imprudent to insist upon such a
slippery point — painting and literature being arts
which employ different means, treat different subjects, and appeal to different faculties of our minds.
Impressionism is not only a study and evocation of

modern life, but a study of light, sunlight, starlight
— even gaslight. It has given us the sunshine of
Monet, the footlights of Degas, the open air of Ma-
net, and also Whistler's nocturnes. Again, the im-
pressionists were influenced by other artists, and
not by men of letters: Daumier, Gavarni and Guys
were their real masters.

Far more important factors than impressionism
were at work: the progressive suppression of average fortunes, due to the steady decrease of income
and increased cost of living; the growing predomi-
nance of the plutocracy and steady weakening of
moral forces; the progress of socialism and of anarchy among men of letters culminating in the words
of a French poet, Laurent Tailhade, ''Qu'importe le
sort de vagues humanités, pourvu que le geste soit
beau?''* In any case the bourgeoisie was taking more and more interest in labor questions:
and that is the explanation of the influence of
Russian writers which was so widely felt at this
moment, the sudden leaping into fame of Tolstoï
and Dostoïewski. In 1886 appeared M. Melchior
de Vogüé's *le Roman russe.* The book was made
up of a series of articles which had appeared in
the *Revue des Deux Mondes,* with a preface which

---

*See *Documents d'études sociales, sur l'Anarchie,* par Alexandre
Bérard, Lyon, 1897.

"Il faut rendre à chacun ce qui lui est dû: or, il est bien certain
qui si l'anarchie a pris le développement qu'elle a pris, on le doit
à une certaine presse boulevardière, aux névrosés et aux sceptiques
de la capitale, qui ont vu dans la nouvelle école une nouveauté
curieuse et dans ses théories des piments pour leurs sens blasés.
Ce n'est point, en effet, parmi les miséreux que l'anarchie a fait
le plus d'adeptes, mais bien parmi les déclassés qui errent, sans
métier déterminé; ce n'est point parmi les travailleurs en blouse
qu'elle a recruté ses soldats, mais parmi les ratés aux redingotes
rapées; Emile Henry et Vaillant étaient de cette catégorie. Que
voulez-vous? des publicistes comme M. Laurent Tailhade célébraient
la *beauté* du *geste*, et des duchesses étaient pleines de sympathie pour
les *compagnons* de la dynamite." (Page 4.)

created a sensation since it proclaimed the bank-
ruptcy of naturalism, the disgust of the naturalistic
novel, and perhaps the fear felt by the bourgeoisie
at this socialism which the Russians had created.
Raskolnikoff's words to Sonia, "It is not before
you that I prostrate myself, but before all the suffering of mankind," words which carried the French
mind so far away from the art-for-art school, were
taken as a watchword by those men who felt op-
pressed, as it were, by the glory of Flaubert and
Zola, or who wished to ingratiate themselves with
democracy. The *Revue Contemporaine* proclaimed
the glory of the Russians and set the ball rolling so
well that M. André Suarès's articles on the Russian
novelists in *les Cahiers de la Quinzaine* many years
later offer a good example of the way in which good
will may develop into enthusiasm.

At the same time English influence was also at
work, and little has been said on this subject in any
just or thorough fashion. Ever since the time of
Voltaire and Montesquieu French minds have been
preoccupied with England; in the Nineteenth Century a veritable anglomania reigned among the upper classes, as the many English words incorporated
into the French vocabulary prove. While the English jockey and the English tailor were conquering
the boulevards, and Longchamps and Auteuil, such
critics as Philarète Chasles, Emile Montégut and,
above all, Taine, were popularizing English literature in the salons. Then very soon Darwin's book
was to be found in every library. Carlyle, of whom
Taine had made a masterly study as early as 1864,
had a still greater influence between 1887 and 1900,
and numerous translations and enthusiastic studies
of his works were published. The ever alert French
mind quickly realized that Carlyle was really "the

founder of modern irrationalism" as Chesterton has
called him. The young Frenchman of that time
wanted poetical and symbolic novels; he was very
eager to idolize something, and Carlyle came at the
right moment, providing him with certain symbols,
and above all with that imaginative power which
awakens the intelligence, and sets the molecules of
the brain a-dancing like the stars in the sky. His
influence was all the greater in that his medium was
history, and he was thus free from the blemish of
the novelist who cuts out bits here and there in life
and makes up a garment in his own fashion which
is often as strange as Harlequin's coat. It is interesting to note that the wide success of Mr. Balfour's
Foundations of Belief (translated by G. Art, with a
preface by M. Brunetière) was in part due to the
influence of Carlyle in France. George Eliot and
Mrs. Browning were also widely read.

This Russian and English influence is well seen in
such works as Paul Margueritte's *Jours d'Epreuve*
(1888), *la Force des Choses* (1891), *la Tourmente*
(1893); Edouard Rod's *le Sens de la vie* (1889), *la
Vie privée de Michel Teissier* (1894); Paul Bourget's *le Disciple* (1889). It appears at its highest
in Paul Desjardin's famous *le Devoir présent*
(1892), a book which marks an epoch.

At the same time other forces, those of the
"Poètes Maudits," were triumphing in literature;
and the curious thing is that, far from hindering
the movement we are considering, they helped it on
its way. The same wind that blew over the heavily
scented streets of Paris, haunted by Verlaine, Rimbaud and their peers, filled the sails of the idealist
ship. Paul Verlaine, repentant, absolved, yet still
a great sinner, ending his days in the workhouse, a
great poet who sings as men pray and who has writ-

ten some of the most profoundly religious poetry
of the Nineteenth Century — its Villon in fact —
Verlaine still appeals to the young writers of France.
Witness this passage from François Mauriac's *l'Enfant chargé de chaines*, a novel published just before
the war: "Jean Paul va doucement cherchant les
allées solitaires. Il se forge un idéal de vie grave et
sérieuse, une vie toute pleine de religion et d'inquiétudes d'ordre social. Une chanson accompagne,
en sourdine sa rêverie; quoiqu'elle chante dans son
coeur, il l'entend distincte et comme éparse dans
l'air. C'est la chanson du pauvre Verlaine assagi:

> 'Elle dit la voix reconnue
> Que la bonté c'est notre vie,
> Que de la haine et de l'envie
> Rien ne reste, la mort venue. . . .' "

Nor must we forget Huysmans, that Flemish caricaturist who somehow strayed into the Nineteenth
Century, with all the power of his extraordinarily
expressive style, and whose influence has not even
yet been counteracted; nor Rimbaud to whom Claudel partly attributes the cause of his own return
to faith.[*]

Then there is M. Téodor de Wyzewa, author of
Valbert, Contes Chrétiens, and *les Disciples d'Emmaüs. Valbert* is a pure masterpiece, little read, it
is true, but none the less a masterpiece. *Ma Tante
Vincentine* is a kind of edition de luxe of Dickens
for the use of pious souls, with a thread of St. Francis running through it. If modern criticism were
really worth its salt, it would long ago have hailed
as one of the finest biographies of the last fifteen
years this story of a "poor relation" living with her
poor relatives, this picture of a saint's life, "créa-

[*]See *Œuvres de Arthur Rimbaud,* Préface de Paul Claudel, Paris,
1912.

ture toute pleine de chansons.'' She knew all the
stories of Poland, and hope, charity, fortitude and
gladness ever flowed from her lips into the heart
of her young nephew. Her beautiful soul was Wyzewa's first teacher and he has fully acknowledged
his debt: ''Ce que ces contes m'ont appris, toutes
les paroles resteraient impuissantes à l'évaluer
justement. Ils ont façonné pour toujours mon coeur
et mon cerveau, m'imprégnant à la fois des sentiments que nulle expérience ultérieure de la réalité
bourgeoise ne devait plus parvenir à étouffer en
moi et d'une foule de notions, de principes essentiels,
qui allaient constituer désormais, si je puis dire, le
fondement secret de ma 'philosophie.' Ce sont eux,
ces contes de mon enfance, qui m'ont enseigné à
admettre toujours la possibilité des choses impos-
sibles, à me défier de toute prétendue science impo-
sant des limites arbitraires aux faits, sous prétexte
de 'lois' et à tenir pour étrangement incomplète et
indigente la réalité de nos sensations présentes en
regard de celle de nos libres rêves.''

Putting aside all questions as to the literary or
philosophic value of this group of books, no one will
deny that they represent the intellectual evolution
of a generation which has passed from positivism
to idealism, from science to the gospel of the humble.
Obviously, these different writers, who themselves
are representatives of hosts of others, may take up
very different attitudes on political and religious
questions.

But, dissimilar as they may be, they are alike in
one thing: they are all convinced that side by side
with the truth of observable things there is another
truth. And the history of that Christianity of
which they are the champions proves them right.
It was the fishermen of Galilee and not the philoso-

phers of Rome who swayed the crowds and propagated the faith. Enthusiasm, then, is one of the great motive forces of the world. *Quantus amor tantus animus.**

From all these debates metaphysics emerges with added lustre. That is the explanation of the present-day rebirth of philosophy. Man's rule of conduct cannot depend on any of these sciences which Renan used to class among *les petites sciences conjecturales.* Renan said one day: "Mes négations ne sont pas le fruit de l'exégèse, elles sont antérieures à l'exégèse." He meant that if he accepted no supernatural story, it was because he conceived a certain world-system. His refusal of belief was due not to the discussion of a text, or reading of a manuscript, but to the whole development of his philosophic "made in Germany" thought.

Scholars who peck away at a text are not prophets — not even among themselves, since part of their time is necessarily devoted to proving the other was wrong; Renan realized that when he said: "Le propre des études historiques et de leurs auxiliaires, les sciences philologiques est, aussitôt qu'elles ont atteint leur perfection relative, de commencer à se démolir." After all, there is nothing surprising in that, when one reflects upon the fashion in which the human mind has never ceased building that it may destroy, and destroying that it may rebuild once more. As Lord Salisbury once said: "Few men are now influenced by the strange idea that

*I have not included Charles Maurras in this group of writers because, although he ranges himself with the defenders of religion and for that very reason might have been classed with Brunetière, he is a true pagan, a disciple of Anatole France and a founder of neo-classicism, which has a holy horror of Bergson and his school. His influence has been considerable.—Cf. Faguet: *Short History of French Literature.*

questions of religious belief depend upon the issues
of physical research.''*

In fine, then, let us not be science's dupe, nor ask
of her more than she can give. If such is indeed the
feeling of the younger French writers, then we must
expect to see poetry reflecting this idealistic evolution,— nor shall we be disappointed. We shall see,
as I hope to show, French poetry rising to new
heights through a rebirth of the care for the Divine.

IV

The general trend of French contemporary
thought before the war might seem to be a return
pure and simple to spiritualism, or rather to Pla-
tonism† (for Plato's Idea is singularly like Bergson's *élan vital*), were it not that other tendencies,
essentially original, took shape at the same time,
harmonizing in a curious way the Bergsonian doctrine with the scientific and social activities of the
times.

Swedenborg's theory that every soul exists in a
society of souls is but a poetical myth for the reality
which exists within us: our feelings and wishes, our
inspirations and premonitions, issue forth from this
fertile and all-powerful soil, the unconscious self, so
long neglected by scientists. Maine de Biran was
the first genial explorer of these mysterious and
undiscovered circles of our ego; and, though Leibnitz
and Perrault, Barthez, Bichat and Cabanis, had
hinted at the presence of wild and hidden forces
within us, Maine de Biran must be considered the
real leader in this emancipation of the human self

*Lecture to British Association, 1894. (Oxford Session.)

†According to Plato, Ideas are dynamic forces, shaping matter
and organizing it, and leading the world to the Beautiful.

which ever strives towards more vitality and stronger personality.

The idea of such a power, wonderful, undefinable, even immeasurable, came to certain minds with the force of an inspiration; for such a theory opens out wide vistas of hope, long avenues of meditation in time and in space, — in time, for in such manifestations of the inner soul we are, as it were, thinking and talking out of all Eternity, and truly Pascal's words have proved to be true when he says, "Toute la suite des hommes, pendant le cours de tant de siècles doit être considérée comme un même homme qui apprend continuellement"; in space, for our brain can radiate and act far beyond the limits of our organism, and nature becomes thus transparent to our new sense. All things are in a flux, and the incessant movement of our mind can take us through all ages to the very first men who, in a great shudder of awe and delight, mingled their soul with the Great Power that encompasses us. Magic was nothing but a very deep presentiment of the powers of our *mental life,* which is to the *cerebral life,* to use a Bergsonian metaphor, what a symphony is to the movements of the conductor's baton.

Numerous nowadays are the writers who have launched out on this sea of more or less bewildering facts, but whilst Germans busied themselves in writing a sort of poetical story of the unknown, French philosophers and medical men, such men as Théodule Ribot, Pierre Janet, Boirac, Dumas (to name only a few), having an extreme impatience of metaphysical conjectures, study above all the diseases of the mind, trying to find the ever elusive will-o'-the-wisp of metaphysics, viz., the law or laws of psychic phenomena.

M. Pierre Janet has more than skirted the borders of this world of bewildering depths, and in his *Automatisme psychologique* he goes as far as to say that there are two ways of knowing a phenomenon: an impersonal sensation, and a personal perception, so that between the personal and clear perception and the purely physical state of the body there is an intermediary state in which unconscious psychological phenomena can exist by themselves and have a life of their own. Wordsworth preached formerly that we were the passive recipients of external influences; and M. Pierre Janet, when he speaks of a patient who recognizes a drawing he has not seen, or remembers a movement he has not felt, declares that the patient becomes then and there conscious of sensations which had seen this drawing or felt that movement. (Cf. *Automatisme Psychologique,* pp. 313-14.)

During the last decades biology, sociology, psychology, have passed from the descriptive to the really creative stage, and the old dream of *anima mundi* has reappeared draped in scientific garments.

We must not, therefore, be astonished to find in *Matter and Memory* M. Bergson supporting his thesis with some of M. Ribot's or M. Janet's theories, and indeed striking is the resemblance between M. Janet's theory of unconscious representation and M. Bergson's fundamental theory of pure memory. If you admit unconscious sensations, you admit *ipso facto* that memories exist within us without our knowing it, and, as M. Bergson says, that the past never ceases to exist. So memory is no longer a weakened perception, an assembly of nascent sensations, but a principle independent of matter, a spiritual web woven, as it were, through and through our being, bearing with it the integral

survival of the past, a miscrocosm more complex
than all solar systems. All these studies of conscious and unconscious life, of primitive and social
life, as exemplified in the works of William James,
of M. Delacroix, or M. Durkheim, have served
Bergsonism, and culture (for the two go hand in
hand), not only by real gifts of scientific knowledge,
but also by suggesting questions which help us to
realize the dramatic interest of religious life.*

But at the same time there is another tendency
of the age: that of a certain skepticism doubting
even that it doubts, a clever Pyrrhonism declaring
that mankind, far from resting on the soft pillow
of *nonchalance,* must needs live and act, for, if it
be true that no virtue is final, we must needs live
and act in order to discover our own ideals. We
must lose ourselves in order to find ourselves again;
and there is no hope for any man who is not un-
settled or even wild. The French mind, weary
of romantic messianism, sick unto death of all the
formal schemes for rejuvenating the world, grown
skeptical after too many political experiences, and
also *né malin,* for some time took a cynical view of
the universe, but its desire of quickening life, of
expanding in all directions, could not long delay
conquering doubt, distrust and pessimism. Mankind
is a damned rascal, said Anatole France's M. Bergeret, but at the same time he praised Demos, who
is wiser than we know.

Now when M. Bergson declared that at times of
choice we decide without any reason and perhaps
even against reason, and "in certain cases that is

---

*We can only refer the reader here to M. Parodi's book, *La Philo-
sophie contemporaine en France,* in which the author dwells at length
on similarity of thought between thinkers as different as M. Durkheim or M. Bergson.

the best reason," the French philosopher was not only instructing the children of men to live in to-day, but he was emphasizing the doctrine which agreed most with the temper of his age: Demos is wild, but there is in him a divine vital fire which flickers at times but still burns and presently bathes all things in an ocean of light.

M. Jean Weber, in a justly famous article in the *Revue de Métaphysique et de Morale,* took up M. Bergson's line, but went further and declared that if Fact is to be our new idol, success then justifies everything.

At about the same time Nietzsche's doctrines were stirring the Parisian imagination, not of course in the nature of a revelation, but as giving a new importance (for it was "made in Germany") to this gospel of Force and success at any cost. Doubtless the theory of a *superman* had fascinated the romantic mind, but no writer in the Nineteenth Century, before Nietzsche, had taken such delight in drawing the picture of a new humanity building up its future on the wrecks of a poorer or weaker humanity.

One wonders whether the student of a hundred years hence will find matter for astonishment in his discovery that such diverse writers as Henri Lichtenberger, Jules de Gaultier, Emile Faguet, Pierre Lasserre, and Daniel Halévy, study and extol a German so cynical and so mordant, so full of self-conceit, and that they hand on his sayings with the divine truculence of an oracle. Doubtless this same student will have already discovered that at the time European minds were more than ever dominated by the *"libido sentiendi, libido sciendi, libido dominendi."* "We are born unjust," says Pascal, "for all tends to self." Nietzsche, the last fruit of the

Renaissance, the scapegoat in the Great War, is essentially anti-Christian: to him Christian morality is nothing but hypocrisy, and yet he is singularly like Pascal in his lifelong struggle to attain perfection. And this very influence of Pascal reinforces that of Nietzsche. Pascal has said: "Being unable to make what is just strong, we have made what is strong just." Nietzsche merely added: "Why justify what is strong? What is strong is just." Success then is the best policy, and action man's first duty. Now, all these writers addressed themselves to minds which after wandering through ancient and remote civilizations arrived at the declaration that no rational, no demonstrable, rules of morality exist, since morals are generated as the climate is, and vary as the climate does. Health is not only the condition of wisdom, but the creator of acts and thus of values which by emerging triumphant from the struggle for life become the Tables of the Law. Such ideas are expressed, for example, by M. Jules de Gaultier, whose books are filled with original thought and with that force which, according to him, participates in the very nature of the world. Any theoretical morality is absurd: the love of power is the greatest instrument of civilization, since it is the desire to acquire command over nature. This philosophy, more or less disguised in M. Jules de Gaultier, is to be found in the writings of M. Lévy Bruhl, M. Pradines, M. Rauh, and M. Chide, and from in between the pages of all their volumes peeps the countenance of M. Bergson. The same ideas are also to be found in the work of that great student of sociology, M. Durkheim. M. Durkheim would not trust conscience out of his sight. Conscience is a bad judge of all that takes place at the bottom of our being, because it does not penetrate there. Moral dicta have value only in so far as they demand our adherence from a social point of view. Dr. Forneval, in *l'Anneau d'Améthyste,* speaks practically the same language. The same ideas are to be found more or less hidden in the writings of Charles Maurras, frankly developed by M. Maurice Barrès. Man, being an animal, must obey social laws which are strong only in so far as they are supported by tradition: by facts or promises of facts which heredity has created in us.

All this worshipping of fact and action would be but an anti-intellectualism were it not that all these men believe in a cosmos moving by progressive scientific method and not by leaps or sallies. But at the same time it would be amusing and pathetic to show how many different doctrines have been born of this respect for fact: the most extravagant individualism, and also respect of tradition; integral royalism, and also anarchy pure and simple. If the secret spring of our action lies never in our intellect but in the more intimate unexplored kingdom within us, that of the subconscious forces which plunge into a mysterious past, poetry as a divine *mania* rules the *universe;* and it would be more worth while to show the pathetic side of such a spectacle — poor humanity overwhelmed with the realization of life's shortness concentrating all its power in a desperate effort to feel and act.

Another tendency very much akin to the preceding ones is that seen in the frame of mind of M. Georges Sorel, who would have us return to a state of society wherein everything would be at the same time instinctive and heroic. Apostle of a warlike mysticism, M. Sorel professes to be Bergson's disciple, and one may wonder whether his inspirations are flashes of the Bergsonian spirit in unison with scientific rationalism, or whether they are simply the outcome of the French desire for a quickened sense of life.

In his *Réflexions sur la Violence,* as well as his *Illusions du Progrès,* M. Sorel adopts the Bergsonian philosophy viewed from a certain angle in order to declare that the *prolétariat* should give free rein to its instincts, that revolutionary movement may be spontaneous and original in the Bergsonian sense; the holy violence of the universal strike pleases his bellicose imagination. Never has M. Bergson's theory of pure duration been put to such use: for this mysticism which believes in a truly holy alliance between our deeper self and the Power directing the Universe, this heroic enthusiasm developed by the most absolute disinterestedness, will give magnificent impetus to our artistic powers, our joys, our enthusiasm, our inventive spirit, all of which are at the summit of the scale of human values. Who knows whether man, finally free, may not triumph even over death?

But one must not be led to making of the disinterested syndicalist the Bergsonian hero *par excellence.* Very few partisans of the universal strike have even a nodding acquaintance with Bergson's writings. He is merely a name for them, just as Jean Jacques was for so many revolutionaries of 1789.

Thus on every side we see the extolling of the deep self at the expense of the superficial self; it is a real revolution in thought, wherein the effort of the human mind constantly strives to find itself in the presence of the Infinite, and like M. Bergeret peopling the universe with seductive forms and sublime thoughts. If it be true that every philosophic system is the work of its author's temperament, it is even more true that every generation collaborates with its favorite authors.   Its great writers, philosophers or poets express each in his own way what is in embryo at the bottom of the mind of the lettered public.   Thus, even if we would not go so far as accepting the theory dear to M. James and M. Boirac,* which would make of our mind something spread abroad outside itself and not enclosed in a cranium, we must confess that the Press by disseminating the ideas of the moment contributes towards making out of the invisible multitude of its contemporaries one vast common spirit which helps genius to bring forth its inventions.

*See *The Psychology of the Future*, by Emile Boirac, translated and edited by W. de Kerlor.   London, Kegan Paul, Trubuer & Co., Ltd.

HENRI BERGSON

W E are told that Madame de Staël, one evening after dinner, asked the German philosopher Fichte to explain his philosophy to her — "in a few words." We are not told how Fichte answered. We may guess. It was really rather foolish of Madame de Staël to make that request, for metaphysics is stranger, more marvellous than the land of Nod. That is why one likes M. Bergson for having made statements that seem paradoxical, or even incredible, and for having written his *Creative Evolution,* the most wonderful poem the French have latterly produced. Systems of philosophy are heroic fictions which appeal to our imagination, but unhappily they are nearly always limited to a few centuries, often to their own, and we must, therefore, often take them with a grain of salt. M. Bergson knows this as well as any one, for his method aims at resembling that of nature which builds organic structures, not after the manner of a manufacturer, but after that of an artist. We are too intellectual, he tells us, and that is clever of him, for thereby he cuts the ground from under his critics' feet.

In spite of all that pedants think and say, philosophy is the art of seeing things as they are, and M. Bergson is a past master in that art. Much will be forgiven him for his book on laughter.*

*Laughter. Authorized translation by Cloudlesley Brereton and Fred Rothwell. Macmillan, 1911.

The man who perceives so nicely that "rigidity, automatism, absentmindedness and unsociability are all inextricably entwined," and all serve as ingredients to the making up of the comic in character, gives us in those words a very solid pledge of soundness. The philosopher who knows the social functions of laughter is a very sane man. "A rogue alive to the ludicrous is still convertible," says Emerson. Let all critics of M. Bergson's doctrine please note the fact: a philosopher alive to the ludicrous is a dangerous adversary.

Newton achieved immortal fame, according to Voltaire, because he one day saw an apple fall off a tree. Let us then suppose that M. Bergson's renown comes from his having one day seen a billiard ball roll along the green cloth of a billiard table. We have all seen billiard balls roll along, without metaphysics being any the better or worse for that. But M. Bergson happened to be thinking of Zeno of Elea whose riddles on motion have kept the philosophers busy for close on twenty-four centuries. Now Zeno of Elea would say: "At every moment the ball you think moving is motionless, for it cannot have time to move, that is to occupy at least two successive positions, unless at least two moments are allowed it. At a given moment, therefore, it is at rest at a given point, since it is there; nor does it move from the point where it is not yet, since it is not there. Motionless in each point of its course, it is motionless during all the time that it is moving. Its so-called motion is a succession of immobilities." M. Bergson reflected that the movement of the ball, which at first glance, as Zeno had said, seemed decomposable *ad libitum,* was nothing of the sort: that, although the moving ball occupied, one after the other, a series of imaginary points on the line, motion itself had nothing to do with a line. To say that the rolling of a ball is a series of points traversed by the ball is to attribute to it a series of immobilities. And how can movement be reconstituted out of these immobilities?

Whenever I imagine a trajectory, my mind always wants to deal with an equation; i. e., my mind wishes to picture to itself the positions occupied by a certain body moving in space; and in the case of the billiard ball my imagination immediately calls up the picture of the horizontal straight line which I have been taught is the shortest distance between two points.

But in reality the ball, though it has created distinct movements by the mere fact of occupying different positions, has made one indivisible movement, which ceases to be a movement from the moment I stop it in my mind, or stop the ball with my hand, or when the ball stops of itself. Of course there is a series of intermediate stages in the path traversed by the ball; but as places of rest they are purely imaginary, since the ball passes on, and its passage is movement.

Let the reader consult M. Bergson's book *Time and Free Will* and his short Treatise *"La Perception du Changement,"* he will see that the Eleatic paradox is M. Bergson's great battle horse. And quite right, too. For it is thanks to Zeno that M. Bergson has made his great discovery, that "duration has no moments which are identical or external to one another, being essentially heterogeneous, continuous, and with no analogy to number."*

Thus Bergson was led to make a great distinc-

Time and Free Will, p. 120. Authorized translation by F. L. Pogson, M.A.

tion between time and space. Space, as represented
by the ball's rolling, is nothing but mathematical
time.   Science, when dealing with movement, sub-
stitutes for concrete movement the trajectory of
the moving object, and conceives it as a series
of positions.   Science is right when foretelling an
astronomical phenomenon, but often wrong when
foretelling a psychological one. *Why?* Because "the
future of the material universe, although contem-
poraneous with the future of a conscious being, has
no analogy to it," or if you like, because our states
of consciousness are processes and not things,
because they are alive and constantly changing.
If the orbit of a planet can be perceived all at once,
it is because its successive positions are the only
things that matter.

"In order to put our finger on this vital difference,
let us assume for a moment that some mischievous
genius, more powerful still than the mischievous
genius conjured up by Descartes, decreed that all
the movements of the universe should go twice as
fast.   There would be no change in astronomical
phenomena, or at any rate in the equations which
enable us to foresee them, for in these equations
the symbol t does not stand for a duration, but for a
relation between two durations, for a certain number
of units of time, in short, for a certain number of
simultaneities: these simultaneities, these coinci-
dences, would still take place in equal number; only
the intervals which separate them would have
diminished, but these intervals never make their
appearance in our calculations.   Now these intervals are just duration lived, duration which our
consciousness perceives, and our consciousness
would soon inform us of a shortening of the day if
we had not experienced the usual amount of dura-

tion between sunrise and sunset. No doubt it would not measure this shortening, and perhaps it would not even perceive it immediately as a change of quantity; but it would realize in some way or other a decline in the usual storing up of experience, a change in the progress usually accomplished between sunrise and sunset."*

After all, the "mischievous genius" would really have the Mad Hatter's conception of time — when he says to Alice, "Now if only you kept on good terms with Time he'd do almost anything you liked with the clock. For instance, suppose it were nine o'clock in the morning, just time to begin lessons, you'd only have to whisper a hint to Time, and round goes the clock in a twinkling! Half past one, time for dinner." — This is mathematical time — "That would be grand, certainly," said Alice thoughtfully, "but, then — I shouldn't be hungry for it, you know." This is real time.

True time, of which we have an intuition, when we watch the ball rolling, is not a mathematical proportion: it is constituted by deep-seated conscious states, and when our ego allows itself to live, and does not separate its present state from its former states, those states intermingle in such a way that one cannot tell whether they are one or several. Our joys, our griefs, for instance, are processes and not fixed enduring objects. And the moment we try to examine them, we alter their nature *ipso facto*. Hence the extreme difficulty of the analytic observation of such mental phenomena.

One wonders whether M. Bergson ever read Coleridge. In any case those who know and appreciate Coleridge's notebooks have already taken the first steps towards a knowledge of Bergson. I know

Time and Free Will, pp. 193, 194.

of no clearer commentary upon Bergson's theory
of duration than this passage from the poet-philo-
sopher of Highbury, and if I quote it, it is not for
the very cheap pleasure of seeking one of the hidden
springs of Bergsonism, but solely in order to make
Bergson better understood on a very essential point
of his doctrine.   Here is the passage:

> "How opposite to nature and the fact, to talk
> of the 'one moment' of Hume, of our whole being
> an aggregate of successive sensations!   Who ever
> felt a single sensation?   Is not every one at the
> same moment conscious that there co-exist a
> thousand others, a darker shade, or less light,
> even as when I fix my attention on a white house
> or a grey bare hill, or rather a long ridge that
> runs out of sight each way (how often I want
> the German *Unübersekbar!*) (untranslatable) —
> the pretended sight sensation, is it anything more
> than the light point in every picture either of
> nature or of a good painter? and again, subord-
> inately, in every component part of the picture?
> And what is a moment? succession with inter-
> space? Absurdity! It is evidently only the *licht-
> punkt* in the indivisible undivided duration."[*]

In this way, as it seems to me, Bergson naturally
came to believe that the life of our mind was a
movement like that of the billiard ball.   Our states
of consciousness become fused in one another and
form the indivisible whole which makes up our
personality.   "Within our ego there is succession
without mutual externality; outside the ego, in pure
space, there is mutual externality without succession."[†] The passage occurs in *Time and Free Will*,

[*]*Anima poetae*, pp. 102-103, from the unpublished notebooks of
S. T. Coleridge.   London, Heinnemann, 1916.   Edited by Ernest
Hartley Coleridge.
[†]*Time and Free Will*, p. 108.

perhaps the most important of all M. Bergson's books, since he explains and establishes in it the difference he marks between scientific and psychological time. Bergson takes his place beside Berkeley, who had pointed out the difference between space as understood by the mathematician and space as understood by the psychologist.

When we speak separately of our desires, our wishes, our thoughts, we fall into the same error as when we imagine the states of immobility in the billiard ball's path. Sentiments, ideas, longings, these are all the artificial inaccurate labels — albeit convenient, if not indispensable — which we place upon an ever moving, ever acting, ever flowing reality. And yet we keep our personality intact, its unity is real. We realize it when, for instance, the smell of new-mown hay or of burning wood, or a glimpse of a river through the willows, sets us thinking of charming moments of our childhood. Thus also the picture of a great master reveals his whole soul. Our gestures reveal ours. Our states of consciousness are each of them the entire mind.

We might say that our mind is a billiard ball, only with this difference, that it is ever changing, ripening, creating, growing larger, as it is pushed along. It is a flux, a *continuum,* a long musical composition ever swelling and broadening, in which the opening phrase recurs, coloring the whole. Hence our personality. If it be objected that we cannot think the reality of the life process, I answer that we can live it. Indeed we do live it, witness the whole history of mankind. Life is a perpetual creation, a perpetual birth. It is for each one of us to evoke his closest personal recollections, and then see if the French philosopher has not sounded the depths of our being.

Life should be a never-ending journey through
towns and books and men and things, because every
new impression penetrates into all the others and
gives new life to the mind. That is why love, which
changes for the lover all that he perceives, is master
of the universe. It is the eternal elixir of youth.
Again, that is why a powerful imagination which
deforms or reforms everything is such a miraculous
thing, consecrating for all time the work of the poet.
"We might ask ourselves whether Nature is beautiful otherwise than through meeting by chance certain processes of one art, and whether art is not
prior to Nature" (page 14, *Time and Free Will*).
That is the secret of the fascination of Bergson's
doctrine; it appeals to those souls who seek in their
solitude for renewal, and who ask of philosophy not
only the meaning of their existence upon earth, but
a kind of satisfaction for their appetite for the
subliminal.

Bergson shows us that it is a great misfortune
that "in the humanity of which we are part,
intuition is almost completely sacrificed to
intellect." But what is intuition? For M. Bergson,
"it is a lamp almost extinguished, which only
glimmers wherever a vital interest is at stake. On
our personality, on our liberty, on the place we
occupy in the whole of nature, on our origin and
and perhaps also on our destiny, it throws a light
feeble and vacillating, but which none the less
pierces the darkness of the night in which the
intellect leaves us."

There is no idea upon which Bergson has dwelt
so much, nor about which he has been so misunderstood, some critics going as far as to see in him
an anti-intellectualist. He was the first to wish to
give a scientific foundation to the old, familiar

word, intuition. All the spiritualistic philosophers
before him had appealed to intuition to establish
those theses which we regard as essential to our
moral well being: freewill, immortality of the soul,
belief in God. They all declared that intuition was
a part of intellect. But Bergson will admit only
that intellect is the knowledge of the relationships
of a given form, "it is a natural power of relating
an object to an object, or a part to a part, or an
aspect to an aspect — in short of drawing conclusions when in possession of the premises, of proceed-
ing from what has been learned to what is still unknown. It does not say "this is," it only says that
"if the conditions are such, such will be the con-
ditioned."

Bergson said that if intuition is intellect, since
intellect only possesses an external empty knowledge, the spiritualistic theses constructed upon
intellect fall down like a pack of cards. But if
intuition is not of the same order as intellect, if
it is a knowledge of the world from within, these
fleeting revelations on our liberty, on our origin,
on our destiny have a real foundation in life itself.
"The great error of the doctrines on the spirit
has been the idea that by isolating the spiritual
life from all the rest, by suspending it in space as
high as possible above the earth, they were placing
it beyond attack, as if they were not thereby simply
exposing it to be taken as an effect of mirage."*

Bergson's declaration that intuition, like instinct, belonged to life, was a stroke of genius. Man
is made up both of intellect and intuition. But it is
by instinct — i. e., intuition — that he comes close
to reality. "The most essential of the primary
instincts are really vital processes." Instinctive

*Creative Evolution, p. 283. Op. cit., p. 175.

processes are, as it were, the continuation of those organic processes which we constantly see in action around us and through which we participate in the Great Becoming. And Bergson thinks of the baby chick which breaks its shell with a peck of its beak, — acting by instinct, carrying on the movement which has borne it through embryonic life. Then he remembers the famous entomological observations of Fabre and others, and thus deep study has convinced him that instinct is not resolvable into intelligent elements, that Aristotle's idea regarding the series of living beings as unilinear was false, and he boldly declares that instinct and intuition are a prolongation of life, are life itself, and that it follows that our ideas of God and destiny are substantial and true.

I may be mistaken, but that is how I see the natural development of Bergson's thought. He first discovered what was real time, he saw that our deep-seated conscious states were like a musical composition being continually amplified; this led him to see that our spiritual life was a perpetual creation, and that the great obstacle to this perpetual birth was that part of the mind we call intellect, but that, on the other hand, we had intuition, a kind of superior instinct, which, far from detaching us from the empirical world, showed us its reality and truth. In other terms, Bergson's idea of time begot his conception of intellect and intuition, his conception of science, his conception of metaphysics, and finally his conception of the universe considered as the manifestation of a spiritual principle.

At any rate it looks as if Bergson had set off from this conception of spiritual life and arrived at this conception of the visible world. The world is like our spiritual life — a flux, it is forever changing. Immobility is only the greatest illusion among the countless illusions around us.

Here, as is his habit, Bergson takes his stand upon science. "Faraday was right who said that all the atoms interpenetrate and that each of them filled the world.' Things and states are only views taken by our mind, of becoming. There are no things, there are only actions.*

Such is the philosophy of children who are not too convinced of the reality of their surroundings. Stevenson knew that, too:

> "Let the sofa be mountains, the carpets be sea,
> There I'll establish a garden for me."

Children do not separate the real from the imagined. They live in a world of their own, which is as real to them as the scholar's or philosopher's is to him. The "grown-up" who accuses the child of lying falls into gross error, for the child is ignorant of falsehood as he is ignorant of truth; he has an inner sense of the world which confuses images with the things themselves. How, then, does the philosopher act towards the universe, towards a table, for example? If I am to believe the Hon. Bertrand Russell, a table is for Leibnitz a community of souls; for Berkeley, an idea in the mind of God; and if I accept what Professor H. C. Jones tells me, a table is nothing other than a collection of electrical charges in violent motion. If that is really so, there was nothing so strange in Alice's seeing the Cheshire cat's grin vanish and appear again alone; the cat's grin is merely a vibration which lasts rather longer than the other vibrations.

*_Creative Evolution_, pp. 214 and 261.

II

The theory of exterior perception is the corner stone of Bergson's philosophy; it is that theory which upholds his theory of knowledge and all that theory of the natural sympathy which makes us penetrate most deeply into the reality with which we are surrounded. In studying Bergson we must always bear in mind that the simple facts of consciousness, to whose pure quality he was the first to draw our attention, are similar to the facts of instinct, as instanced, for example, in certain kinds of wasps who attack and paralyze their victim with a knowledge and skill possessed by few human surgeons.

Bergson in his acute study of Berkeley* has given us the example of what the study of a philosopher by philosophic intuition should be. After having indicated the various influences undergone by Berkeley, he penetrates into his doctrine like the wasp which looks at its victim from within, and he shows us Intuition guiding the Bishop of Cloyne in his researches and meditations. He rails in pleasant vein at those who, in order to reconstruct externally Berkeley's doctrine, seek its origin among the neo-Platonists, Hobbes, Descartes or Malebranche, and we might follow his example and, borrowing his own image, gently tease those who speak of the Bergsonian salad and declare that the oil of his wonderful style, the vinegar of his impatience with the materialism of his times, are useful only for adding flavor to a mixture of the herbs of neo-Platonist and German philosophy, dusted over with a salt of Ravaisson and William James.

*L'Intuition philosophique, Revue de Metaphysique et de Morale, 1911.

If we in our turn are to discover the image or concept directing Bergson in his researches, we must first put on one side all the images with which he embellishes his works — such as the shell bursting into fragments which are again shells, or the reservoir filled with boiling water from which steam is issuing. These are the tricks of the poet, mere illustrations of his thought, but they are not its starting point. Bergson has understood Berkeley's thought so well because he has lived it; and the study to which we refer, and in which he has put the best of himself, is vivified by that Intuition which must serve us as guide. Not only do we see only what we have eyes to see, as Bergson teaches us, but we see well only when we "put back our being into our will." "Is it not patent," he asks, "that the philosopher's first step, while his thought is still uncertain, is to reject definitely certain things? Later he may vary in what he affirms, he will not vary in what he denies."

So that with Mr. Bergson the first impulse was a movement of reaction against contemporary naturalism, because of his inability to accept a blind mechanism as efficient cause of our knowledge of reality.

The profound intuition he had of our psychic states was this: they do not constitute a numerical multiplicity. We attribute that to them as we project them symbolically into space. But in themselves they are pure quality and, as such, incommensurable. There is no fixed quantity of spiritual energy in the world. We break up our inner life into a multiplicity of fragmentary states which we imagine to be fixed and which are not; and we act in the same way when we perceive the external world. We cut reality up into slices when we situate it in space.

Or, to express the same idea differently, we might say that the explanation of the problem of knowledge is not to be found in the idealistic theory wherein the spirit does not emerge from itself, nor in the materialistic theory which declares that all objects are independent things able to exist without the mind.

How does Bergson perceive matter? In the same way, I think, as Berkeley perceives it (I purposely use Bergson's own words), "as a thin transparent film situated between man and God." Whatever differences there may be between Berkeley and Bergson — differences upon which Bergson has dwelt in *Matter and Memory,* and although Bergson has not yet composed his theodicy — these two philosophers have the same conception of the world. The one will call bodies *ideas,* the other will call them *images.* And both will mean by that, firstly, that things really are what we perceive them to be, that our senses do not deceive us and that there is not behind the sensible qualities of things a matter impossible to conceive; and, secondly, that the vital Force (the one will call it God, the other the Impetus of Life) has created Intellect to know the world of matter, and has given to matter the appearance of an existence spread out in space. Berkeley in this way arrives at saying that Nature is the language in which God speaks to man. Bergson is not so very far from Berkeley in spite of appearances. When he declares with great insistence that "intellect and matter have progressively adapted themselves one to the other in order to attain at last a common form," he places God near at hand, in the time which we feel to be the very stuff of our life.

The worlds and beings we see around us have

their origin and life in the single force which Bergson calls supraconsciousness, above matter and beyond it. For him the idea of creation is merged in that of growth, "God having nothing of the already made." As for inert matter, its immobility is an appearance, purely and simply. Since everything is movement, since movement is reality itself, "what we call immobility is a certain state of things identical or analogous with what happens when two trains run with the same speed, in the same direction, upon parallel lines; each train seems motionless to the travellers seated in the other — immobility being that which our intellect desires, we make a reality of it, an absolute, and we see in movement something adding itself thereto." And a little further on he adds: "All the mechanism of our perception of things, like that of our action upon things, has been regulated in order to here arrange, between the external and internal mobility, a situation analogous to our two trains, doubtless more complicated, but of the same kind."*

Matter then resolves into vibrations: for that is all Bergson leaves to matter, and it was rendered equally bare by the philosophy of Berkeley. Bergson then is not a realist, because, in his view, the realists break up, for the greater convenience of practical life, the continuity of the real. They set up as absolute that division of matter "which, in our view, is hardly anything but an outward projection of human needs." "Pure intuition, external or internal, is that of an undivided continuity;" . . . "the divisibility of matter is entirely relative to our action thereon."†

This brings us back to Berkeley's point of view,

---

*Perception du changement, p. 20, u. & seq.
†Matter and Memory, pp. 215, 239, 292.

as expressed by Bergson: "La matière est inextensive à notre représentation, elle n'a pas d'intérieur, pas de dessous, elle ne cache rien, ne renferme rien, elle ne possède ni puissances, ni virtualités d'aucune espèce, elle est étalée en surface, etc."*

Bergson will say there are no things, there are only actions. This once grasped, it is easy to understand Bergson's theory of perception. We are in whatever we perceive. I am part of the scent of the lilac as it comes into my window. I exist in the organ vibrations which pierce the cathedral walls. My being is prolonged in things, and I possess the universe in my sensations. Venus rising from the ocean waves, such is the image of the awakening of ourself in the bosom of all things. I know of no better paraphrase of Bergsonian perception than Claudel's famous passage in his poem *"L'Esprit et l'Eau"* (*Cinq Grandes Odes*):

"Où que je tourne la tête
J'envisage l'immense octave de la Création!
Le monde s'ouvre et si large qu'en soit l'empan, mon regard le
    traverse d'un bout à l'autre.
J'ai pesé le soleil ainsi qu'un gros mouton que deux hommes forts
    suspendent à une perche entre leurs épaules.
J'ai recensé l'armée des Cieux et j'en ai dressé état,
Depuis les grandes Figures qui se penchent sur le vieillard Océan
Jusqu'au feu le plus rare englouti dans le plus profond abîme,
Ainsi que le Pacifique bleu-sombre où le baleinier épie l'évent d'un
    souffleur comme un duvet blanc.
Vous êtes pris et d'un bout du monde jusqu'à l'autre autour de
    vous
J'ai tendu l'immense rets de ma connaissance†
Comme la phrase qui prend aux cuivres
Gagne les bois et progressivement envahit les profondeurs de
    l'orchestre
Et comme les éruptions du soleil

*Revue de Metaphysique et de Morale. 1911. L'Intuition Philo-
where except in man consciousness has let itself be caught in the
net whose meshes it tried to pass through." Also p. 213: "Mind uses
space like a net . . . which thrown over matter divides it. . . ."
sophique.

†A Bergsonian image.   Cf. *Creative Evolution*, p. 278: "Every-

Se répercutent sur la terre en crise d'eau et en raz de murée,
Ainsi du plus grand Ange qui vous voit jusqu'au caillou de la
  route et d'un bout de votre création jusqu'à l'autre,
Il ne cesse point continuité non plus que de l'âme au corps."

But not only is there *union* between object and
subject in perception, there is *unity*, declares
M. Bergson. His metaphysics demand that. The
spiritual forces working in the universe are within
us. The beneficent reality in which we bathe is
itself consciousness, and our perception, aided naturally by our memory, makes us penetrate into that
creative force which has succeeded, by traversing
matter, in arriving at something which is realized
only in man.

In this way may be explained the phenomena of
telepathy, suggestion, second sight, which show the
spirit breaking through the bonds of the body. So
also may be explained the fact that man guesses
the secrets of nature; his presentiments, his intuitions, are flashes of illumination sent by the Great
Reality. So again may be explained the interpenetration of different consciousnesses, and the fact that
old married couples grow alike in face and mind, or
that the words of certain great mystics have been
anticipations of future truths.*

On the other hand, our nature, as Pascal finely
guessed, is only a first habit; our feelings, our concepts, our gestures, have become in time a force
which acts within us, which creates an incessant
novelty and in this way is stronger than matter in creating in its turn; "the living being
is above all a thoroughfare." Life is always
free, spontaneous, incalculable. Carlyle's *Essay on*

---

*"An identical process must have cut out matter and the intel-
lect, at the same time, from a stuff that contained both. Into this
reality we shall get back more and more completely, in proportion
as we compel ourselves to transcend pure intelligence." *Creative Evolution*, p. 210.

Cromwell is an excellent explanation of this doctrine.

Consciousness, then, is the great, the only reality. Since Descartes we have been taught that mind and matter were two realities of different nature and irreducible to unity. But Bergson separates himself from such doctrine, which leads either to a *naïve* realism according to which mind is only an epiphenomenon or to a subtle idealism which declares that all reality is only mental. Reality is movement, indivisible Duration, Universal Becoming. It is the common origin whence come matter and intellect, and intellect was evolved only to deal with matter.

Perception is, therefore, action's tool used by our body to cut into the future: it is the point of the knife dividing the universal flow. The resulting slice is what we call matter, that is to say, a selection and contraction of images in duration. What constitutes the image in each case is the selection and contraction effected by memory. This spiritual activity which prolongs the past into the present plays then a most important part: it renders perception possible.

Without wishing to try to summarize the well-packed pages of *Matter and Memory,* nor to enter into the discussion of details, we may here remind the reader that for M. Bergson perception is the great act of Life. We are only to resign ourselves to conception, when perception is lacking.* Happily Art is there to show us that an extension of our faculties is possible. The poet, painter and musician have perceived in nature a host of aspects which we have doubtless seen but which we have not really noticed. Bergson's book on *Laughter* is

Perception du Changement, p. 5 et seq.

entirely based on this intuition that Art is a more
direct vision of reality, because the artist places
himself back within the object by his *sympathy*.
Never was M. Bergson better inspired than in his
passage on music, because music is the expression
of thoughts so profound that words are powerless
to express them. Here again, like Berkeley, Bergson shows the greatest distrust of language. Abstraction has created a veil of symbols which hides
Reality from us. Music is one of the dynamic
schemes, motive rather than representative, a natural outpouring inexpressible in itself, the very manifestation of the activity which pushes the world
forward, vibrations laden with pure emotion which
enable us to recover contact with Life. And M.
Bergson has constant recourse to music to make
us understand his theory. "Let us listen to a
melody, letting ourselves be lulled by it: have we
not the clear perception of a movement which is
attached to no mobile, of a change without anything
changing? The change is self-sufficing, it is the
thing itself."*

Samuel Butler, in his *The Way of All Flesh*, has
an amusing passage which always reminds me of
certain passages in *Matter and Memory*. I mean
the advice given by the Doctor when consulted for
the cure of Ernest Pontifex. "I have found the
Zoological Gardens of service to many of my
patients. I should prescribe for Mr. Pontifex a
course of the larger mammals. Don't let him think
he is taking them medicinally, but let him go to
their house twice a week for a fortnight, and stay
with the hippopotamus, the rhinoceros and the
elephants till they begin to bore him. I find these

Perception du Changement, p. 24.

beasts do my patients more good than any others. The monkeys are not a wide enough cross; they do not stimulate sufficiently. The larger carnivora are unsympathetic. The reptiles are worse than useless, and the marsupials are not much better. Birds again, except parrots, are not very beneficial; but he may look at them now and again, but with the elephants and the pig tribe generally he should mix as freely as possible.''

Readers of Butler will remember how beneficial the treatment proved, and how the hero drank in great draughts of these animals' lives to the regeneration of his own. We may seem to be some way from *Matter and Memory,* but in reality we are not far. For Bergson, as for Butler, the line separating things from their surroundings is in no wise clearly defined. Just as within ourselves no sensation can be detached, or isolated from the states of consciousness with which it is linked, so in the universe there is no such thing as an isolated object: between the world of mind and the world of matter, there is contest, of course, but first of all there are action and interaction. Consciousness and matter arrive at an understanding, for matter contains a kind of elasticity which its adversary, life, turns to its profit. Matter is indivisible like consciousness, and sensation is extensive like matter.

If this be the case (and Bergson founds his *Creative Evolution* upon this contest between consciousness and matter), it is quite comprehensible that the Zoological Gardens should be an excellent school of psychotherapy. We have only to look back upon our childhood to understand this saying of Bergson's, which Butler might have signed: ''Spirit borrows from matter the perceptions in which it feeds and restores them to matter

in the form of movements which it has stamped
with its freedom." The child does not separate
himself from his surrounding objects. His representation is, to begin with, impersonal. It is only
later that he externalizes his concepts in relation to
one another. But we become as children again in
our day-dreams, in those states of the soul in which
the external world is not distinct from us, but in
which life appears a series of wonderful possibilities.

On the whole, with Bergson we are in the world
of Change. We are constantly changing, and each
of our changing states is in itself a change. There
is a continuity in our discontinuity, and discontinuity in our continuity. Bergson has been called
the modern Heraclitus, but we must be very sure
what is meant by that. Certainly he would say that,
supposing our earth were destroyed by fire, the
conflagration of the universe would be nothing but
a transition to a new universe. But he is a Heraclitus who has read his philosophic predecessors and
has reflected and consequently thinks of safeguard-
ing truth from this flux. He saw clearly that, when
he declared nothing was fixed, he was giving himself
up, bound hand and foot, to the mercies of the
skeptic. Therefore, as soon as he has overthrown
the temple of truth built by human intellect, he
orders at once a more mysterious one to be made by
intuition.

Intellect can give us only very relative, if very
practical, ideas of an object. Intuition enables us
to enter into that object. Since reality is all change
and flux, we enter into it for a moment of this flux;
so that in the end we are only taking part in the
Eternal Becoming, mere artisans, conscious or unconscious, of the divine which creates itself in every

age. "In the Shakespearean drama," Coleridge writes, fresh from the schools of Germany, "there is a vitality which grows and evolves itself from within." Substitute universe for Shakespearean drama, and you have Bergson's doctrine in a nutshell.

It is clearly more than easy to ridicule this conception, and the famous passage in the third book of *Pantagruel* comes uninvited to mind, when Panurge, under pretense of praising debtors and borrowers, laughs at all the "doctrinaires," all makers of systems, all those who think that they have discovered in a Word the master key to all the locks of nature, the Open Sesame to all its doors. And where Panurge uses the word *debt*, I can imagine an Anatole France using the word *duration*. "*Debt* is the great soul of the universe. . . . A cosmos without debts! . . . Then among the planets would be no regular course; all would be in disorder. Jupiter reckoning himself to be nothing indebted unto Saturn would go near to detrude him out of his sphere. . . . . The moon will remain bloody and obscure," etc., etc.

But it must be admitted that for all those who do not accept the doctrine of a revealed religion, the Bergsonian system offers an excellent solution of most of the difficulties of contemporary philosophy.

When Kant asks himself whether the *categories* of the human mind do not mutilate reality on a Procrustean bed, Darwin and his disciples, far from refuting, support his argument by showing that human reason and animal instinct are only adaptations of human organism for the furtherance of life in given surroundings. Then, at that point, Bergson intervenes and shows us that intuition, though it is like instinct in one sense, differs from it in that it is not a biological but a spiritual instrument, enabling us to see the world in a simple flux.

The great writer of whom one is reminded here and whose influence was, and is, greater even than that of Bergson in Anglo-Saxon countries is William James. If we wish to measure the sum of our indebtedness to these men we have only to examine, in perusing our daily papers, to what extent our ways of thinking are moulded, consciously or unconsciously, by their universal touch. It will be one of the tasks of the historian of the future to apportion to each of these writers not only his particular share of influence upon us, but also the exact imprint they had on each other. Briefly, and in order to avoid paying to the one tribute which might appear to be criticism of the other, let it be said of both that their common sense, their catholic sympathies, their love of energy and life and human endeavor, their sense of individual as well as relative values, their wide and scientific outlook upon life, have led them to see that Darwinism was at bottom a doctrine of life and freedom, spontaneity and spirituality.

Of the two William James is the clearer, being more human and taking Philosophy by the hand as a child in leading strings. James loves to talk with the man in the street, to harass him with words of wisdom and vituperate against the flesh and the devil. He is dominated by a Puritan ardor, intrepity and the love of virtue, together with a touch of the spirit of the Norman adventurer. Bergson is more academic, more aloof, more *amoral,* yet underlying the coldness of the philosopher we can see blazing up countless mingled Gallic and Hebraic creations and inventions, and can feel their warmth. William James's philosophy is like a boy's running away to sea with all its wonderful possibilities. Bergson's audacity of thought, great as it is, does not prevent his sometimes seeing the Absolute in the shape of a Professor of the "Collège de France."

Still, when all is said and done, their philosophy, by placing Spirit above intellect and declaring that above reason there is a more direct source of consciousness, intuition, and leading as it does directly to ethics, is singularly alike. It consists, above and before all, in admitting that there are limits to our faculty of comprehension: limits laid down by ourselves and by Nature; and it insists upon our making a serious effort to enrich our ethical consciousness. James asks us first and foremost to act and work; Bergson declares that creative energy is insight. James demands that we should be dead to reason in order to become perfect Christians. Bergson demands that we should be dead to the "categories" of our intellect in order to become perfect philosophers. James declares that we are created to act rather than to chop logic, and Bergson in his turn affirms that we are made much more for action than for thought. But both agree, "We must take things by storm; we must thrust intelligence outside itself by an act of will."

Both thinkers react against a certain science of their age and at the same time against a certain literature made up of rebellion against laws and order. It is of the greatest interest to watch how these two thinkers, after having exalted energy and boldness, affirm that ethics and not temperament are the supreme facts to which allegiance must be owned, and how in this way they pass from the narrow philosophy of subjectivism to the wide field of objectivism.

This is not the place to follow up a parallel which imposes itself upon every reader who knows the two writers, but it is interesting to note that James's presbyterianism had the same result as Bergson's amoralism: it silenced the sentimental whimperings of temperament and bade them act in manly fashion. The doctrines which admit the omnipotence of a superior and awful Being are also the doctrines which lay greatest stress upon the importance of energy, of courage, and the heroic virtues, as are also those which declare that creation "is not a mystery; we experience it in ourselves when we act freely." None acquainted with the play of our intellect will be surprised at this attraction of contraries.

What scientific feeling revealed to James, æsthetic feeling revealed to Bergson: the absolute error of scientists in claiming to measure the scope of our sensations; the folly, in a word, of the science called psychophysics. Every sensation as it grows becomes transformed. It is no more possible to conceive the sum of our difference between two sensations than it is to draw a boundary line between memory and consciousness.

Bergson realized that very clearly, and was led thereby to see and to teach that the body was utilized by the mind, or rather that "The spirit overflows the brain on every side, and cerebral activity corresponds only to an infinitesimal part of mental activity."* His famous thesis *Time and Free Will* is devoted to showing that mathematical laws, though they may explain the material universe, are powerless to explain the world of our soul. Our Psyche is not merely the interpreter who translates by

---

*Cf. *L'âme et le corps. Conférence faite par M. Bergson. Le Matérialisme actuel.* Paris, Flammarion, 1914.

thought and feeling the things which our body expresses in extent and in movement. Our Psyche is original, is free, is capable of creating: above all, she is the mistress of the body which she makes her slave.

But, whether we will or no, moral questions will have themselves asked in philosophy. If existence is not one great struggle for greater good, it is of no more worth than those plays which delighted our childhood, wherein virtue was always rewarded and vice duly punished. But a philosopher like Bergson who has reflected upon Reality is forced in spite of himself, even though his work aims at being or seeming entirely a-moral,— into the poignant realization of a war to the knife between the powers of good and evil, between barbarism and liberty. Within us all is a spiritual power in which we can take refuge and meditate at ease: it is there that are to be found the deep roots of our personality communicating with all nature.

That is what Bergson realized so fully, and that part of his philosophy will always appeal to a spirit with a passion for the ideal.

It is very interesting to see in what light many Frenchmen have considered Bergson and stripped him of his Anglo-Saxon garments. Most of Bergson's admirers have affected to see in him only the philosopher for whom our reason is a mere collection of scraps, a heap of rubbish.

After all, Bergson's book on laughter is the best commentary on his doctrine. The philosopher who is always crying, "Automatism is our great enemy," is the apostle of elasticity of character. When a man becomes a man of one idea, a pure mechanism, he should be laughed at. Spirituality is a progress to ever new creations. Let us praise the poet or writer who, intoxicated with the heady wine of his own imagination, writes poems or novels full of daring thoughts. That is the explanation of Bergson's influence upon so many of his contemporaries, in particular of his influence upon Georges Sorel,* and his disciple, Edouard Berth. Indeed, both these men appear sometimes to be juggling with Bergson's doctrine. The idea that since motion is an indivisible whole, a general strike must be an indivisible whole, only proves that, if one puts one's mind to it, a theory of violence and *sabotage* can be deduced from *Creative Evolution*. Bergson cannot be held responsible for such disciples, whose banner bears the strange device, "Down with intellectualism."

Bergson offers us the curious spectacle of a philosopher of Jewish origin who has had the singular fortune of bringing to Catholicism such men as M. Maritain (who later, of course, attacked him),

*M. Georges Sorel, an idealist and pragmatist and an inconsistent socialist, in his book, *Reflexions sur la Violence,* has not failed to notice the resemblance between Cardinal Newman and Bergson. "It is impossible to read Newman without being struck by the analogies between his thought and that of Bergson: people who like to make the history of ideas depend on ethical traditions will observe that Newman was descended from Israelites."

The passage quoted by Sorel is the following: "Assent, however strong, and accorded to images however vivid, is not therefore necessarily practical. Strictly speaking, it is not imagination that causes action, but hope and fear, likes and dislikes, appetite, passion, affection, the stirrings of selfishness and self-love. What imagination does for us is to find a means of stimulating those motive powers; and it does so by providing a supply of objects strong enough to stimulate them. It will be our wisdom to avail ourselves of language, as far as it will go, but to aim mainly, by means of it, to stimulate, in those to whom we address ourselves, a mode of thinking and trains of thought similar to our own, leading them on by their own independent action, not by any syllogistic compulsion. Hence it is that an intellectual school will always have something of an esoteric character: for its aim is an assemblage of minds that think, their bond is unity of thought and their words become a sort of *tessera*, not expressing thought, but symbolizing it." (*Grammar of Assent*, p. 302. Burns & Oates, 1870.).

M. Joseph Lotte, and, most famous of all, Charles Péguy. At the same time he has as antagonists the orthodox believers, thomists or cartesians, like Mgr. Farges and the Abbé Piat, and the rationalists for whom M. Bergson's philosophy is pure verbiage. M. Julien Benda has given himself a good deal of entertainment in pointing out the chinks in Bergson's armor, and it is, of course, obvious that when the philosopher declares that the Real is the ineffable and inexpressible, he condemns us to silence.

Of all the French disciples, M. E. Le Roy is the one who has studied his master with most devotion and greatest profit. One wonders whether the distinguished mathematician is to become the new Malebranche of a new Descartes. It would certainly seem that the reading of Bergson was for him a mystic experience: "Truth known by the heart."

No reasoning can prevail against such immediate experience. The man who has arrived without the aid of dialectics at understanding that "Spirit is the immediate cause of all the phenomena in nature," can afford to laugh at ironical logicians.*

Bergson is above all a great poet. I give him the title to do him honor and not at all in the deprecatory sense in which certain critics use the term. After all it is the poets who are the true immortals, and they have an advantage over the philosophers in that they make every one take an interest in spiritual moods and imaginative passions.

*Berkeley 3rd Dialogues between Hylas and Philonous.

MAURICE BARRES

A PERSONALITY as complex as M. Barrès' is well calculated to attract and defy criticism, for he unites in the highest degree the faculty of contemplation with the talent for action, combining the idealist and the practical man, the mystic and the realist, being at the same time President of the League of Patriots and a great parliamentary figure. Politics, of course, is a serious and rough-and-tumble game requiring a quick wit, but little deep or impartial intelligence. In a world of partisans misunderstanding must reign supreme. Common sense bids you stick to your party, when self-interest counsels a palinode. Besides, in this region poetical and lofty ideas are very dangerous explosives. Treading the clouds must be left to the tight-rope dancer. The best politician is evidently in this mad world the city contractor, or financier, or soap manufacturer. It is not for us to be wiser than life: we must accept it as it is. M. Barrès's success is, therefore, all the more interesting in that his soaring imagination, his avidity for ideas, have never been checked by the materialism of a changeable Parisian World.

A greater artist than Disraeli, whom he recalls so often, he is not so successful a statesman, because he is a lesser cynic, and because French political life is not, or was not, so nicely arranged as English. Yet the fact that his virile style and heroic sentiment made the *Echo de Paris* during the war one

of the most popular newspapers in France, seems
to show the elevation of mind of a nation whose
speculative faculty is seldom divorced from the
practical. Again, Barrès's indomitable will reminds
his reader of Disraeli, as well as his outlook on life,
and that easy spanning of enormous distances of
thought which characterizes both the Oriental and
the French mind. Art for both of them is the great
force which takes men out of themselves and in so
doing directs them to the one and only path of
eternal truth. "To rule men, we must be men," as
Disraeli said one day; "to prove that we are giants,
we must be dwarfs, even as the Eastern genie was
hid in the charmed bottle." Barrès holds such doctrine essential. His mind is never dazzled by his
own fancies. At bottom, like your true Lorrain, he
is of the earth earthy, but his poetic power is like
the skylark which, springing from the soil, breaks
up "the tiresome old roof of heaven" into enchant-
ing and melodious forms.

Bergson realized that there is a power other than
mere intellectualism, whose impetus leads mankind
through life. Study Barrès, his books and his
polemics, and you will see how this stormy petrel
of politics plays in the fiercest tempest, with a
feeling that he is part of the force which controls
the hurricane.

The interest of a study of Barrès lies in the fact
that, whenever his spirit took a step forward, it
ranged itself in a wider sphere than the one left
behind. The æsthete became member of Parliament,
the editor of the *Cocarde* in due time succeeded Paul
Deroulède at the head of the League of Patriots.
The inexhaustible discontent of a Byron, a Chateaubriand or a Benjamin Constant changed in Barrès'
soul into a nationalism which is for him above all

good breeding, and which forces the agnostic in
him to appreciate the order and tradition of the
Church of France.

We see him at twenty in 1882 coming to Paris
from his Lorraine, anxious to know and understand all. Nature had endowed him with a peculiar
modesty always on stilts, and with a hero-wor-
shipping faculty beginning perhaps too often at
home; and in addition she gave him the same gift
she gave to his fellow countryman, Callot, that of
seeing things at once in their true and in their
grotesque lights. These gifts, together with his
unslumbering curiosity, his unerring instinct for
unmasking a countenance and his youthful super-
ciliousness, led him to adopt that ironical pose
which is so entertaining both for himself and for
his reader. It is true, the author sometimes pays
too dearly for his pleasure and ours, too often his
mind is merely a dull kaleidoscope and demands
a constant change of amusement of which he is
the first to recognize the vanity. Continual change
is no change. He seems to believe that it is positively immoral not to be cosmopolitan, and so, at
every turn of the road, he presses furiously forward
to find a new God, hoping to enjoy the discovery
with the "child's first pleasure" of Wordsworth
and the daffodils. But, as he pitches his tent not
by the side of a lake, but under the shadow of the
nihilism of Renan or Stendhal and the pessimism
of Baudelaire, he cannot hear the birds singing
merrily while Pippa passes. Yet the stars shine
out at times overhead, and good is in his heart.
Then the idea dawns upon him that what is truly
wonderful in him is his very mind able to conjure
up all the beauties he aspires to possess.

And so at the end of his literary pilgrimages he

is left to whistle by himself, and he realizes that only one thing really exists, and that is self. The universe is a great palace of delights, which self creates and destroys at the bidding of caprice, and wherein the gods with whom you feast are your own thoughts. But at the same time the universe is the Great Whole, living, thinking, speaking to the mind of man. Subjective Pantheism, in the hands of an artist such as Barrès, is like a futile game of cup and ball: mind and matter play with each other without intermingling with each other. Life has no meaning. You spend it in endless wishes, and in knowing that your wishes will never be satisfied. You long for eternal emotions, and are in reality only a series of successive states of mind.

Your temperament is all-important in your eyes, yet what a tiny thing it is in the hard and stern mechanism of the universe! However, this dualism of fervent feeling and cold intellect, these antinomies of temperament, represent the hunger for beauty which cannot but be appeased, and which must be fostered at all costs.

Barrès has himself told us that those idealogical novels, *Sous l'oeil des Barbares, l'Homme Libre, le Jardin de Bérénice, l'Ennemi des Lois,* are the outcome of "une prodigieuse susceptibilité cérébrale." But this susceptibility must be cultivated by study, it must be cared for, it needs a soul-hygiene.* There is no reason for spurning the methods of pious men of the past, even though their ideas no longer appeal, — men like Saint Ignatius, for example. Indeed, there is every reason why a skeptic, or a pagan, should use these spiritual exercises, for by so doing he will show the breadth of his mind.

*See *Trois Stations de Psychotherapie.* Perrier. Paris, 1891.

The positivists acted in the same way when they recommended the reading of the Imitation while attempting to substitute Humanity for God. Humanity being an abstraction, Barrès thought of replacing it by self which is Reality, and for his new religion he laid down the following precepts: "We are never so happy as when in a state of exaltation. The pleasure of exaltation is enhanced by analysis. We must aim, then, at feeling as much as possible while at the same time we analyze as much as possible."

Comte dreamed of a cult of Humanity, but Barrès thinks only of an extension of Self; and in this way dilletantism becomes a sort of religion, a new form of holy narcissism.

This religion is practised by Barrès in three ways. In the first place he mocks his contemporaries. Everyone knows his extraordinary pamphlets on Renan with their superb self-confidence, their amusing juvenile ferocity, and their power of hitting the mark. *Huit Jours chez Renan* and *Renan au Purgatoire* will live as long as some of the malicious tales of Voltaire. Secondly, he plunges into politics and the attractions of Parliament. The spice of Parliamentary life is battle, and Barrès has had his fill of it with his Boulangism and his Nationalism. "For God's sake," said Stevenson, "give me the young man who has brains enough to make a fool of himself!" But Barrès never went so far; his sense of humor was too keen. Finally, he travels, and we meet him in Italy or Spain or Greece, in those antique-laden lands where the dust on the roads is the dust of human bones. Nature can only speak to him insomuch as she is Clio's dwelling place. The sermons he finds in stones are the history of humanity. A landscape tells him no speaking

story until the day on which man suffered there.
Thus is intensified his passion for sharing in all
men's passions. Disraeli's saying, "Every moment
is travel if rightly understood," was Barrès' motto,
and he went to Aigues-Mortes, to Venice, and to Toledo in order to saturate his every moment with
eternity. If Venice enchants him, it is because, to
his mind, no place lends itself so well to analysis of
shades of feeling, and because Goethe, Chateaubriand, Byron, Georges Sand, de Musset, Théophile
Gautier and Wagner have lived there in their time.
Toledo attracts him inasmuch as it was the haunt
of Greco. "J'y respire une volupté dont j'ignore
le nom, et quelque chose comme un péché se mêle à
tout un passé d'amour, d'honneur et de religion.
C'est le mystère de Tolède et nous voudrions le
saisir." At Ravenna thoughts assail him on every
side as if they had been left behind there by all the
men who have passed through the city, with their
passionate desires and hatreds.

Barrès is like the traveler who knows all the echoes
of the mountain passes on his way and who amuses
himself with hearing his own words return to him
in mysterious and multisonous thunders. His writings on criticism, or travel, or philosophy, are really
an interpretation of German metaphysics, and that
is why the English writers he most recalls are
Disraeli, Coleridge and Carlyle. The magnificent
pages which the great Scot devotes to Dante, for
instance, are Barrès *avant la lettre,* and perhaps
the advantage is with Carlyle. Honors divided;
for both men have the true taste for the divine,
and both have drawn from the same German
romantic source.

When we want to get at the young Barrès, we see

that after all the most important things about him are his childhood in Lorraine and his German culture.* All his early books are either the sensual application of the doctrines of Kant or Fichte, of Hegel's notion of universal becoming, and his idea of the identity of contraries, or else the outcome of a most ardent patriotism. And for a long time this patriotism drew its weapons from Germany.

*"My early childhood was spent at Strasbourg and in Alsace as well as at Charmes and in Lorraine. When I was three years old I was sent to a religious establishment where the good sisters could not do enough to spoil me. I was often taken to Strasbourg cathedral, and the hours I spent in that mystic atmosphere have left very happy impressions upon my mind.

"But the memory which dominates my childhood is that of the events of 1870. I was eight years old when war broke out. First of all I saw convoys of French soldiers pass by. For lack of room, the men were put on the roofs of the carriages when the inside was full and the poor wretches were scorched by the burning August sun. Wine in plenty was brought to them, although most of them were already drunk. Some time after, hidden in a hay cart, I saw the lamentable rout of du Failly's army corps, defeated at Froeschviller. The regiments were driven back in disorder, and blocked up the road to such an extent, that I had to stay in my hay cart all day. They were ordered to encamp in a meadow near Charmes.

"At home we had some officers dining with us. I was not allowed to appear at table, for the sight of a child might have been yet another sorrow for these defeated men. But I could not help watching through the door when the dishes were brought in and I saw how emaciated my parents' guests were.

"Before daybreak the soldiers left in disorder, for it was reported that the Prussians were approaching rapidly. Some days later the Prussians arrived and occupied Charmes, conducting themselves in their usual manner. They forced the notables of the place to climb on to the engines, as hostages, so that, in the event of an attack, they would be massacred at the first shot. I remember the Prussians compelling us to put lights in our windows every night to prevent fire being opened upon them. These illuminations had nothing festive about them for they often lit up tragic scenes. All gatherings had been forbidden, and the sentinels in their zeal shot even isolated passers-by. Sometimes they fired on our windows, through the doors, or into the cellar windows.

"Yes, they have indeed committed atrocities, and for this reason there is not a single antimilitarist in Lorraine. The Prussians are still our most obvious and determined enemies, and those who are never absent from our thoughts.

"Their occupation, which was very long, for it lasted from the

Barrès is deeply imbued with German philosophy.
That goes with his milieu, Kant-laden, Hegel-laden,
as well as Marx-laden. His life might be summed
up as a contest between the romantic inspirations of
a student of things German, and the patriotic instinct of a Lorrain who has suffered from the
Franco-German war. And as the influence of Germany may be called Romanticism and that of France
Classicism, it is obvious that the contest has a very
wide bearing, and is the battle between two civilizations, two geniuses.

The serious reader of *Les Déracinés* is at once
struck by the influential rôle played by M. Burdeau,
the professor of philosophy at the *lycée* of Nancy.
Barrès himself speaks of the philosophy class "où
son adolescence s'enivra d'une poésie qui ressem-
blait à de l'épouvante." But Burdeau himself is
only a representative man of the élite of the professors of Philosophy in the University of France,
before the coming of Bergson, men who made their
students swallow a German pill by putting it in the
jam of those magic words, Categorical Imperative.

In their pride of believing in a moral law, applicable to all men, at all times, and in all places, they
ignored the point that *conscience* is a strictly human
fact, and Barrès, later on when master of himself,
was to declare in *Les Déracinés*, "il y a dans cette
règle morale un élément de grand orgueil — car elle
équivaut à dire que l'on peut connaître la règle
applicable à tous les hommes, — et puis encore un
germe d'intolérance fanatique, — car concevoir une

outbreak of war until the complete liberation of the territory, made
on my childish mind a deep impression, and one which I put to
immediate use, since I was elected nationalist member at twenty-
five years of age. The memory of the unfortunate heroes of Froeschviller and Reichshoffen commanded me to fight for the French cause
on every field, and it is for the same reason that later I opposed
the Dreyfus party."

règle commune à tous les hommes, c'est être fort tenté de les y asservir pour leur bien; — enfin il y a une méconnaissance totale des droits de l'individu, de tout ce que la vie comporte de varié, de peu analogue, de spontané dans mille directions diverses.''

It will be a long time before enough is said about the influence of German philosophy on Nineteen Century France. Barrès, in undergoing this influence, is only following such illustrious predecessors as Madame de Staël, Victor Cousin, Michelet, Quinet, Pierre Leroux, Proudhon, Taine, Renan, to choose only a few names.

This German influence on Barrès is in reality merely the influence of Rousseau in another form. A disciple of Descartes would call it voluptuousness, or perhaps the product of an Asiatic temperament. This strong instinctive bent towards making feeling the source of all truth, a wonderful land ''beyond good and evil'' ruled by that vital force which Fichte calls *Ego,* Hegel *die Idee,* Schelling *Nature,* Schopenhauer the *Will-to-live,* and Hartman the *Unconscious;* many labels but only one opiate!

Mr. Yeats* tells us that the work of a great poetical writer is ''the man's flight from his entire horoscope, his blind struggle in the network of stars.'' But Barrès did not tumble — at all events not at first — amidst the meteors of heaven. The sensuous languor of his nature, together with his humor, and his deep conviction of the flowing nature of things, keep him from kicking against the planets and escaping from himself. He, too, is of the opinion—

Per Amica Silentia Lunae. Macmillan, 1918. Cf. *Le Chant de Confiance dans la Vie: les Amitiés françaises,* pp. 237-67.

". . . that even saddest thoughts
Mix with some sweet sensations, like harsh tunes
Played deftly on a sweet-toned instrument."

Consequently the world with all its wondrous virtuosity pleases him, because the artist is a still greater virtuoso!

His two books *Du Sang, de la Volupté et de la Mort* (1st edition 1894, new edition 1903) and *Dolori et Amori Sacrum* (1903) will always be read by the philosopher as well as by the artist. Not only does Barrès carry on the sentiments of youth, a child's sense of wonder, a feminine desire for novelty, into the realm of manhood, but his voluptuousness is so physical, his power of thinking in images so great, that he far surpasses Rousseau and the Romantic artists on this point. Nobody before him had shown to such an extent that just as the deep self of a great writer is, as it were, a musical phrase full of the poignant sensitiveness of our consciousness, so his style gives us the intuition of that wonderful world of the mind whose emotions "are instinct with a thousand sensations, feelings or ideas which pervade them."[*]

Barrès is, to borrow once more from Bergson,[†] the writer who "tears aside the cleverly woven curtain from conventional ego, and shows us under this appearance of logic a fundamental absurdity, under this juxtaposition of simple states an infinite permeation of a thousand different impressions which have already ceased to exist, the instant they are named."[‡]

[*]Bergson, *Time and Free Will*, pp. 17-18.
[†]Bergson has often been reproached with feeding a German thought.
[‡]Op. cit., p. 133.

Thus when Barrès writes: "La volupté et la mort, une amante, un squelette sont les seules ressources sérieuses pour secouer notre pauvre machine,"* he gives us Hegel's doctrine of the identity of contraries: love of life being synonymous with love of death, in a way that brings it down to the level of all.

But we can never be quite sure that Barrès is not laughing at us. This egotist in Asiatic dress harbors a free and daring spirit which is always full of energy, and is sometimes as biting as Swift's. The starry remoteness of his philosophic standpoint did not prevent his entering the world of politics. As early as 1889 M. Barrès was elected one of the deputies of Nancy, and from that time onwards he has never ceased to try and prove Disraeli's famous saying, "The world was never conquered by intrigue, it was conquered by faith."

"We want an Ideal," wrote Barrès in his *Cocarde* (15th September 1894), and he found this ideal in patriotism. Before 1914 it was easy to call such feeling jingoism: but to-day the salvation of civilization is that steady flame of patriotism which burns in every soldier of France.

Barrès gets his love of action from the state of modern society in which he lives. Life in French society is an incessant struggle.

In England it is not sufficiently realized how the French Revolution of 1789, and the different revolutions of the Nineteenth Century, by breaking up the molds of society, let loose all kinds of ambitions, showed the citizens countless possibilities, stimulated every kind of activity, offered every imaginable temptation. To ignore the fact is to be incapable of

Du Sang, de la Volupté et de la Mort.

understanding Balzac and his heroes, while Stendhal on the one hand and Jules Vallès on the other are filled with the frenzy of the ambitious man determined to arrive at all costs. Taine, in his *Origines de la France Contemporaire*, wrote the now famous words, "Faire son chemin, avancer, parvenir, telle est maintenant la pensée qui domine les hommes,"* and that Barrès realized the same thing is abundantly shown by the series of studies called *De Hegel aux Cantines du Nord*. This little book is indeed an admirable commentary on the Barrès of 1894, and shows how his dilletantism was really stoicism in disguise.

"Le cynisme confine à la chasteté," Flaubert wrote one day to Georges Sand.† "Innocence and uncleanliness may go together," Meredith remarks in *Rhoda Fleming;* and these sayings of two great novelists are far-reaching: they prove La Rochefoucauld's theory that it is impossible to disentangle our vices from our virtues; they confirm the theory of William James and Bergson on the continuity of our subjective states. There is in our personal continuum such a medley of good and bad, of foolishness and wisdom, so many possibilities, "silly fancies, grotesque suppositions, utterly irrelevant reflections,"‡ by the side of reason, that once we realize it, all the psychological theories of former times fall to the ground, the theory which divided our mind into so many faculties as well as the theory which accounted our mental life as nothing but a multitude of separate sensations.

But if that is so, if the mind is at every stage the

*Maurice Barrès. *De Hegel aux Cantines du Nord avec une Preface et des Notes d'E. Nolent*. E. Sansot. Paris, 1940.
†*Correspondance entre Georges Sand et Flaubert*, p. 17. Paris, Calman Levy. Préface de H. Ames.
‡See William James, *Elements of Psychology*, Vol. I, pp. 552-553.

playground of simultaneous possibilities, ought not literary criticism to take it into account? M. Barrès compares himself to a dramatic cast.*

Just so! "Who but a Hegelian historian," asks William James, "ever pretended that reason in action was *per se* a sufficient explanation of the political changes in Europe?" And in our turn we may ask, Who but a literary critic nurtured in the school of Taine will pretend that the *faculté maîtresse* is an explanation of the works of a writer? And if that is so, who can doubt the prevalence in the long run of the man of action over the artist? Feeling exists for the sake of action. That feeling will be victorious which makes for efficiency, and which has been strengthened by years of habit. That is the theory so dear to William James and so much truer than La Rochefoucauld's: habit. It is the habits of Barrès as a child, his childhood's impressions, which will conquer: habit, which with him is merged in the Unconscious.

And one must not neglect the influence of Paris upon him. The spectacle of Paris always seething with excitement, the toy of every political passion and fashion, with its population of Balzacian adventurers all out for personal aggrandizement, or of charming little persons such as Bérénice, strengthened Barrès in his subjective philosophy, and steeled his heart. In order to understand his own self, dense with multitudinous being, he needed an excitable, impetuous, hypercritical and sensuous society. He gained thereby a vivid and practical comprehension of the meaning of the Subconscious, the *philosophie des unbewusten,* and became inspired

---

*"L'homme qui me plaît," says André Mallère, "je le compare à une belle troupe dramatique où divers heros tiennent leur rôle." (*L'Ennemi des Lois.*).

with that love and enthusiasm for the spirit which are deeper than our intellectual being, the great primeval force running within us like a living sap.* Meredith's Mrs. Lovell thinks of the French as a streaming banner in the jaws of storms, with snows among the cloud-rents and lightning in the chasms. Barrès would welcome an imagination so akin to his own. There is a magic power in the idea of a great vital impetus, *énergie créatrice*, pushing man blind-folded through life towards a better self. Behold, then, our egotist transformed into an altruist, our decadent into an heroic stump orator and belligerent politician who braves the slings and arrows of contested elections. The universe is a great adventure for him, because he is the troubadour of the Subconscious, a true Bergsonian. "The invisible breath that bears him on is materialized before his eyes."

There was a time when Barrès's friends feared he would fall a victim to the so-called æsthetic movement of 1890. True, he did not wear a sunflower in his buttonhole; rather his own heart for daws to peck at. But life is not like the heroes of French romance, interesting only when wicked: life is the test of the best of our soul — like the woman we love.

And such was the love of heroism within Barrès that he made a projection of it outside himself: he invested with all the rare qualities of genius a man who at best was a kind, gentle fellow, for Geneneral Boulanger was nothing but a puppet in the hands of certain peculiar fates. But, let it be said to Barrès' eternal honor, he never ceased to defend his former hero, his political chief, when he was

---

*See *Le Jardin de Bérénice*, pp. 77-78, and also *De Hegel aux Cantines du Nord*.

maimed and terribly bruised in the political *mêlée*.
Barrès is therefore a symbolic figure. His story
is the history of countless young men who began
with subjective idealism and individualism and
ended in collectivism or nationalism; that is why
the evolution of his books has so much significance.
It is from the desert of his own soul, from the home-
lessness of his philosophical world that Barrès
turns to the conception of another world, a world
of moral, spiritual and at the same time physical
agencies. Nature is for him not only a wonderful
mother, but also the spiritual tie between ourselves
and our ancestors. Our union with nature is our
union with them. "J'ai trouvé une discipline dans
les cimetières où nos prédécesseurs divaguaient,"
wrote Barrès, with a sly dig at the Romantics.

II.

The study of a writer as Protean as Barrès leads
to the conclusion that all *static* criticism, *i.e.*, all
criticism which aims at fixing a mobile writer in
one attitude, cannot but be false criticism. In
any case, as Bergson taught, if there is time which
passes, there is also time which lasts. In our spiritual life there is a permanent self as well as a
successive self. The history of the stages of a
writer's development must take into account both
the durable and the changeable.

The critic is helped in his task by the fact that
the study of any great writer is also the study of
the ideas which move the universe. Plato and
Saint Augustine, Plotinus and Descartes, are our
contemporaries. The moral powers of the universe
surround and protect us: they burst the setting
which confines the thinker and the poet and be-

hind which stretches the infinite perspective of the world — just like those pictures of the old masters in which we see nature painted to show the "streaks of the tulip" and the wonderful distant landscape.

Barrès has been in turn active and acted upon. His surroundings have weighed upon him and he has still more reacted upon his surroundings. Even as reason and faith are mingled in the Christian life, so in Barrès' mind is there incessant exchange between the world and himself, between the intellectual and the subconscious parts of his soul.

If we read M. Barrès works in strict chronological order without taking into account the articles he published between them, or the continual influence of politics upon his mind, we pass from *l'Ennemi des Lois* (1892) or from *Du Sang, de la Volupté et de la Mort* (1894) to *les Déracinés* (1897), and the ordinary reader is, to say the least, surprised at what appears to be a remarkable metamorphosis. For the Enemy of the Law, the man who used to say: "Je m'accuse de désirer le libre essor de toutes mes facultés et de donner son sens complet au mot exister," has emerged as the convinced nationalist, the hero-worshipper, defender of tradition. The man who was once so proud of his isolation now longs to return to the atmosphere of his native Lorraine. The man who seemed to be the very embodiment of a-moral ambition has but one desire — to continue by speeches and propaganda the work of those ancestors whose blood flows in his veins.

Les Déracinés, one of the best of Barrès' books, describes the adventures of seven pupils at the Nancy lycée who set out to seek their fortunes in Paris far from their native Lorraine, all victims of the uprooting philosophy of M. Bouteiller.

Barrès brings the French Revolution into court
again exactly as Taine had done. The most interesting chapter in the book is the one on Taine's visit
to Roemerspacher. This visit, as a matter of fact,
really took place; it was Charles Maurras whom
Taine went to see on account of the former's article
in the *Observateur français*. The famous passage
contains the French philosopher's eloquent words
as he stops to look at a plane tree in the square of
the Invalides. A nation is like a tree. Just as the
vitality and development of this plane tree are
ordered by its roots, the soft warm earth, then by
the sun, then by the shade cast by the buildings
round it, just as the tree obeys "that sublime
philosophy which consists in the acceptance of the
necessary things of life," even so the development
of the individual or nation, who, like the plane tree,
aims at "une belle existence," depends upon the
ineluctable laws of heredity and environment.

No more individualism! For suppose your
neighbor also sets out to give its fullest sense to
the word existence, there will be strife between
him and you. No, there must be a federation among
men, for the intellectual individualist who follows
the bent of his instincts must needs tend towards
solidarity, and tend therefore to become a unit in
a far wider form of individualism.

The solution offered by Barrès is that we should
strike deeper root into our native soil. Franco-
German philosophy impels the young men of France
to retire within their shell of self, and thus hands
them over to that individualism towards which they
are already by their nature too strongly drawn.
Such doctrine of self has not much importance in
Germany, where men own a sheep-like obedience
to their bad sheep-dogs. But a Frenchman, with

his instinctive repugnance for discipline, is naturally attracted by a philosophy which appeals to his strongest feeling.

Barrès' solution is a *ruse de guerre.* He takes our instinctive selfishness and converts it into patriotism, for in order to achieve his end he has recourse to another potent feeling, our desire to endure forever among our fellow men, to perpetuate our self in our species. "Let us return to the place where we were born and where our dead lie buried, for there shall we find the truth which will comfort us."

It is impossible not to be reminded here of Comte, whose real doctrine is expressed in the words: "Ce qu'il nous faut chercher, ce sont les vérités qui nous conviennent," and of Disraeli, the English writer most often quoted by Barrès. "The truth is," says Disraeli, "progress and reaction are but words to mystify the millions. They mean nothing, they are nothing; they are phrases and not facts. *"All is race."*

A very deep saying which seems blazoned in lurid letters upon the sky by the World War. Barrès has much in common with the statesman who wrote that, and who said another day, "There is a class of political philosophers . . . . who think that they will elevate a nation by degrading it into a mob."

Both Disraeli and Barrès, votaries of the Beautiful, sought in literature the means of expounding the same political wisdom, and which, more powerful than their egos, or rather springing from their deeper selves, forced them to dedicate themselves to the worship of practical wisdom and order. "Chacun de nos actes qui dément notre terre et nos morts nous enfonce dans un mensonge qui nous stérilise."*

*Amori et Dolori Sacrum, pp. 273-282.

There is a famous passage in *Contarini Fleming* expounding this same political wisdom, and which Barrès would have signed "with both hands."

"Before me is the famous treatise on Human Nature by a professor of Königsberg; no one has more profoundly meditated on the attributes of his subject. It is evident that, in the deep study of his own intelligence, he has discovered a noble method of expounding that of others. Yet when I close his volumes, can I conceal from myself that all this time I have been studying a treatise upon the nature — not of man, but — of a German? What then? Is the German a different animal from the Italian? . . .

"The most successful legislators are those who have consulted the genius of the people . . . one thing is quite certain, that the system we have hitherto pursued to attain a knowledge of man has entirely failed. . . . To study man from the past is to suppose that man is ever the same animal, which I do not. Those who speculated upon the career of Napoleon had ever a dog's-earned annalist to refer to. The past equally proved that he was both a Cromwell and a Washington. Prophetic past! He turned out to be the first. But suppose he had been neither; suppose he had proved a Sylla?" . . . etc. (*Contarini Fleming.* Part the Sixth, Ch. I.)

Anyone who reads M. Barrès' pilgrimages to Domrémy or to Saint Odile, *All Souls' Day in Lorraine, Au Service de l'Allemagne, Collette Baudoche,* fresh from the perverse subtlety of *le Jardin de Bérénice,* or the anarchist declarations of *l'Ennemi des Lois,* will easily understand how ill-meaning critics seized upon his attitude in the Dreyfus case as a means of attack upon Barrès himself and as an instrument for reproaching him with the instability of his doctrine.

And yet Barrès made no recantation: it is merely the normal development of an extremely rich and complex personality, whose very richness and complexity were bound to lead from cult of self to cult of ancestors, from individualism to nationalism by way of determinism. ("Je lui ai exposé quelques-unes des thèses déterministes, connues aujourd'hui sous le nom de nationalisme." *Voyage de Sparte*, p. 123.).

But just as nationalism is a form of exoticism, as Nietzsche put it, so Barrès' traditionalism is a form of his Germanism. He was the first to point out the danger for the French mind of being towed into the great unknown sea of thought by German philosophers. And if he thundered so finely against certain doctrines of Kantian philosophy, it was because he knew by experience the dangers of these so-called transcendental truths which have nothing to do with reality.

The analytic power of his mind, his insatiable curiosity, his passion for understanding everything, together with a strong perception of the vanity of all things in this world, have become fused in an enlightened patriotism, and a deep-rooted civic sense, because his intelligence and his temperament showed him that here on earth nothing is isolated, nothing finite, but that each one of us is merely a phase in a scheme of indefinite development. The enterprise may appear paradoxical, for by using self-love, which is necessity, and Taine's theories, which are pure determinism, Barrès succeeded in creating for himself "an instrument of freedom."

Feeling, then, in the depths of his being, that all

things but race fade and pass away, above all obedient to that great contemporary French movement, that so much more than socialistic social growth of France, seeking by every means in his power to restore that equilibrium of mind lost in 1789, Barrès is far from wishing to impose immobility upon the world. The aim of his nationalism is to respect the divergencies of men, and to organize the social relations between his own personality and the personality of others. His nationalism is the true intuitiveness of the poet in whom lies fermenting the living intellect of a whole race. When, as a kind of explanation of his so-called conversion, he says, "Penser solitairement, c'est s'acheminer à penser solidairement," the saying, for all its neatness, may be taken literally.

It is hardly necessary to point out the strong resemblance his thought bears to Bergson's philosophy. Bergson writes: "Que sommes-nous en effet, qu'est-ce-que notre *caractère* sinon la condensation de l'histoire que nous avons reçue depuis notre naissance, *avant notre naissance même,* puisque nous apportons avec nous des dispositions prénatales? Sans doute nous ne pensons qu'avec une petite partie de notre passé; mais c'est avec notre passé tout entier, y compris notre courbure d'âme originelle, que nous désirons, voulons, agissons."

That is to say, we are determined by our ancestors — they are the well-springs of that subconsciousness upon which we must always draw if we would live in beauty. Geologists tell us that there sometimes exists under the bed of a stream (which is often the creation of man) another deeper stream which never runs dry, while the first is easily exhausted by the sun. Even so with the two personalities of Barrès. Under the superficial, somewhat artificial Baudelairian, impeded by rather ill-matched qualities, there flows that deeper feeling which is the accumulated gift handed down from generation to generation. Barrès saw that his mind was covered with scraps from Michelet, Saint-Beuve, Baudelaire, Stendhal or Renan, not to mention the German philosophers and foreign scenes; but through the very comprehension of so many different souls, he felt the more strongly the strength of the bonds holding him to his own country. On the one hand were books, and activity of mind, on the other the uninterrupted flux of feeling; on the one hand deductive logic, on the other intuition — intuition in its true sense, a kind of mercy not strained and twice blest, which goes beyond the ordinary forces of the intelligence.

To study a writer with documents in hand and a pince-nez is but to pursue delusion. Truth can only be found if knowledge is sought by love. "L'intelligence, quelle petite chose à la surface de nous-mêmes!" That is the *leit motiv* of Barrès' writings.

There again he reminds one of Disraeli. "Man is born to adore and to obey" — Sidonia looks for hope "in what is more powerful than laws and institutions, and without which the best laws and most skilful institutions may be a dead letter and the very means of tyranny, in the national character." And again: "In this country since the peace, there has been an attempt to advocate a reconstruction of Society on a purely rational basis. . . . There has been an attempt to reconstruct society on a basis of material motives and calculations. It has failed. It must ultimately have failed under any circumstances. . . . How limited is human reason, the profoundest inquirers are most conscious. We are not indebted to the reason of man for any of the great achievements which are the landmarks of human action and human progress. It was not Reason that besieged Troy; it was not Reason that sent forth the Saracen from the desert to conquer the world, that inspired the Crusades, that instituted the monastic orders; it was not Reason that produced the Jesuits; above all, it was not Reason that created the French Revolution." (*Coningsby.*)

So many unexpressed and unexpressible feelings regulate our actions. Life is not literature; life runs underground, as it were; and the best reasoning in the world is the impudent dragoman of the mystery of reality. Plato's cave-dwellers, who turn their backs upon life, are the emblem of all those who see the world only through the cinematograph extracts made for them by their minds.

Barrès is not one man but a multitude: the mass of all those Lorrains who for centuries past have defended their possessions against every invasion. His greatness, his humor, are the greatness, the humor, of all those fine men, his ancestors, who were individualists, too, in the best sense, since it was their business to hand down intact to their descendants the land which they had ploughed and shielded from the barbarians.

This is by no means saying that Barrès' personality establishes the truth of Taine's famous theory of environment creating character. Not every Lorraine is a Barrès, and the explanation by means of climate and soil is far too simple to contain complete truth. The complex nature of such a man as Barrès is due to numberless causes which will always remain mysterious. It may be disputed whether he was created by Lorraine, but there is no doubt about his having created Lorraine for us. However strongly we may be formed by our dead, we always bring with us some original element, something free, which all the reasoning in the world cannot create or destroy.

The importance Taine attaches to race and climate could be much more readily attributed to intellectual environment, the literary atmosphere of a given time which influences you as you breathe it in, everywhere you go. The Parisian atmosphere of 1885 to 1895 was Marx-laden, Hegel-laden, and Napoleon-laden. That is the explanation of the socialism of the time and of Boulangism. Barrès seems to sum up all these influences in his person with an added indefinable characteristic which gives him a place by himself in his nation, I mean that acute sensitiveness which the baseness and pettiness of life forces to take refuge in preaching traditionalism. So, for once, Dr. Johnson, Patriotism is not the last refuge of a scoundrel!

Barrès hymns energy, respect of tradition, Corneille's honor, Pascal's thought, Racine's love: noble themes all of them and well suited to touch our hearts, but at bottom ambiguous formulas and which may be understood in a different light by the various worlds reading them. Neither love nor the cult of energy are moral forces, properly speaking. The honor so dear to Corneille is a convenient ticket for pasting over several rather villainous actions. And traditionalism amounts to saying that the salutary errors which have turned out well in the past have become truths. Barrès' triumph is the triumph of Pragmatism. The man who had so much to say in praise of the beauty of the laws of decadence and death has ended by building an altar to energy as manifest in the defense of Motherland. There are certain truths which are necessary to the human mind. Pragmatism

is a need of the mind which must be satisfied.
But our nature has another need, that of believing in the objectivity of truth. Are two thousand years of Christianity founded upon an halluci-
nation of Mary Magdalene? What foundation can
we give to morality when we separate it from the
religious ideas to which it has been attached for
centuries past?

Hence, then, the hero-worshipper in Barrès and
his hatred of all that is energy-sapping. One has
only to look at his face, its pallor, its energy, the
eagle-like nose, the firm chin; the whole breathes
disdain for all those arm-chair politicians who have
had no influence upon their time, for all those poets
who have died in their garret, and for the so-called
heroes who have never conquered anything, not
even their own ego. One realizes the pleasure that
such a man must get out of electoral committee-
meetings, political fights, and even out of the public-
houses wherein votes are brewed. Persons in
drawing-rooms may be pitch-forked into high places,
but not into high resolutions. In order to be strong,
a man must be battered and buffeted by the storms
of political life. Every faith implies a determina-
tion to believe, a *parti-pris*. There is no doctrine
in existence which can resist the dialectic of the man
who is resolved not to accept it. Principles are
affairs of feeling and it is for them that men lay
down their lives. "We have an incapacity of proof
insurmountable by all dogmatism. We have an idea
of truth invincible to all skepticism."*

*   *   *   *   *

Is there a poetic view of the world? That question has been lately asked and brilliantly answered
by Professor Herford. A study of Maurice Barrès

*Pascal.

confirms the English scholar's affirmative; not only there is, but there needs necessarily be, a poetic view of the world. Feeling is of more account than logic; enthusiasm is the true core of reality. Our constantly straying reason is in its essence incapable of facilitating in any way the achievement of that superior being which we are striving to attain, and of which logic cannot even suspect the existence. Barrès is convinced that syllogism and analysis are valuable only in a certain restricted sphere of art, and this has led him to take the road leading back to his own Lorraine, to the cemetery where his own dead lie. In reality his cult of the dead is his way of saying "Charity begins at home." So "The Enemy of the Law" has become the Defender of Tradition. The philosophy of the communion with the dead, profoundly poetic as it is, brings us near to the philosophy of Comte on the one hand, and of the mystics on the other. The self, that indispensable factor in the world's organism, depository of the life of its forefathers, sees at the same time a creation so deeply saturated with the spirit of God, that even the presence of evil does not prevent its hymning the Eternal Wisdom, which, despite appearances, triumphs in the end.

It is in this light that we must understand a much criticized passage in one of his later books, *"La Colline inspirée,"* "L'univers est perçu par Vintras d'une manière qu'il n'a pas inventée et qui jadis était celle du plus grand nombre des hommes. . . . Vintras exprime chez eux le sens du supranaturel. Il renverse, nie, les obstacles élevés entre l'instinct des âmes et le mouvement spontané de l'esprit. Il fournit à ses fidèles le chant libérateur."[*] These lines show the latest, though I think

La Colline inspirée, p. 209.

not the last, stage in Barrès' mystic development, where he believes in primitive inspiration of humanity.

All that distress of the analyst who declared that life was meaningless, has faded into the joy of the sensitive artist who declares that feeling is not only the best guide through life by reason of its intuitive action, but the best interpreter of that divinity which has ever appealed to men by the ineffable spectacles of nature and by the still more baffling mysteries of genius and liberty. As Barrès himself wrote in *La Mobilisation du divin:*[*]

"Arbres fatidiques, dames Fées des prairies et des sources, mystérieuse respiration des bois, vent du soir qui passe à travers les taillis, ô sentiments fragmentaires! Je ne vois pas dans la nature les dieux tout formés des Anciens, mais elle est pleine pour moi de dieux à demi défaits. Toute une végétation subsiste au fond de nos cœurs, tout un univers submergé. Ames du purgatoire, aïeux qui réclament des libations sur leurs tertres, génies des lieux et mes propres sentiments réveillés, toutes les épaves de la vieille race m'appellent. . . . Il faut dégager et unifier tout le domaine du sacré . . . c'est l'heure d'achever la réconciliation des dieux vaincus et des Saints. . . . Pour maintenir la spiritualité de la race, je demande une alliance du sentiment catholique avec l'esprit de la terre."

NOTE.—Barrès was born on September 22nd, 1862, at Charmes sur Moselle (Vosges).

On his mother's side (Mlle. Luxer) he belongs to one of the oldest families of Lorraine. His father's family is of Auvergnat origin. From 1550 the Barrès name is to be found in the registers of Blesle (Haute-Loire). For generations, father and son, the Barrès were royal notaries. Barrès's enemies have found pleasure in calling him a Portuguese Jew. The Portuguese ending Barrès, together with the writer's profile seem to be the most important factors in this

[*] *La grande pitié des églises de France*, 1914.

attempt at genealogy, together with a desire to wound a national writer. The Barrès family takes its name from a little commune of Mur-de-Barrez — and for those who are interested in questions of atavism and eugenics, it is as well to add here that the country of Auvergne is old Celtic territory which, like so many regions in the south of France, bears the marks of Saracen infiltration. Many are the villages in this district where the men and women are an Arab type. The partisans of the race theory may explain in this way the mystical philosophy of Barrès, for it was the Arab philosophers of the Middle Ages who analyzed with such wonderful precision the mysterious communion of the soul with God.

The novelist's great-grandfather, *officier de santé et conseiller général* of la Haute Loire, published in 1801 a topographical description of the Canton of Blesle. He had three sons. The youngest of these, J. Baptiste Auguste Barrès, who was born on the 25th July, 1784, enrolled in the *corps de vélites* which Bonaparte created in 1804.

Travelling in the east of France, he married at Charme-sur-Moselle, Mademoiselle Barlier, whose father and grandfather had been members of the Council of that district. Of this marriage was born Auguste Barrès, who, after taking his degree as civil engineer in the Ecole Centrale, and after two years of travel, returned to settle at Charmes, where he married Mademoiselle Luxer. These are the parents of Maurice Barrès.

PAUL BOURGET

AMONG modern French writers no one has suffered more at the hands of his critics than M. Paul Bourget. It may be that the general public, in crying out for individuality, has impaired, or rather debased, the critical faculty of our literary judges. Certain it is that our modern Aristarchs seem to care more for adorning and gilding their own self-made halo than that of the writers they depict. Authors are no longer reviewed for their own sake, but "ad majorem critici gloriam." But nothing could be further from the truth than such a rhetorical, self-satisfied, self-seeking criticism. All writers are not martyrs broken on the wheel of style, — far from it, — nevertheless they must be studied with piety and touched with reverential hands.

To call M. Bourget a regenerated infidel, to compose a diptych in which we see him — on one side a pagan worshipping a Parisian Venus, and on the other a Father of the Church, a miter on his head and a crosier in his hand, may appeal to our sense of antithesis. But to one for whom life is a mystery at every moment, and whom the conditions of human existence fill with anxious gravity, such criticisms appear less than futile.

The truth is that M. Bourget is a firm believer in science to-day, just as he was twenty years ago. Genuine, open-minded investigator as he is, his great, his poignant, originality consists in accepting the scientific dogmas of our time, while clinging to his spiritual convictions. The writer he reminds one most of is Taine, Taine in the last years of his life. He began by casting a philosophical doubt over all things. He adores facts, science, and medicine, which he studies with tireless ardor. Besides, he himself declares he is a fervent disciple of Taine and in his preface to the final edition of his *Essais de Psychologie Contemporaine* he places his collection of studies under the patronage of the great positivist philosopher. All his strength and all his weakness come from that. Paul Bourget is far too often inclined to show us the works of the human machine and set them moving while we watch; he too often allows himself to be impressed by the mask of gravity worn by doctors and scholars; he likes to wear it himself sometimes.* It would be good for him to read Molière frequently. He has an immense respect for abundant medical erudition; no doubt a good thing in itself, but which at times becomes really comic when brought into play at the most interesting point in his books. He runs it too hard, just as formerly he ran Spinoza too hard, as if that great philosopher had diagnosed once and for all the maladies of the soul.

Bourget quotes Taine somewhere, speaking of this religion of science and how it thrilled him: "In this use of science and this conception of things, there are new art, new politics, new religion, and at the present moment it for us to seek them." And Bourget cries, as he transcribes these lines, "Even now, at this moment, I do not copy these lines without emotion. They were the creed of my youth, they

---

*Cf. his comparison of *le mal romantique* with Graves' Disease. *Pages de critique et de doctrine*, tome I.

were the watch-word to which I subordinated all my efforts.'"*

II

M. Bourget began his literary career by claiming to be a disciple of Stendhal, and much that was purely instinctive in Henri Beyle's novels has attained definite maturity in Bourget's writings. He was, after Taine, one of the first to recognize Stendhal as the great psychologist who could describe the mechanism of grief and joy susceptible of being played upon by love, and the succession of feelings that such and such a person must needs experience in such and such a moral state. According to Stendhal we are sensitive mechanisms acted upon by circumstances; and therefore the only legitimate way of writing a novel is to show the series of sensations or memories in man's mind (each of which is a mental impulse), which in their conflicts with one another drive the human being hither and thither, to the amusement of the cold observer. Stendhal discovered and tried to prove that in the human mind there are no two successive sensations which do not contradict each other. William James merely echoes him on this point, though it remains to be proved whether James had read Stendhal or not.†

According to Stendhal the human mind is always

*Paul Bourget: *Les Témoignages de l'expérience:* Revue Hebdomadaire, 18 juillet 1912, pp. 307 et seq.

†Speaking generally, our moral and practical attitude, at any given time, is always a resultant of two sets of forces within us, impulses pushing us one way and obstructions and inhibitions holding us back. "Yes! Yes!" say the impulses: "No! No!" say the inhibitions. Few people who have not expressly reflected on the matter realize how constantly this factor of inhibition is upon us, how it can train and mould us by its restrictive pressure almost as if we were fluids pent within the cavity of a jar."—*William James, Varieties of Religious Experience,* p. 261.

a chaos of sensations following one upon the other with vertiginous rapidity. Julien Sorel, for example, the hero of *le Rouge et le Noir,* traverses every possible state of emotion, from egoism to sacrifice, hypocrisy to perfect frankness, with a facility which has roused the ire of the logicians. It is only upon reflection that one realizes the depth of Stendhal.

Thus the novel, as defined by both Bourget and Stendhal, should contain nothing but descriptions of states of mind. Analytical acuteness then becomes the greatest faculty of the novelist; soliloquy his chosen instrument. As the characters are more or less marked in the "passage d'armes" of life, they match with morbid introspection the rounds which succeed one another in their souls. These characters seem to wear their hearts on their sleeves, that they may examine them the better. They act, and watch themselves acting: they feel and examine themselves whilst feeling.

Hence a worship of analysis for its own sake, and a longing for endless sensations; hence the portraiture of exceptional creatures, for Worldly Wiseman does not like to adumbrate himself; hence also the pursuit of criticism of the tragedies of love, for they are the only ones that can be analyzed *more geometrico.* (The mechanical nature of cerebral action is never more aptly illustrated than by jealousy, for instance.) Hence, also, a moral world of fine gradations, of subtly-linked conditions shifting intricately as circumstances change around us.

In order to obtain all these subtleties of effect the novelist must himself be a Proteus: argus-eyed, hundred-handed, able to cope with his own surging, swelling miscellany of facts, and a quick-change

artist, who has to play as many parts as his fancy
bids him. Thus we find M. Bourget saying one day
to M. F. Chevassu: "To be perfectly happy one
ought to live five or six lives: to know the joys of a
monk in the cloister: those of a worldling in a
drawing-room: those of a great general: one ought
to taste all the emotions of active life and all those
of intellectual life."*

"To be perfectly happy"! The day was to come
when M. Bourget was to say that the sweetest words
he had learned in the wilderness of his sensations
were Rest and Peace; for a man who is all things
to all men may be a very great critic, but is a sad
nihilist at heart. Stendhal rather liked his own in-
credulity: too many people around him believed;
and a desire for self-portraiture was his real motive
in writing. But M. Bourget adopted his method not
so much for love of himself as for love of truth.
He honestly believed that the ordinary novel of the
Nineteenth Century was untrue to life. Balzac, for
instance, in spite of his knowledge of the human
heart, overdraws his characters, the lights are
heightened, the shadows deepened. Le Père Goriot,
and le Père Grandet have much of the caricature
in them. As for the novelists of the Sand school,
they are too romantic, too free and easy in plucking
this fortune here and that circumstance there and
tying them rashly to their characters. They pander
to their readers, flatter them with childish success,
or scare them with shocks of tragedy. But life has
other means by which it fits the man to his circumstances and makes them the fruit of his character.
The eyes of an analyst opening on Parisian life:
such is the genesis of his early work: and his pessimism is positivism filtered by a poet's imagination.

Les Parisiens by F. Chevassu, p. 172.

But the moment was not far distant when the moralist was to appear, declaring that psychology is to ethics what anatomy is to therapeutics, and holding it his duty to prescribe after having diagnosed.

Paul Bourget has been reproached with lack of imagination. On the contrary, he has an extremely powerful imagination, which occasionally plays him tricks. Doubtless the documentation of his novels is carried out with scrupulous care: but just as in his early books, *Un Crime d'Amour, André Cornélis, Mensonges,* he was hindered by his romantic fancy, which made him consider it *chic* in the highest degree to possess thirty-two pairs of boots and a dozen dress coats, or showed him as arbiter of elegance a man like Casal, who is an almost perfect snob; so in his second manner Bourget, still in pursuit of his will o' the wisp, constructs his characters far more in accordance with the decrees of a system in which he still believes, than in accordance with reality. He is *always* the man who wrote the *Essais de Psychologie Contemporaine.* He has lingered too long in the company of Baudelaire, Taine, Renan, Flaubert, the de Goncourt brothers and Amiel: he has borrowed their way of looking at their fellow countrymen. He has considered them with a disdain which is apparent in all his works, less profound perhaps than that of Flaubert, because M. Bourget is more Christian, but deep enough to confuse his vision of things. I will not say that M. Bourget execrates the Philistine, but he sees in contemporary France a collection of moral maladies. He says and believes that Taine's method and the study of Darwin led him to Royalism, and made of him one of the companions of Charles Maurras, the new Rivarol of France, who for the last twenty years at least has tried to prove daily that the monarchist solution is the only one in conformity with the teachings of positivism.

It would be probably more correct to say, as Maurice Barrès believes, that the human mind is all linked up in such a way that we each follow on in the steps of others, and that consequently M. Bourget has elaborated judgments and works which are the reaction of his thought upon its surroundings. The fact that he has traveled further than his masters along the road of religion shows that he has followed the evolution of his day. The French spirit had its metamorphosis before the war, and M. Bourget, by force of circumstances, found himself in the front ranks, fighting for what he believed to be truth and science. He himself declares that it was the most systematic positivism which made of him a traditionalist. However that may be, M. Bourget had learned that the moral and the physical law are ever in contact, that character not only merges into temperament but plays the most important part in life, that the world of the mind, while it rests on the foundations of the nervous system, yet brings us into communication with the Infinite. The novel must therefore be as complex as life itself, or rather it must perceive and express the relations between humanity and its environment and customs. And alas for France, according to M. Bourget, where such relations are inharmonious! Thus his great novels such as *l'Etape, Un Divorce, l'Emigré,* or his dramatic works *la Barricade, le Tribun,* are political tracts which would come very close to true contemporary history, were it not that a certain love of emphasis and effect on the part of the writer produce in the reader a feeling exactly opposite from the one the novelist wishes to create. This is hardly the place to study the

misunderstanding which has endured throughout
the Nineteenth Century in France between the intellectual *élite* and the commercial movement of the
middle class.   The works of the romantic poets, the
satires of their contemporary caricaturists, the dishevelled romantic dreams of a Petrus Borel which
have an analogy in those of Flaubert, or Gautier or
Baudelaire, the creations of Henri Monnier, and
Daumier or Forain, the types of Joseph Prud-
homme, Homais, Bouvard et Pécuchet, all these
bear witness to the uneasiness arising from manifold causes, but which is above all the product of an
education directing youth to the study of letters
rather than to the cult of action.   In England, —
one may make bold to say, — where the methods
are different, you do not find that *naïve* intellectualism which from time to time disfigured pedagogy
in the Nineteenth Century.

Mind is played upon by a thousand causes, by
the character of our age, as well as by the various
characters of our ancestors, by economic and social
factors, by the influence of foreign countries, by the
ever-increasing discoveries of the time, so that it
behooves political writers and novelists not to sit
at a great distance from their fellow men nor
patronize them, but to forgive, humor and even
admire them.   That is why the reading of the likes
and dislikes of such men as Flaubert, Taine or Bourget, is an inexhaustible source of astonishment.
Not that their criticisms were without foundation!
The exclusive cult of Abstract Reason by a part of
the French nation may excuse some over-coloring
of the picture.   Over and over again in M. Bourget's work you find the most just and logical criticism of rationalism — of that blind confidence in
reason held by the Eighteenth Century, of that

fanaticism which furnished the guillotine with so many victims. No one, not even Taine, has more vigorously combated the Eighteenth Century ideas upon man *in abstracto,* Rousseau's man born free and good. No one has shown better that the individual cannot be studied separately, since the human being is essentially a social being, existing only in and by society, that is to say, in and through religion.

Such a way of depicting life may appear to many a reader of Bourget profoundly tedious, cold, bald and even meagre. To gild the pill is a popular and approved art. But it is only right that this lack of interest, of which so many complain when reading Bourget, should be ascribed to the touching sincerity of the writer towards his own art, to his conception of truth. Indeed we have only to look at Paul Bourget's portrait to realize the vigor and surprising trenchancy of his intellect. In his so-called master, Henri Beyle, one sees a sensual mouth, greedy eyes, a most fleshly, earthly countenance, a big burly fellow with something boisterous in his manners. M. Bourget's face is that of a philosopher, thin, penetrating, sad, the face of a man endowed with an intense natural acumen, who is fond of bending ideas with visible effort.

"Anatomists and physiologists, I find you everywhere!" cried Sainte-Beuve after reading *Madame Bovary.* This intense acuteness of Bourget's is his prime characteristic. But his moral preoccupation must never be forgotten. For his wit is the servant of a moral sense so highly developed that it seems to many of his readers to have brought him into self-contradiction: Bourget, the psychologist, convinced, as he appears to be, by his study of man, of the mechanism of the mind, parts company with

Bourget the deeply religious Christian intent on leaving a higher idea of man in the minds of his contemporaries. The first places man in the midst of nature, or of Parisian life, and studies him as a natural product subject to natural laws: the second separates man from Nature and makes him read the laws of morality to an immoral universe. Man is no longer merely an intelligence obedient to logic, but a will conscious of moral obligations.

But in reality Bourget treads the same path as William James. The great American philosopher realized long ago that Darwinism, far from enthroning mechanism as a universal principle, obliged us on the contrary to "remodel the fashionable mechanical interpretation of consciousness."*   And M. Bourget, coming from another direction than William James, and going another way, saw quite plainly that our moral ego, that our "heart," as Pascal says, instead of being a source of error, was a living fountain of truth. The "heart" had had no place so far in the great philosophic systems. Yet there is no reason for refusing to come to the help of this poor relation, no objection to trying to emerge from moral nihilism by restoring some of its dignity to human conscience. Our knowledge, being only a collection of *soundings,* as Bergson says, is not the complete image of the real. The universe is nothing but wax we fashion as we will. It *becomes.* Reason yields to Will. Truth it is which makes men noble. *Fiat justitia, ruat coelum.*

In the eyes of Bourget, the positivist, the Latin maxim is meaningless, for a disciple of Comte cannot but laugh at such idols as Perfect Justice, Perfect Liberty, Perfect Equality; in the eyes of Bourget,

*See *William James,* by Howard V. Knox, p. 25. London, Constable, 1914.

the Christian, it is only just. The history of Bourget's evolution is as curious as that of Taine. Taine at the close of his life dared not end as he had begun, and asked for a Christian burial, because he realized that scientific laws could never give more than an aspect of truth.* He had already written: "The difficulty of governing democracies will always gain partisans for Catholicism: the underlying anxiety in sad or tender hearts will bring it recruits always, always the antiquity of possession will keep some men faithful to it. Those are its three roots, and experimental science does not teach them, since they are composed not of science but of feelings and needs."† M. Bourget has lived long enough to realize the truth of these words of Taine, he has seen the upgrowth of the philosophy of Bergson and William James.

Indeed Taine and Bourget are living examples of the truth of William James's words, "Man needs a rule for his will, and will invent one if one be not given him."‡ Even children love fights, and flying flags, and beating drums, as well as a general building and storming of castles. Children show us that instinct in which striving is nature's favorite game; their conception of nature legitimates the emotional, poetical and practical tendencies of their natures so as to become a real fulcrum for their minds. Bourget saw that perfect truth is *successful* truth, truth which can be applied to life and tested by life; and the history of mankind as well as the facts of our daily life proved to them that truth is that which satisfies not only our reason but our

*Cf. the letter written by Taine to M. Bourget on the publication of *le Disciple*. Correspondence, tome IV, p. 292. Paris, 1907.

†Taine, *Voyage en Italie*, Vol. I, pp. 388-389.

‡William James, *Principles of Psychology*, p. 315.

whole nature, and that the beliefs we cannot do
without are those which must be adopted at all
cost if we are to progress. To Bourget they certainly appear as the best proof of the divine
effort which built man. For him and his disciples
truth is, as it were, an inborn necessity which com-
pels them to adopt such views as will develop our
"impulse to take life strivingly." And, from the
moment Bourget felt he was thus in harmony with
the universe, he dedicated his labors to the development of the idea which gave him access to the divine
and highest Powers. Indeed he could not but be
confirmed and settled in this vatication of his mind
by the teaching of William James that such an
attitude was an intelligent comprehension of
Darwinism: vital utility is the only criterion of
truth. Herein again we are reminded of Bergson.

III

Let us now make a rapid survey of M. Bourget's
work. First of all he was the novelist of Parisian
love. No one can describe the order of such shifting
states of mind as flit through a soul dying with its
curiosity unsatisfied, any more than the scientist can
describe the order of variable winds. Yet the manner
in which M. Bourget depicts love betrays the secret
workings of his soul; for love is but a condition of
one's mind:

> "The blot upon the brain
> That *will* show itself without."

Love is for him the most subtle and dangerous
deviser of our decadence, and the symbol of anarchy.
It leads to crimes such as that committed by Armand
de Querne on the adorable and unfortunate Hélène

Chazel; it even hardens sinners like Julien Dorsennes to final impenitence. Love, that great cosmic force, appears to be laid by the heels, as it were, in a sponging house, vilified by the eternal question of money. Think of the life of Suzanne Moraines in *Mensonges!*

On the one hand the immoderate love of luxury has unsexed most of his heroines, on the other his heroes know but two states — desire and satiety. It must not, however, be thought that M. Bourget's ethics are those of the Restoration Comedy, nor his standard of honor that of the betting ring. It is because purity is for him a type of Divine energy, that he has called one of his most typical books *Mensonges.*

No nation can endure which does not sanctify love, the source of life, peace and happiness. According to Bourget, the very foundations of society were never shaken as they are at the present day; not by pressure of famine nor by the sting of envy, but by the ugliness and immorality of so-called love. Never have the French upper class led such a wolfish life! *Crime d'amour* is a crime only because Armand de Querne believes in a moral responsibility. *Cruelle enigme* is an enigma because the author thinks that foulness is painful as indicative of the withdrawal of Divine support. *L'Irréparable* is the story of a girl who dies of the gnawing remembrance of a stain upon her honor. Nor is M. Bourget merely dressing dolls for us: he knows his Parisians because he knows himself. His characters are for him typical of their circumstances. What they are implies what is around them; the relation in which they stand to the rest of the world is as important as their own qualities. They are the children of a century of romanticism

which has given free rein to their impulse and thus
destroyed the tone of their character.

Then — and it is here that he finds the greatest
opposition to his views — M. Bourget goes a step
further. If anarchy reigns in the family through
selfishness and luxury, anarchy must necessarily
reign in society. How can it be otherwise? Others
are affected by what I say, what I do, what I am.
These others have their spheres of influence; so
that a single act of mine may spread in widening
circles through a nation.

"There is no sort of wrong deed," writes George
Eliot, "of which a man can bear the punishment
alone; you can't isolate yourself and say that the
evil which is in you shall not spread. Men's lives
are as thoroughly blended with each other as the air
they breathe, evil spreads as rapidly as disease."
And throughout M. Bourget's novels, as throughout
George Eliot's, there prevails this idea, that the
influence of our actions extends to the remotest
generations. M. Bourget's critics aver that this
is but a postulate of our nature. But is not such a
postulate in the hand worth two in the bush?
Skepticism may be excellent in Venus or in Jupiter,
but in the universe we inhabit we need a strongly
built spiritual fortress, a real castle of the soul.
Even supposing life to be a succession of dreams,
and bad dreams at that, yet poetic justice is done
in dreams; our minds will have it so. Speak as you
will, do as you please, morality must conquer. Our
inmost self tells us that there is a moral law: "when
the master of the universe has points to carry in
his government," says Emerson, "he impresses his
will in the structures of minds."

There are few words so pregnant with meaning.
We bow like children before the spiritual because

it is invisible, with perhaps an afterthought that it
may be unreal: but the spiritual is reality — the
only reality. It works within us and around us.
We talk of morality as something external, something to put on at certain hours. We talk of God
as of some poor schoolmaster whose orders can be
laughed at. We talk of destiny as of a blind and
deaf person acting at random. But morality is our
very life. We entertain angels unawares at every
hour.

However apparent such truths may be, yet half
of mankind is busy denouncing them: their self-
chosen part is to deny all commonly accepted
creeds and traditions, and M. Bourget is bent on
showing them that their wilfully disconnected spirits
disport themselves in a vacuum apart from realities.

For such a truth-hunter, this question of morality
must be upheld by good solid foundations, and M.
Bourget appeals to science for the test of his arguments and method. Thus science is the author of
what seems to so many of his critics to be a re-
gression.

Far from sweeping away the questions and
answers of his old catechism, science forced him
to believe in the vitality of good and evil, in the
ennobling influence of virtue. Nature from the very
beginning of the world shows us the progress of
mankind inscribed in the mind of the first men (the
very gestures of the grandfather re-appearing in
the actions of the grandson) — and for the improvement of the race. Innumerable generations devote
themselves to the well-being of those who come
after. Thus natural selection affords us the best
examples of love or tradition.

From science M. Bourget learned that reason in
man is built up of sensations and images, and con-

sequently borders on the dreadful realm of madness. Man is not a reasoning animal, but an impulsive one. Not only does love make him blind, but his passions make him squint: which is far worse. He even has fangs. Let us beware of rousing in him his wild instincts. Let us not play with ideas, which are real forces and cannot be brushed away like trifling cobwebs of the human intellect; their effects never fail to show themselves sooner or later; hence the responsibility of the novelist.

Again from science M. Bourget learned that man is a slave to his environment. Our ego which we so carefully cherish has not suddenly risen out of space or time. Our ancestors lived on a certain plot of ground; they had grown used to it; the color of its river and of its sky passed as it were into their eyes; the quality of its earth passed into their blood; their temperament resembled its soft or hard soil; customs and laws were fashioned by these manifold influences.

The destiny of man is ephemeral, if we consider the short moment of his life; it is eternal if we think of the lineage of his ancestors. Thus according to science every human action gains in honor and grace by its regard to things of the past as well as to things that are to come. But the only links which connect forgotten and following up ages are chastisement of our low passions and discipline of the intellect: they are the same links which weld parts of empires together and make them last for ever. We can now understand the attitude of questioning awe of the writer in the face of the infinite past, pressing on us all round and invading our life like a tide felt inland.

M. Bourget's first wish to be everybody and everything had led him to desperate nihilism; his temperament had been paralyzed by too many systems of philosophy, his will was inert in the face of many possibilities, and his soul was an arid desert.

But the human mind wishes to act and to believe, and M. Bourget, realizing that there are rules of conduct that can be ascertained from results of experiments made by men in other times and other countries, found a faith, to whose service he was willing to sacrifice his personality.

M. Paul Bourget is a great admirer of English institutions and English customs. It will always be to the honor of England that so far she has given to the world the form of an ideal government, a government of which it might be said, as Wotton said of Sir Philip Sydney, "His wit was the measure of congruity." The English gentleman is the perfect product of civilization. In the eyes of M. Bourget the best government is formed by a healthy and wealthy governing class, a body of men placed above the vulgar temptation of enriching themselves, whilst by their established social rank they acquire an *esprit de corps* that prevents them from ever entertaining the idea of bribery and blackmail.

French aristocracy, on the other hand, having cast away all power and all duties, in a fit of enthusiasm on the famous fourth of August, 1789, lacks that sense of superiority, that reserve of dignity, that eagerness to be in the thickest of the fight, and abandons to cliques of politicians the glorious task of governing France. The activity of the French, their brightness, their enthusiasm for symmetry and simplicity of arrangements, their passion for equality, have been harmful rather than beneficial to them. They believed that they had the right to rebuild society, but, as they were not well versed in the practical conditions and difficulties of government, while at the same time they were filled with inspiring ideals, such novices in the art of practical politics played havoc in the ancient and complex fabric of France.

The sovereignty of numbers is not necessarily supreme morality nor sound policy, for such a sovereignty likes change above everything; hence every now and then new governments and numerous small "affairs," which, though not very important in themselves, tend nervertheless to show that France is, or was, suffering from that subtle disease which was fatal to Athens.

Now it is easy for us to see that M. Bourget's love of England had led him astray, in so far as it rendered him blind to the fine qualities of his countrymen. An Englishman who knows his Paris as well as his London, Mr. Richard Whiteing, could have taught him (had M. Bourget read his book, *The Life of Paris*) that Paris and France were animated by an immense vitality. But there it is, England appeared to Bourget, as she did to Taine, a land of marvels: here was a country in the hands of a land-owning, wealthy, governing class, and extremely prosperous. (If his idea seems a little out-of-date it must be remembered that he has not visited us lately.) "What I am, I owe to traveling," says M. Bourget. In England he saw that politics cannot be a science of abstract ideas, but is an empirical art.

IV

"Habit is nature improved"; that might well be taken as the motto of M. Paul Bourget's later novels, above all of *L'Etape*. Science, conceived as an exalted branch of morals, year by year drew

this ever young novelist closer and closer to the
Ancien Régime, and exalted him with a deep sense
of moral obligation towards his ancestors. If such
is the alliance between science and Old France,
M. Bourget is surely not alone in his own camp.
Indeed, well thronged is the school of reactionists,
if we may call reactionary men who with a somewhat revolutionary mind demonstrate the imperfec-
tion and weakness of the Revolution. After Renan,
whose dreams of aristocracy are well known, the
name to cite is that of Charles Maurras, the leader
of the *Action Française* group. But side by side
with the young disciples of Maurras, many of whom
must have been killed by now, and who combined
a free lance spirit with great literary talent, mention must be made of other writers in other schools.
We must include such men as the Vicomte de Vogüé
(his book, *les Morts qui parlent,* is only written to
prove the power of tradition): as the poet, Jean
Moréas, a great traditionalist, and all the greater
traditionalist in that he was born a Greek; as the
critic, Emile Faguet, who in his book upon the Eighteenth Century did not hesitate to speak his mind
to a century which was "neither Christian nor
French" and thus wrote the sequel to the critical
studies of Taine. I have chosen the names of three
writers as different as possible, in order to show
clearly the tendencies of the modern French mind,
at least in the greater part of France.

It is generally recognized that James and Bergson have a great influence on contemporary youth,
but it is only fair to say that the study of Auguste
Comte's Positivist Philosophy gave the young minds
of 1900 their taste for facts and individuals. In
this sense one may say that Comte's influence is
merged in that of Bergson; both men teach that

life overflows the framework in which philosophical
systems would encase it. The influence of Bourget
reinforced once more that of Comte. All agree on
this point, that no human progress can be made
unless the poor human plant avail itself of the hus-
banded resources of a race and a country.

Comte, with his utter contempt for all metaphysics, included in his hatred the work of the French
Revolution, which according to him had failed to
recognize the laws which maintain society. He believed that man had a natural horror of order, and,
further, that he was led by his imagination to attribute an extraordinary power to his own dreams.
Comte's thought is not very distant from that of
the pragmatists: though he would develop our self-
control by some religious system; that is the explanation of his admiration, expressed in the latter part
of his life, for Catholicism, since in his eyes the
individual exists only in and through society. His
influence upon Charles Maurras, from this point of
view, cannot be over-estimated.

In the same way one may discover among the contributors to the *Revue critique des Idées et des
Livres** a certain number of *soi disant* agnostics who
nevertheless profess the profoundest respect for the
religion of their childhood, and in the same temper
as Comte, through love of order and harmony.

It might be as well here to remind the reader of
Madame Adam's book *Chrétienne* (1913) which is
in absolute contradiction with her first book *Païenne,*
or of M. Louis Bertrand's early *St. Augustin* and

---

*The *Revue Critique des Idées et des Livres*, justly famous for
its admirable energy and enthusiasm for classic France, had gath-
ered round it before the War a brilliant *pléiad* of young writers, the
greater number of whom fell on the field of honor. Distinctions here
are invidious: but perhaps one may say that the most talented were
Pierre Gilbert (author of *la Forêt des Cippes*), Jean-Marc Bernard,
and Lionel des Rieux.

his last book, *Sanguis Martyrum:* with their underlying idea that it is Christianity which makes us
realize more completely than any other doctrine the
ideals of our true nature.

So then M. Bourget is well in the contemporary
stream. The finesse, the acuity, of his mind make him
like those insects (and the comparison, I am sure,
would not displease him) whose antennæ bring them
into contact with certain of the minute vibrations
by which space is traversed, so completely are they
attuned to the world's harmony. There are pages
in the *Démon du Midi* which seem quite prophetic,
breathing an organic sympathy with the whole
frame of society. That, however, is explicable,
since, after all, society is our own intellectual con-
struction. The war novels of M. Paul Bourget are
cast into the world of thought not so much for our
delight as for our instruction and improvement.
Before the war his profound religious convictions
gave great authority to his work, but now his theories are based upon reasons which we understand
unfortunately all too well. War is a reality which
lends its force to the novelist's thesis.

It may be that formerly such books as *l'Etape*
(1902), *Un Divorce* (1904), *l'Emigré* (1908), sometimes seemed like so many satirical pictures con-
taining a certain disproportion caused by the whims
of the painter, and M. Bourget's brush exaggeration
may have wearied us more than once; but to-day his
latest novels, *le Sens de la Mort, Lazarine, Némésis,*
(not to mention the *Démon du Midi*) appear to
speak absolute truth seen in the lurid light of present events. In the serene sunshine of the years
before 1914 we could not imagine that our world
was a bankrupt one, and all the vigor and splendor
of Bourget's intellect could not outdazzle the light

of reality which showed us every man managing to work out his own salvation from the errors and follies of his age. We were even haunted by the thought that this epoch, which seemed to us so awful and decadent, would appear to our grandchildren delightful and even venerable, in proportion as the mist of distance and the dimness of their sight would weave garments for the past, like the Emperor's new clothes of fairy story. To-day the consciousness that we live encompassed about by incalculable world forces, that man must be fortified by bravery, purity, temperance, is borne in more and more heavily upon our minds, and prevents our shutting our eyes to the infinite which embosoms us. M. Bourget's war novels are hymns of praise to self-sacrifice. And indeed, surrounded as we are by men who die for us, we feel that if Time can hush the tumult of contemporary opinion, it cannot stay the preaching of a Truth which makes life worth living. To quote his own words: "Une loi aussi mystérieuse qu'universelle veut que la guerre, cette sanglante épreuve, soit la forme inévitable de cette contrainte que les individus comme les nations doivent subir. D'un bout à l'autre de l'Histoire nous constatons que les peuples qui ont voulu, enivrés de leur civilisation, s'en faire un instrument de jouissance et de paix, ont été livrés comme des proies aux peuples plus rudes. Ils ont été envahis et asservis. Leur renoncement, la largeur et l'opulence de leur hospitalité ne les ont pas sauvés, ni même leur supériorité de culture, s'ils n'ont pas su la défendre les armes à la main. Nous ne possédons rien qui ne soit menacé, dès que nous n'avons plus l'énergie de maintenir cette possession par la force. Toute propriété n'est qu'une conquête continue.''

Of course no writer is perfect, and a critic might find in *Némésis,* as in *le Sens de la Mort,* certain defects. M. Bourget reminds us sometimes of a mystic giant-killer; his characters attitudinize too much, and the last day, in the Palazzo di Valverde, in *Némésis,* is really like the Day of Judgment. But we must be grateful to a novelist who descends from his tripod into the actual present, and who never wearies of preaching that all the evils of the present time are the outcome of the false and selfish aims of man, and that their remedy lies in honesty and in Christianity. Such simple truths, yet so hard to realize!

Bourget is the reconciling link between Taine and Bergson. In fact, Taine had already prepared the way for Bergson by his attack upon Reason.

"Not only is reason not natural to man nor universal in humanity, but its influence in the conduct of man and humanity is such. Save in a few cold, lucid intellects in which it can reign because it meets with no rival, it is far from playing the principal part; that falls to other powers born within us and which by right of being first occupiers keep possession of the dwelling. Reason's place therein is always limited and the duties it fulfils always secondary. . . . Man's masters are physical temperament, corporal needs, animal instinct, hereditary prejudice, imagination, in general the dominating passion, more particularly personal interest or the interest of family, caste or party." (*Ancien Régime,* p. 59.)

Further, Bourget's aim is to be above all a physiologist, as is well brought out by M. Jules Grasset's book, "*L'Idée médicale dans les romans de M. Paul Bourget.* Every reader of Bergson knows the importance he attaches to calling our attention to biological problems. But at the same time, as Dr. Grasset shows, Bourget wishes to escape from "the fanaticism of Science" in exactly the same way as Bergson's disciples, and he opposes the order of mind and the order of heart to that blind impassible universe which can crush us, but can only do that.

At the close of 1914, on the death of M. de Meun, Paul Bourget took this writer's place for a time on the staff of the *Echo de Paris*. Those who read his articles were able to realize the influence Bergsonian ideas had upon Bourget, though here again we are reminded of Taine, who was always teaching that abstract ideas could be verified only by the results they gave, when applied. But Bourget, faithful to living psychology, never describes the brutal objective fact: he paints it as reflected through the souls of his characters, being convinced that the most exact, most precise description of any scene is the description of a soul-state. M. Le Roy, in his acute treatise on Bergson, has shown us that this was exactly the Bergsonian method. And this amounts to saying that the artist must find in Reality that hidden inner thing which is not apparent to the eye of the man in the street. Brunetière, in his *Renaissance de l'Idéalisme,* speaks practically the same language as Bergson in his *Perception du Changement:*—

So that direction of thought influences a whole country's actions, modifies its spirit and helps to mold its destiny.

Once again we come back to the humanist point of view; the importance of a truth is measured by its utility to a nation. And the test of a truth's utility is Will, the active soul; not intellect, the passive soul.

ANATOLE FRANCE

IN a certain country churchyard, fair as are all English country churchyards, one tombstone stands out from all the others, as a noble thought from the passing impressions of every day. I love it because some artist has engraved on it a sheaf of corn, and this perfect simplicity is rendered the more touching by the commonplace pretentiousness of the surrounding stones made to order by the stone-mason of the neighboring cathedral town. Some good husbandman died — his name is already effaced by yellowing lichens — but the symbol of his energy and work stands erect among the meadow flowers which bloom there every year. Its classic nudity, its homely decoration, are a perpetual lesson in taste to the modern mind, unbalanced as it is by so many different impressions, buffeted by so many incoherent images. In the very midst of the desolation wrought so remorselessly by Time around the little church, that sheaf of corn speaks of the eternal youth of Life, and so speaking robs Death of his terror, forcing him to abandon his sting. Fertility and joy reign in the spot where sorrow thought to rule, and this vision of the immortal wheat serves to restore its Greek serenity to the mind, as it dwells upon the miracles of germination, earth's fecundity, and the tomb's purification.

Anatole France, in the midst of the modern tangle of ideas, is like that tombstone. Everything about him is simple, clear, ordered: everything is harmoni-

131

ously balanced. Greek serenity and charm, grace and pliancy: such are the qualities of all his work. Not for him those limitless aspirations such as ruffled the locks of three generations of romantics. Anatole France is concerned only with the sentient forms which surround and delight us; his dreams are only of order and harmony, transporting on to paper what eye and ear can seize. So great is his art that in reading him one is irresistibly reminded of Joubert's remark about Rousseau, when he said that no writer so well gave the impression of flesh wedded to mind and the delights of their union. In every book of Anatole France's there are magnetic sentences which make us well realize the physical voluptuousness of style. All the ardor of life finds in him its best interpreter. Curiously enough, his is the most deliberate of arts, and some critics have found considerable entertainment in counting up his borrowings; yet at the same time it is the very art of the *unconscious*. Its author has the power of calling up all the subconscious powers which exist in us, with exquisite skill selecting and grouping beautiful sound with subtle thought, setting side by side the rarest and most homely words. He is the interpreter of that "ordinary" soul which he himself qualifies as "desolate and longing, gentle, innocent, sensual, sad, dragging after it its weariness in its pursuit of illusion and hopes." So that it would be quite wrong to study Anatole France merely as an icy intellectual. His imagination is an emotional imagination. Man carries the world in his mind, but M. France seems to carry all the emotions of the world in his heart. That is why he, skeptic though he is, has seen so clearly into the Christian heart. A man cannot tie his shoelace without recognizing all the laws of nature, and M. Anatole France, by that sensitiveness of intellect which makes him all things to all men, leads us into the magic circle wherein genius is really a larger imbibing of the common heart.

The life of reason is only one part of our life. The life of feelings, which has nothing to do with logical reason, does not change with the course of centuries. That is the real torch handed on by one generation to the next, and Reason seems to exist only for the purpose of protecting the flame from draughts.

To what extent, then, is Anatole France, with his protests against the abuse of rationalism, an anti-intellectual? Nothing, certainly, could be better calculated to please the French classical mind than the fine order of his deductions, the clearness of his method, and the limpidity of his style. Again, it may be said that all his works tend towards the triumph of reason. Yet the self he lauds in his books is after all an indecent self, cynical and non-moral. Now, if I am to believe M. Albert Bazaillas,[*] that self is the Unconscious.

M. Anatole France is never tired of telling us that he follows only his own inclinations, for morality is non-existent and truth ever eludes us. "That *know thyself* of Greek philosophy is a great piece of foolishness" (*Le Jardin d'Epicure*). "Oh, yes, morality! I know — Duty! But duty is the very deuce to discover" (*Le Lys Rouge,* p. 37). Similar passages abound.

But it is precisely on account of the thousand shades of his ever mobile temperament that Anatole France has been able to reflect human feelings. Boring down through the changing complexity of passions, he has arrived at the bedrock of all feel-

---

[*] Cf. *Musique et Inconscience*, par Albert Bazaillas, Paris, 1908.

ings, and acquired a wise knowledge of humanity which brings him near to the Greeks. The Greek Sophists and Protagoras declared long since that there is no such thing as truth, but only opinions — that which is shameful in one man's eyes may be honorable in another's. Such is the opinion of Euripides in his famous line, when Æolus accuses his son Macareus of the crime of incest, and the latter replies, "Where is the shameful action if its author judges it not so?"

M. Anatole France merely repeats the words of the Greek poet in a thousand variations.

M. Maurice Barrès once wrote: "One thing is quite certain: that life is aimless and that man nevertheless needs to pursue some dream."*

Anatole France, who knows, none better, that life is aimless, dreams of reincarnating in himself the soul of a Greek, of the age of Phidias, and of arriving, through love of order and true proportions, at that perfect beauty of which the Parthenon furnished a type to the Universe.

But Anatole France is a Parisian with an Angevin father, which means he has a double share of the mocking, delicate, sensual spirit; and the soul reincarnated in him is that of Lucian or of Meleager rather than that of Plato. His irony has sometimes the cruel immobility of the masks of Greek actors; and his lips part in a sneer to give passage to bitter poisonous words lashing the odious — or ridiculous — sides of our existence. Yet his irony is pity's daughter; as he himself says, "That same nervous sensitiveness which makes us weep over many things, makes us laugh at many others." And he can discern the wondrous dawn of a new humanity: if the marvel of Greece existed, it can exist again.

*Voyage de Sparbe.

Minerva, who was once the incarnation of wisdom, perfection, beauty and taste, cannot die. Besides, he can find consolation for everything at the feet of the Venus of Milo — not infrequently the Venus is not even of Milo! We remember why his Brotteaux des Ilettes in *The Gods Are Athirst* believed that "Nature was not entirely bad."

This ardent neo-hellenism, this belief that the Greeks were the artists of the world and that with them all was grace, harmony, moderation and wisdom, which never failed to support Anatole France in the highly heterogeneous society in which he moved, comes to him from several sources; not only from a certain milieu in which he lived, but also from himself, from his true foundation, — that is to say, from certain ancestral habits, not of thought, but of feeling.

In order to understand Anatole France one must first be acquainted with the efforts of an important group of French writers who, some in order to be rid of what they call the Semitic virus, others aiming at creating a society or, if that be impossible, a literature based on the ancient model, others again striving to arrive at a type of beauty or reason which should rise superior to the variations of centuries, practised the religion which upheld Théophile Gautier, Taine, Renan, or Leconte de Lisle, and which may be most conveniently called neo-hellenism. If only one could really penetrate to the depths of these men's minds, it would be curious to analyze what they understood by neo-hellenism. The feeling is eminently vague, since it is nourished upon ideas culled from every age, every philosophy and every town of Greece and Asia Minor; and yet, at the same time, the feeling is profound and violent, since it is also nourished on all the cares and all the

hatred experienced by these men. If the Sixteenth-
Century scholars and men of letters saw in the study
of Greek writers a means of reacting against the
Middle Ages and their religious teaching, and of
thus propagating a fertile belief in the goodness and
wisdom of nature, it is equally clear that the Nineteenth-Century writers with whom we are for the
moment concerned aimed at declaring war upon
French Society as constituted by the Revolution of
1789, and at the same time upon Christianity, that
religion which Anatole France calls "exterminator
of all thought, all science, and all joy."*

As a matter of fact, a Ronsard in the Sixteenth
Century can join with his friends in ceremonious
sacrifice of a goat to Bacchus without thereby ceasing to be a Christian. His cult of antiquity is merely
the guiding faith of his *literature;* that of his life is
the Christian religion. We have to wait till modern times, that is to say till an age when the writer
would fain direct not only letters, but society itself,
to see the artist's literary piety transformed into a
veritable cult of Greece, into a living, vital religion.
The Greece which existed and exists only in men's
minds has been made living by the fervor of these
French writers. The Nineteenth Century will ever
be the century in which the Greece of Phidias was
most adored, and in which the belief was held that
there had once really existed a happy land in which
men were guided by Reason. Any text-book of
French literature will give you an account of the
return to antique art which characterises the close
of the Eighteenth Century. It is perhaps unnecessary to remind the reader of the Pompeian paintings
in the salon in the *Rue Chantereine* where Bonaparte wooed Joséphine. There is no better proof

*Vers les temps meilleurs, II, 78.

of the hellenic atmosphere of a certain part of society than the fashions during the Directory and First Empire. Athens and Rome were then two wellsprings of powerful energy, and it may be said that many a Frenchman carefully composed his "sensibility" on the lines of an antiquity he found in André Chénier, Winckelmann or even Goethe. Indeed, the extremely complex movement of Romanticism could not succeed in destroying Classicism, for the simple reason that French culture is a direct descendant of Greek and Latin tradition. There is no better proof of that than the ever-fresh fame of a man of genius who died in 1839 at the early age of twenty-nine: Maurice de Guérin. His poem *le Centaure*, steeped as it is in a passionate feeling for Nature, is a better commentary than any learned dissertation on the enthusiasm felt then for antiquity and the love for the forces of nature.

Théophile Gautier, influenced by André Chénier, and still more influenced by his own passionate desire for voluptuousness, was able to endure his existence of galley-slave of journalism only because he was upheld by his conception of Greek beauty. His contemporaries, Paul de St. Victor and Théodore de Banville, were fanatical worshippers of a Greece they liked to Italianize. Renan's prayer to Pallas Athenê is only surpassed by that of Charles Maurras to the same goddess. Taine forgets his Anglomania to muse upon Greece as the only country in which a man may harmoniously develop his faculties.

The desire of the true neo-hellenist to work for the happiness of man by freeing him from the shackles of religious superstition is perhaps best seen in Leconte de Lisle's *Poèmes Antiques*. It is true that one day master and pupil, Leconte de Lisle and Anatole France, were to quarrel; but even the noisiness of their dispute should not make us forget that the favorite poet of both is Lucretius because he, even as they, declared war upon religion, begetter of all evils.

Louis Ménard, Leconte de Lisle's friend, had none of this fierce hatred: he believed that all religions were true since they were successive affirmations of an eternal need. Anatole France makes his Gallion (*Sur la Pierre blanche*) express the same idea: "You must know, dear friends, it is not enough to tolerate every religion, you must honor them all, believe that all are holy, and all equal by reason of the good faith of those who profess them."

The last comer to this school is M. Charles Maurras, whose *Anthinea* is the purest expression of that cult of Reason which the Greeks alone realized.

Among all these neo-hellenes — and my list is necessarily far from complete since for that a whole volume would be needed — Anatole France shines in the front rank in enthusiasm and his care of style. The great gods are not propitiated by analysis and devotion, and M. Anatole France must needs know it as he makes his examination of conscience; for he is one of those who are convinced that reason plays a very small part in the life of man, and that the great impulse which keeps the world moving is sentiment. And yet he worships an independent Reason existing in each of us and allowing us to come near to the august Truth seated on the summit of the Universe.

M. France is as much of a determinist as Barrès, although both speak a different language and dwell in hostile camps. M. France is well aware that his reason is fettered by certain habits of thought contracted in his youth and in particular among the Parnassians. Nor does he forget that he has put his

likes and dislikes, his revolts and anxieties, his whole
temperament, in fact, into his neo-hellenism. He
does not deceive himself; and that is, after all, his
greatest characteristic in the modern world of letters. The last of the Pagans of Paris is perhaps
the most elusive of them all.

Once again we see that the real interest in studying a man of letters is a dramatic interest, a question of contest between the conflicting forces of that
writer's soul. With Anatole France it is not merely
the contest which exists in the thinker desirous of
composing for himself a would-be-hellenic vision of
the universe, and who by nature is a sentimentalist
disillusioned before taking action, yet wishing to act.
Nor is it merely the contest in the inner soul of every
man seeking his true self, but who can only lend himself and never wholly give, and who tries to find consolation in mocking heroism and ridiculing morality.
Nor is it merely the contest which sooner or later
must arise in the mind of a man who is at one and the
same time an idealist and a determinist; of the epicurean who at one moment preaches that man wars
upon man by an eternal immutable law, and the next
that if men fight it cannot be through the laws of
a mechanistic nature, since war is a transitory state
whose ideal termination is peace. No, the dramatic
contest is deeper laid. With Anatole France it is
the outcome of the profound disagreement existing
between his physical temperament and his intellectual aspirations.

In thought M. France is the freest and most audacious of writers: to prove that would be merely to
stave in an open door. But at the same time he is
the least pugnacious of men: such is the testimony
of those who know him best. His enemies would
suggest that he is afraid of receiving blows.

M. Fernand Calmettes, who knew M. France in-
timately, has devoted some most interesting pages to
him in his book *Leconte de Lisle et ses Amis*. M.
Calmettes notices, too, this discord between Anatole
France's two selves, and tells us how the habitués
of Leconte de Lisle's salon were disconcerted by
these alternating movements of advance and retreat
— by the ardent protests of an out-and-out republi-
can, followed by the retreat of a writer utterly hostile
to violence and careful mainly of nothing but his
own personal comfort. M. Calmettes has some very
penetrating passages when he charges Anatole
France with fleeing from that simplicity in which
his mind was most at ease — "just as some women
leave the man they love for another who gives them
no pleasure" — and a little further on M. Calmettes,
grouping together Renan, Jules Lemaître and Anatole France in an eloquent passage, accuses them
all of yielding to the needs of the moral weakness
of their age. "There is nothing in the world or
in life worth taking seriously or tragically. Every
violent gesture is imbued with the ugliness of all
exaggeration. True elegance dwells only in the gentleness of irony, in the serenity of indifference."
It is true that sometimes Anatole France seems to
attach so little value to his ideas that we realize he
loves them for their charm rather than for the truth
they may contain. His voluptuous intellectualism,
product of a sinuous mobile soul, plays around ideas,
convinced that revolutions are as useless as words,
and that everything happens in the world by means
of "forces which are blind, deaf, slow and irresistible, bearing all things away." But while we may
admit with M. Calmettes that some of M. France's
writings have been too indulgent towards the moral
inertia of his day, it must always be recognized that

he is a false skeptic playing a dilettantism like an instrument, ear-tickling for his contemporaries, but playing it only so long as his heart of hearts remains unconcerned.

He is a true Frenchman, never ceasing to fight for the ideas dear to the heart of every Frenchman: first, the idea of freedom and in particular freedom of the pen (on this point it is sufficient to read his polemic with Brunetière in 1889 on the subject of Bourget's *le Disciple*); secondly, the idea of justice which at the time of the Dreyfus case brought the skeptic from his study, or if you will, the cynic from his tub, to plead fervently in the cause of justice; thirdly, the idea of the classical spirit, for our dilettante has shown in every one of his writings that the individual worth of every Frenchman is due in great part to the collective worth of his Roman-Greek ancestors. To these I would add the idea of patriotism, the love of France, — *France, mère des arts, des armes et des lois,* — which inspired such eloquent pages from his pen during the World War.

Anatole France is the son of eminently pious parents, as he himself has been often pleased to tell us. When the time comes for relating his real biography, it will be seen that this skeptic has been guilty of more than one virtuous action.

Those who have read *le Livre de mon Ami, les Désirs de Jean Servien,* and certain pages of *la Vie Littéraire,* may have noticed to what an extent Anatole France is a Chateaubriand who has turned out badly, but a Chateaubriand who is far more sincere than his prototype, far less vain, utterly ignorant of the lower feelings of Chateaubriand; with nothing to fear, that is, from the criticisms of a future Jules Lemaître. It would be amusing to imagine a dialogue between these two epicureans in whose souls the battle between Christianity and paganism had such widely differing results. Certainly both men put into practice the saying which Stendhal attributes to an Italian lady: "What excellent sherbet! and how much more delicious it would be if it were a sin to drink it!" Only, from this point of view Chateaubriand would appear to be the greater epicurean, for he does really believe in sin. M. France, far more critical and more malicious, is entirely of Emerson's opinion. "What flutters the Church of Rome, or of England, or of Geneva, or of Boston, may yet be very far from touching any principle of faith." True, he declares, when studying Sainte-Beuve, that religion is a seasoning which improves the taste of voluptuousness; and again he writes that George Sand and Chateaubriand knew the value remorse adds to pleasure; but his epicureanism, complicated as it was by skepticism, deprived him of a pleasure which religion alone can give. No unbeliever can really know the joys of sacrilege; God is not blasphemed by a man who declares God does not exist.

M. France is so convinced that mysticism pours its blandest perfumes over epicureanism that he has founded some of his books (*Thaïs, Sur la Pierre blanche, La Révolte des Anges*) on the idea that religion strengthens passions by the attraction it lends them by condemning them. When his sinners confess their sins, or make their examination of conscience, M. France is determined his reader shall realize the intense pleasure such psychological exercises can give. And in this way, with supreme skill, he makes us collaborators of Saint Theresa and Ignatius of Loyola.

It is a kind of sorcery, and his chapter of fascina-

tions is very long. He loves the marvelous, he loves
to relate fantastic legends or pious chronicles; so
much so that it has been truly said that his thought
is haunted by the mysterious. A child will put a
mask over his face to frighten himself, but M.
France leans over his own mirror in order to be horrified at his own countenance which he distorts at
will — and his toys are numerous.

So that in reality there is no reproach he so little
deserves as that most frequently hurled at him — of
wallowing in the obscene. M. France has his sensu-
alism exceedingly well in hand: it is intellect rather
than anything else which is spent in his *grivoiseries*.
The greatest pleasure of his so called immorality
lies for him in its wit, and his love of order and moderation does not abandon him even in his most singular ebullitions. His sensuality and his curiosity
should never be separated. They are two different
aspects of a mind "which is a born spectator," and
which wants to preserve "the ingenuousness of the
lounger whom everything amuses and who in an
age of ambition can still adopt the disinterested
curiosity of small children." He is not so easily
amused, after all!

Sensual he doubtless is, like all those who are
born curious, and in particular scholars. He speaks
somewhere of the "silent orgies" of meditation;
and wise is the poet who prefers to sup in dreams
with Greek beauties rather than with the flesh-and-
blood ones of his own time.

Anatole France is an artisan who well understands his own fortune; or rather he avails himself
of a certain twist of his mind, of a certain flaw in his
constitution which he knows how to use. If his intellectual boldness knows no bounds it is because he

is at bottom an Eighteenth-Century philosopher —
of the earth earthy. His aim is to reinstate the
senses in the highest place, and he therefore recognizes, affirms and preaches their rights with all
the ardor of a Diderot. Nor does he shrink at
times from contradicting so great a psychologist
as La Rochefoucauld, who wrote: "La plupart
des femmes se rendent plutôt par faiblesse que par
passion."

No other man has related his own life as has Anatole France. From his early youth he seems to have
realized Montaigne's wisdom in describing our most
fleeting impressions. We see him growing up in
his father's old bookshop on the Quai Malaquais between the Academy and the Rue du Bac opposite the
Louvre, in a piety-laden atmosphere. His father,
M. Noël Thibault, was a highly respected bibliophile
who sold rare editions for the publisher Bachelin-
Defloreune. M. Roger le Brun, in his biography of
Anatole France, tells us that the shop in question
was at No. 9 Quai Voltaire: the establishment now
occupied by Messrs. Champion. M. Thibault *père*
had served in the *gardes du corps* of Charles X and
naturally held eminently royalist opinions. One
must have lived in provincial France and known in
one's childhood old gentlemen who were devoted to
the cause of the Comte de Chambord to understand
the fidelity and loyalty which the elder branch of the
Bourbon family kindled in the hearts of their followers. Anatole France's mother, "a woman of
gentle, serious piety," as he says, was a native of
Bruges, while his father was of Angevin origin; and
it seems to me that his parents can be often seen
looking through the windows of his eyes. It appears, too, that he had a very Eighteenth-Century
grandmother; and he is most of all what that grand-

mother made him, since our tastes so often skip a
generation. Very often that Voltairean grandmother plays naughty tricks on the pious mother in
his brain. On one page we read the counsels of the
good master to Jacques Tournebroche: "My son,
fear women and books for their weakness and their
pride. Be humble of heart and spirit. God grants
to the humble a clearer understanding than to the
learned." These words, which might be culled from
the Imitation, heighten the effect of the following
pages which seem to express much what Apollonius
of Tyaneas says to Saint Antoine in Flaubert's
book: "He is a simple soul, he believes in the reality
of things!" All the facts of Nature are Eleusinian
mysteries.

One wonders whether there is any truth in the
theory that at Stanislas College Anatole France suffered at the hands of a priest. Some critics have
endeavored to explain his hatred of the *curé* by that
reason. I think his hatred of religion comes rather
from an antipathy in his nature. The more one
reads Anatole France, the more is one impressed
by his terror at the irresistible flight of time. In
his eyes the only value of life lies in the idea of
death threatening it at every turn. Christianity, on
the contrary, while admitting the fugitive character
of life, far from teaching us that we must therefore
extract all possible pleasure from it, tells us to disdain it since it is but the troublous pilgrimage to
an eternal existence.

It is not my task here to analyze each of Anatole
France's books, from his critical study of Alfred de
Vigny in 1878, his two volumes of verse, *Poèmes
Dorés* (1873), and *les Noces Corinthiennes* (1878),
Jocaste and *le Chat maigre* (1879), *le Crime de Syl-
vestre Bonnard* (1881), *les Désirs de Jean Servien*

(1882) to *les Dieux ont Soif* (1912) and *la Révolte des Anges* (1914).

Anatole France has always been what he is to-day, convinced that Christianity is the enemy of all social and philosophic progress; convinced on the other hand that mankind has nothing to gain from revolutions. It is enough to read the four volumes of his *Vie Littéraire* (1888-92), which had considerable influence upon the young minds of the day, to see that Anatole France has really always been the same. Of course there are degrees in his work, just as on his changing countenance; witness his attitude, already alluded to, during the Dreyfus affair. The love of a fight is a very characteristic trait of the Angevine race, and it comes out in M. France's skirmishes with his one-time master, Leconte de Lisle, and his literary adversary, Emile Zola. While he was engaged in writing *la Rôtisserie de la reine Pedauque* (1893), *les Opinions de Jérôme Coignard* (1893), and *le Jardin d'Epicure* (1895), his love of a fight led him to break a lance with writers who really belonged to the same party as he.*

A foreigner once asked Stendhal what was the best way to get to know France. "I only know one way: and it is not very pleasant. Spend six or eight months in a provincial town unaccustomed to receive foreigners." And then Stendhal added, "Best of all would be to have a law suit!" M. France accepts Stendhal's view rather differently, though at bottom everything turns on the Dreyfus affair. Those who want to see what M. France's imagination is should read these volumes rather than *Thaïs*

---

*Anatole France became a member of the French Academy in December, 1896, but I do not think he has often attended its meetings: the academic arm chair would hardly seem easy to him. It was at this period that he wrote his four volumes of *Contemporary History*: *le Mannequin d'Osier* (1897), *l'Orme du Mail* (1897), *l'Anneau d'Améthyste* (1899) and *M. Bergeret à Paris* (1901).

or *le Lys Rouge*. Critics are never tired of maintaining that Anatole France has no imagination; they take him at his word, which is scarcely wise when dealing with such an ironist. On the contrary, Anatole France has an exceedingly powerful imagination which transforms and magnifies the external world. He is for ever discovering anew that the things we look upon as substances have value only as symbols and are only "images changeantes dans l'universelle illusion." If that is not imagination, may one ask what is? "Every healthy mind is a true Alexander or Sesostris, building a universal monarchy." And each of us is a sensitive being endowed with unknown powers.

Anatole France, I repeat, is very like Lucian, but he surpasses the Greek in the depth and pathos of his philosophy. In this way he is well able to understand the aspirations of the new world which is now in its birth throes. His socialism is the comprehension of the state of soul of a people about to produce something fresh, something better, something higher and nobler. M. Calmettes gives us, in his book, a rather charming scene where Anatole France pushes the perambulator of one of his friend's children to enable that friend to enter into free discussion with M. Paul Bourget. I like to read something symbolical into this friendly act: even so would Anatole France wheel the perambulator of infant humanity, avoiding the jolts and ruts of the way, so as to allow his friends to hurl themselves into the ardent contests of politics with even more energy than he. Contact with the populace is by no means repugnant to him, as is proved by his political speeches; but man of letters, *homme de cabinet* as he eminently is, he loses something of his weapons before a rather stormy crowd.

Those who seek an antidote to Anatole France's subtle poisons will find it in the writings of a great royalist writer who long considered himself a pupil of Anatole France, and who has always kept for him a boundless admiration. I mean M. Charles Maurras, the author of *Anthinea*. He too is, or once was, a true pagan: readers of *Anthinea* realized how enamored he was of Greek art when they saw him embracing the first column of the Prophyleum, or when they read the famous passage describing his last impressions of the Athens Museum. The neohellenism of these two writers has led to very different results, because in Maurras it is intellect which predominates and in Anatole France feeling. Maurras believes in a Reason which rises superior to the variations of history and nature, and thereby believes in a hierarchy in art, and thereby in another hierarchy. While contemplating his country given over to parliamentarianism founded on incompetent and irresponsible electoral committees, he dreams of a new French government, founded no longer on selfish appetite but on Reason and Order, and he sees salvation only in a good king. Such a dream can but awaken laughter in an Anatole France who is in temperament much closer to the realities of politics and of life, and who is distrustful of dialectics and pure reason.

To tell the truth, the French writer of whom Anatole France most reminds us is Rabelais: like Rabelais he is a scholar, a monk in the guise of a man of the people. The very simple feelings which every critic has noted are the same in both: the spirit of liberty so engrained in every dweller on the banks of the Loire, together with a sociable kind of instinct made up of gentleness and kindness. It is quite easy to imagine future generations annotating and commenting upon the works of Anatole France just as today we annotate and comment upon the works of the immortal Tourangeau.

Anatole France, though older than Bergson, has contributed far more largely than he himself would be inclined to believe to the influence of Bergsonian philosophy. So true it is that a great spiritual current carries with it other streams and makes them tributary to itself. At first sight there would seem to be nothing in common between Bergsonism which has brought so many minds to a religious conception of existence, and which in the eyes of some seems to sanction the ideal of the Catholic Church, and the philosophy of Anatole France with its foundation of almost incredibly perverse skepticism ending not infrequently in militant anarchy.

But — as M. Bergson himself said when writing of M. Ravaisson-Mollien — what makes the agreement of two minds is less a similitude of opinion than a certain affinity of intellectual temperament. This affinity really does exist between Anatole France and Bergson: it is to be seen in a profound humanism, in their philosophy of flow and mobility, and again in that mistrust of human reason, which is also part of the spirit of their age. Those who have not read the French classics and do not know their Pascal and their Montaigne cannot really understand these two writers. Port-Royal appears more than once on the horizon of our memory: when the abbé, Jérôme Coignard, attacks all that Pascal attacked before him while proving the vanity of human institutions and expressing his disgust for the *trognes à épée* and *chats fourrés* of justice; or when M. Bergson declares that intuition is far superior to Reason, and puts us on our guard against words which distort reality.

M. Bergson's conception of instinct, his theory
that reality which is continuous, durable, and creator
of the universe is to be found not only in conscious thought but above all in the unconscious
thoughts and instinctive actions of animals, is
also clearly seen in Anatole France, as for example when Jérôme Coignard declares he would
never have signed a line of the declaration of the
Rights of Man because of the excessive and unjust
separation established therein between man and the
gorilla.

The conception of history and historical method
which Anatole France has developed in the Preface
of his *Vie Littéraire,* in *Le Jardin d'Epicure,* and
les Opinions de M. Jérôme Coignard, is the same we
find in Péguy, as he doubtless had it from Bergson's own lips. A fact is an essentially complex
thing; its causes are older than the hills, so that
no historian can flatter himself that he can present
it in all its complexity; life is far too subtle, too
elusive — it will always escape him!

The fact that Anatole France has contradicted
himself from time to time, especially when writing
his *Jeanne d'Arc,* matters little. It is evident that
that historical arrogance which calls itself scientific history, with its pretension at arriving at the
only real truth, exasperated Anatole France, even
as it exasperated Péguy, and the close of *l'Ile des
Pingouins,* where he shows us history as a perpetual
beginning again, contains the essence of his thought
on the subject. Moreover, everything in his writings is the outcome of the conviction that life is
not a series of syllogisms and rational deductions,
since our most important actions confront us suddenly without our seeing their why and wherefore,

and impose themselves upon us despite the objurga-
tions of logic.

Must we here recognize a mystical tendency of
a rather German fashion as Bergson's enemies have
declared? On the contrary, these writers are nourished on the very essence of the great French moralists, and if they arrive at a mistrust of deductive
reasoning it is by other roads than those trodden
by the German Romanticists.

Doubtless Bergson as he grows older becomes
more and more spiritualistic, while Anatole France
seems to grow more and more of a skeptic. It would
seem that from the moment when Anatole France
laid bare the cruel attitude of God towards man
he fell into the ironical state of mind of a Swift
and arrived at absolute antimoralism. Bergson on
the contrary, carried away by his fine conception
of the vital impulse, feeling in the depths of his
own self the mainspring of universal life, has risen
through his enthusiasm to the Hellenic conception
of personal immortality. In reality his work is
rather like the atmosphere: whatever its final
unity, there are holes in it. Critics and aviators
know that. In any case *Time and Free Will,* with
its famous theory of concrete duration by reacting
against abstract thought, might bring the reader
to the cultivating of feeling for feeling's sake, and
thus to an essentially Francian vision of the world.
Pleasure is and must be ruler of the universe: and
that is what the heroine of M. France's *les Dieux ont
Soif* shows us. It cannot be denied that the morality
of *Time and Free Will* has nothing in common with
the wise ancestral morality which governs us, because it is the product of the experience of centuries. We know to what the insatiable desire of

life leads. We find it in the books of M. Georges
Sorel, who, like Anatole France and more than he,
dreams of better days when the disciples of Marx
and Proudhon shall hold despotic sway over the
earth. M. Georges Sorel intentionally grafts his
theories, and in particular his theory of the general strike, upon the Bergsonian theory of the
deeper self in contradistinction to our superficial
ego.* It would be quite easy to marshal a long series
of texts to show that the French soul as expressed
by the French moralists from Montaigne onwards,
has ever been struck — when it analyzes itself —
by the fact that we feel within us multiple beings,
and have as it were the recollection of many ex-
istences. There are moments when the consciousness of our identity which is founded on the testimony of memory seems to us a mere illusion, and
in our rarer moments we find ourselves in the presence of desires and velleities so numerous, thoughts
so complex, that we feel we have lived several lives
and flatter ourselves that we embrace all existence.
The finesse of thinkers like Montaigne, Pascal, La
Bruyère, La Rochefoucauld, is shown above all in
their perception of the simultaneity within us of
contrary feelings, and the subtlety of the great modern psychologians has ever sought to note more
and more the combination of our former with
our present states, and the repercussions between
the two.

One may say that Bergson has built the solid part
of his philosophy upon such ideas. For if the sensation of this instant does not destroy those which
went before, we get the impression of a *continuum*,

---

*Cf. his books: *Reflexions sur la Violence* and *les Illusions du
Progrès*.

of a duration of moral life. On the other hand, if
we exist only in a certain point of time, if our impressions are constantly variable, and our moral
being ever enriching itself, if we are incapable of
foretelling the future, we arrive at the other
Bergonsian idea of the imponderable quality of
mind, in opposition to the measurable quantity of
matter.

The impressionism and egotism of Anatole France
are based upon similar convictions. That alone
would suffice to show that in Bergson's theory of
intuition there is an ardent mysticism issuing from
those mysterious regions where the superhuman
alliance of the human being with the great Principle
of all things flows out over the ruins of Dogmatism.

The socialist in Anatole France is not far removed from the socialist in Sorel. That Cornelian
accent we hear in Sorel is distinctly audible in certain pages of *la Vie Littéraire* and proves that the
æstheticism of Anatole France can wield a lance
at need, and fight for a humanity with whose blem-
ishes and flaws he is well acquainted: for he is far
from sharing the naïve Eighteenth-Century philosophy, with its faith in man's natural goodness.

However that may be, whatever the judgment future generations reserve for Anatole France, he
cannot be denied the virtues of a disinterested curiosity and passion for Faith. Thereby this work has
a moral significance. He wants to force us to conquer our liberty by throwing open to all our faculties, to unconscious feeling as well as to conscious
reasoning, a field of action hitherto too often
neglected. The intuition he receives of universal
life saved him from what might have been a dis-
tressing egotism: and in the end the lesson we get

from his work, as from Bergson's, is a lesson of confidence in the human mind, which, by its continual efforts, its slow but sure progress, can ever call up new horizons before it.

All the same, after reading much Anatole France it is good to take down *Cranford.*

PAUL CLAUDEL

ONE may say without exaggeration that in the English-speaking world of those who attentively follow the literary movement in France, M. Paul Claudel is considered a very great, if not the greatest, French poet of the present day. His great merit lies in his being rather difficult, for the Anglo-Saxon public likes books over which it can ruminate, books which are somewhat oracular. Carlyle won immense renown by the way he had of emerging from the sybil's cave. Another great quality of M. Claudel's is that of recalling in his intuitionism, in his love of sensible and discordinate images, in his lyric joy, the great English writers such as those of the Cambridge school — Platonizing or Plotinizing — and those philosophers who, like Berkeley, unable to conceive anything abstract, took refuge in that idealism — realism which alone satisfies their desire to know God.

In France, M. Claudel has been so fortunate as to have disciples who are not only enthusiastic, but distinguished for their originality and moral insight, such as M. Georges Duhamel and M. Jacques Rivière. The terms in which these two very representative writers speak of Claudel remind me of M. Le Roy's homage to Bergson: "The curtain drawn between ourselves and reality, enveloping everything including ourselves in its deceiving folds, falls of a sudden, as if some spell dissipated, and displays to the mind depths of light till then undreamt of, in which reality itself, contemplated face to face for the first time, stands fully revealed.''

M. Duhamel means practically the same thing when he says: ''Tout dans les écrits de M. Claudel semble étranger au monde des proportions courantes.'' So does M. Jacques Rivière when he assures us that the poet can explain the world, not by giving reasons, but by calling them up by his voice in their true order: ''Il *légifère,* il ordonne aux êtres de surgir en les appelant et il fait sentir leur relation profonde.'' So that in Claudel we are confronted not merely by a man, but by a mind-movement of first importance: the fermenting action produced by M. Claudel in his own land, the land *par excellence* of intellectualism. When we see the worship M. Claudel receives in certain literary circles, we wonder if we are witnessing a brilliant 1830 romantic movement. We are reminded for a moment of the magnanimous, if dishevelled, battalions of *Hernani.* But M. Claudel would wield his authority only in favor of the religion to which he is a convert. This aspect of him must, therefore, be explained.

In the *Revue de la Jeunesse,* M. Claudel has himself told us the story of his conversion, on the 25th December, 1886, in *Notre Dame,* at Paris:

''Alors se produisit l'événement qui domine toute ma vie. En un instant mon coeur fut touché et je crus. Je crus d'une telle force d'adhésion, d'un tel soulèvement de tout mon être, d'une conviction si puissante, d'une telle certitude ne laissant place à aucune espèce de doute que, depuis, tous les livres, tous les raisonnements, tous les hasards d'une vie agitée n'ont pu ébranler ma foi, ni, à vrai dire, la toucher. J'avais eu tout à coup le sentiment dé-

chivant de l'Innocence, de l'éternelle enfance de
Dieu, une révélation ineffable. En essayant, comme
je l'ai fait souvent, de reconstituer les minutes qui
suivirent ces instants extraordinaires, je retrouve
les éléments suivants qui cependant ne formaient
qu'un seul éclair, une soule arme dont la Providence
divine se servait pour atteindre et ouvrir le coeur
d'un pauvre enfant désespéré. Que les gens qui
croient sont heureux! Si c'était vrai pourtant!
C'est vrai! — Il m'aime, Il m'appelle! Les larmes
et les sanglots étaient venus et le chant si tendre de
l'*Adeste* ajoutait encore à mon émotion.''

Claudel was then eighteen years old, having been
born in 1868; and the sublime vision had come not
to a pure and simple soul, but to a fastidious Parisian artist.

Every conversion is the secret of a conscience;
psychologians are powerless to discover its mechanism, for the simple reason that critic and convert
are separated by an abyss. As Claudel says so
justly: ''Connaître une chose, c'est la co-naitre en
elle.'' If, as Bergson and the spiritualists affirm,
the soul is not an organ but animates every organ,
not a function but master of every function, if
it is a ray of light emanating from supreme and
eternal Reality, then it is quite clear that every
conversion must be above all a mystery, we are
faced with the problem of divine grace. Even William James, as he draws up his list of converts, can
only state, he cannot explain. The most acute
analysis has never led to more than a realization
that every explanation hitherto offered of the birth
of our feelings is incomplete. The flash of intuition only serves to show us that something which
will always escape us. ''En un instant mon coeur
fut touché et *je crus*. . . . Dieu existe, il est là.

C'est quelqu'un, c'est un être aussi personnel que moi.''*

Nor would we venture to discuss the most important fact of M. Claudel's life were it not that he is a literary artist having himself tried to explain, not so much certain of his states of mind as his feeling of walking always in the presence of God.

And at once we are checked by a fact which will always astonish the enlightened public and which we know has deterred more than one sane reader. I mean the extraordinary influence M. Claudel himself acknowledges of a young man who, in spite of his admirable end, was frankly a wretched abnormal neurotic. William James had the courage to create an agreement between neurasthenia and religion. One wonders whether M. Claudel felt fortified by reading William James, when he dwelt on the influence exercised by Arthur Rimbaud on his mind. William James had spoken of the religious experiences realized by the use of chloroform. Are we to believe that the spiritual intoxication produced by reading Arthur Rimbaud's *Illuminations* so stimulated Claudel's mind that it was for the moment identified with truth?

''D'autres écrivains m'ont instruit, mais c'est Arthur Rimbaud seul qui m'a construit: il a été pour moi le révélateur en un moment de profondes ténèbres, l'illuminateur de tous les chemins de l'art, de la religion; de sorte qu'il m'est impossible d'imaginer ce que j'aurais pu être sans la rencontre de cet esprit angélique, certainement éclairé de la lumière d'en haut. Principes, pensées, forme même, je lui dois tout, et je me sens avec lui les liens qui

Ma Conversion. Rev. de la Jeunesse IX. 1913-1914.

peuvent nous rattacher à un ascendant spirituel.''*

Truly the spirit bloweth whither it listeth. If ever there existed a precocious abnormal genius, it was Rimbaud! Studies of him are not lacking, and it is easy to see in M. Paterne Berrichon's *Life of Rimbaud,* for example, that we are nowise in the presence of a Swedenborg or a Blake. With these we can at least understand their fascination for a certain type of mind nourished on a reading of the Bible and finding in this other reading, in moments of really emancipating emotion, the idea of a sublime part to play upon earth. But in Rimbaud there is not the slightest trace of these powerful imaginations who boldly venture forth to explore the realm of the oversoul. The more one reads M. Paterne Berrichon's sympathetic memoir of Rimbaud, the more convinced does one become that Rimbaud was a poet only for a few years in his life, and that he was mainly a neurasthenic, the prey of all the suffering, hallucinations and caprices of a morbid nature. ''Il exaspéra son système sensoriel par le vin, par les poisons, par l'aventure'' (P. Berrichon).

It is not our desire to undertake here a medical study of Rimbaud's temperament nor of his wandering mania, his hallucinations nor his relations with Verlaine, but, considering him solely from the literary point of view, one may say that he is the direct outcome of an extremely turgid literary Baudelairism, with the added complication of that venomous bitterness we see in unproductive men of letters. His imagination is like the vacillating flame of an electric lamp which is running out — now and

L'oeuvre de Paul Claudel, par Joseph de Tonquédec, p. 134. Letter from M. Claudel to M. Paterne Berrichon.

then a dazzling flash, then utter, profound darkness.

M. Claudel is well aware of all this. And yet if he persists in seeing in Rimbaud an angelic spirit, he must have very potent reasons for blinding himself and trying to blind us. I think these reasons are of various kinds. It may be that Claudel sees in Rimbaud a Claudel who has turned out badly. There, but for the grace of God, goes John Bunyan. Such a state of mind is perfectly comprehensible in a man of powerful imagination, such as Claudel. Again, on going deeper into Claudel's work, one realizes that Claudel the writer has been and still is influenced by Rimbaud, or by the literary group among whom Rimbaud takes his place. This exceedingly curious phenomenon can only be explained by Claudel's artistic vision. But it should be at once pointed out that Bergsonism brought tremendous reinforcement to theories which in a Rimbaud or a Mallarmé were little more than instinctive stammerings or the supercilious *pose* of an over-refined, self-conceited artist.

Rimbaud then has two aspects: the external, which everyone can see: the *poseur*, the frenzied hysteric, the side those who drank with him in tenth-rate cafés may have seen. That is the false Rimbaud. Then there is the inner man: a delicate spirit dreaming of spiritual purity — an angel struggling in earthly mire, the Rimbaud the absinthe-drinkers did not see and who is probably the true Rimbaud, as true at any rate as the other, who is comprehensible only to those who, like him, seek a divine — and always elusive — vision.

It is this latter Rimbaud whom Claudel understood because of that spirit of justice existing between loyal minds, because of a secret affinity between their two imaginations, and also because both their temperaments had been cultivated and widened by the literary and philosophic theories of their time.

Rimbaud, and Claudel at first, are above all dominated by their sensations, and, as always happens in such cases, are therefore inclined to hypostatize these sensations. They are born idolaters, like Bunyan or Shelley. In another age these writers, whose lyricism seemed instinctive to ordinary readers, adapted their precious impressions to the forms of feeling of their time. The life they communicated to their abstractions came to them from their emotions which, however direct or sudden they might be, had their root in their spiritual *milieu,* by which I mean their reading and their readers, rather than their surroundings. That is the explanation of the masterpieces of a Bunyan or a Shelley.

Rimbaud and Claudel, at a later date, appear in an age which, far from adding restraint to their genius, on the contrary countenanced their most extravagant flights of fancy. In spite of the silence of a certain University party about Baudelaire, sooner or later justice must be done, not perhaps to Baudelaire himself, but certainly to his book, *l'Art Romantique,* that inexhaustible mine of information for the generation after. It is by reading this book that one realizes how the German influence worked on artists in the direction indicated by Baudelaire.

"La nature qui pose devant nous, de quelque côté que nous nous tournions, et qui nous enveloppe comme un mystère, se présente sous plusieurs états simultanés dont chacun, selon quil est plus intelligible, plus sensible pour nous, se réflète plus vivement dans nos coeurs: forme, attitude et mouvement, lumière et couleur, son et harmonie. La musique des vers de Victor Hugo s'adapte aux profondes harmonies de la nature, sculpteur il découpe dans ses strophes la forme inoubliable des choses; peintre, il les illumine de leur couleur propre. . . ." (Page 315, *L'Art Romantique.*)*

From this triple impression, says Baudelaire, results the morality of things. Another result is the preoccupation about the unconscious which has always held so many minds; and with it goes hand in hand that hatred of logic, that worship of nature as being the symbol of another world, "nature certifying the supernatural body overflowed by life," and finally the conception of art, not as the art of reason, but as the art of the unconscious.

"Beyond this universality of the symbolic language, Emerson says, we are apprised of the divineness of this superior use of things, *whereby the world is a temple* (italics are mine: — Baudelaire had used the same words — La nature est un temple) whose walls are covered with emblems, pictures, and commandments of the Deity, in this, that there is no fact in nature which does not carry the whole sense of nature." (The Poet.)

It is possible now, on reading Rimbaud and Mallarmé, as well as Huysmans or Villiers de l'Isle Adam (to name the most original writers of this group), to understand with what ardor and frenzy young enthusiastic minds endeavored to find solution to their own souls' questions. It must be compared with those religious experiences we hear of in America or in England. "The rapture of the Moravian and Quietist, the opening of the internal sense of the word, in the language of the New Jeru-

---

*I need not say here that Baudelaire, in trying to explain Hugo to the French reader, expounded his own theories.

salem Church; the *revival* of the Calvinist churches, the *experiences* of the Methodists,'' are other forms of this mystic tendency we find in French Literature. This shudder of awe and delight with which the individual soul always mingles with the universal soul puts on different figures or shapes: here trances or illuminations, there extraordinary lyrics, a dithyrambic turbulence and often — with the realization that the universe is but one thing of which any proposition may be affirmed or denied — a tendency to insanity.

"What is a poet," asks Baudelaire, "if not a translator, a decipherer? With the excellent poets their is no metaphor, no comparison nor epithet, which is not of a mathematically exact adaptation in the actual circumstances, because these comparisons, metaphors or epithets are taken from the inexhaustible fund of *universal analogy.*''*

These words at once remind us of Bergson's famous passage when he wants to elicit a certain active force which in most men is likely to be trammelled by mental habits more useful to life. "Many different images, borrowed from very different orders of things, can, by their convergent action, direct consciousness to the precise point where there is a certain intuition to be seized," etc. (Introduction to Metaphysics). And here Bergson echoes Schopenhauer.

One has only to read Claudel's poems or wonderful odes to realize how the poet, in trying to re-construct before us the inner secret workings of his temperament, has succeeded in plunging us into that inner stream in which we move when unfettered by intellectualism. The identity running through all the surprises of the universe is the

*Page 315, *"L'art Romantique."*

thread which guides his mind out of the worldly labyrinth.

Ne dis point que le ciel est bleu!—Il est quatre heures.
Point d'air, point de soleil! Le ciel est blanc et bleu.
Ne dis point que je suis ici!—Un enfant pleure.
Je sens l'odeur des fleurs une à une. Il pleut.

Donc c'est cela le monde et c'est cela la vie!
C'était cela, la Mer! et le reste est ceci.
Passé, présent, tout est comme en photographie,
O le hasard, ô l'amertume d'être ici!

Est-ce toi, mon âme? Ecoute. Dis: *Je suis seule.*
—Et puis encor? L'ennui! L'ombre qui fait son tour.
—Et puis?—La paix. Plus rien. La paix. Dis. *Je suis seule*
—Amour—Pas amour! Ne dis pas amour!

Amour! parce que je suis grandement malade!
Amour! Dis: *Je suis seule.* Ne dis point amour!
Hier! demain! La chose à faire? **Tout est fade!**
Il me dure et de moi et de vivre et du jour!

J'aime! Et puis! J'aime! Et qui? Je n'aime rien, chut! J'aime!
J'aime! Tout le monde est rentré, voici le soir.
La lampe se rallume et ce lieu est le même.
—Que la mer était triste et que le ciel est noir!
                          (Vers d'exil. Tome IV. Théâtre.)

And now if we turn to the *Cinq grandes odes* and plunge into *L'Esprit et l'Eau* with the poet, when he is carried away by his thought and forgets the public, the critics and the authors, we worship the liberating god.

"Je sens, je flaire, je débrouille, je dépiste, je respire avec un certain sens.

La chose comment elle est faite! Et moi aussi je suis plein d'un dieu, je suis plein d'ignorance et de génie!

O forces à l'oeuvre autour de moi,

J'en sais faire autant que vous, je suis libre, je suis violent, je suis libre à votre manière que les professeurs n'entendent pas!

Comme l'arbre au printemps nouveau chaque année

Invente, travaillé par son âme,
Le vent, le même qui est éternel, crée de rien sa
feuille pointue,
Moi, l'homme
Je sais ce que je fais.
De la poussée et de ce pouvoir même de création,
J'use, je suis maître. . . ."
How truly Bergsonian all that is!

Here we may hear the wings of the poet beating
against all the sides of the solid old lumber of the
world, but in the first poem, written under the influence of Mallarmé or Rimbaud, we have that side
of the human soul which Sainte Beuve describes in
his Preface to *Volupté* as "languissant, oisif, at-
tachant, secret et privé, mystérieux et furtif, rêveur
jusqu'à la subtilité, tendre jusqu'à la mollesse,
voluptueux enfin"; whilst in the second poem the
same fire has been spiritualized, and by the side of
that love of novelty and of the *manyness** there is
a desire to live forwards and to carry the whole
universe in one Thought.

"Ptolemaic astronomy, euclidean space, aristote-
lian logic, scholastic metaphysics, were expedient for
centuries, but human experience has boiled over
those limits, and we now call these things only rela-
tively true, or true within those borders of experience."†

In the end we must always come back to that
theory dear to William James and to Bergson which
considers all psychical existence as of the form of
consciousness only, for both declare or assume that
consciousness exists independently of the physical
world in some vast ocean of consciousness. Souls,
Bergson declares, are continually being created,

**Pragmatism*, p. 179.
†*Pragmatism*, p. 223.

which nevertheless in a certain sense pre-existed. They are nothing else than the little rills into which the great river of life divides itself, flowing through the body of humanity.''[*]

Claudel has lived some time in America and in China, in surroundings where the theories of James and Bergson were widely discussed; and unless he should himself contradict us, everything inclines us to believe that if he declared Rimbaud was his master, it is because he saw him in and through a certain philosophy. Rimbaud revealed the supernatural to him simply because others than Rimbaud, metaphysicians who had passed their lives in ''going into the river and moving up and down to discover its depths and shallows,'' had revealed to him that the absence of link between such and such landscape, I mean between idea and image, the absence of ordinary logical process, put us into communication with the real foundation of the universe.

Mais que m'importent à présent vos empires, et tout ce qui meurt,
Puisque je suis libre! que m'importent vos arrangements cruels?
Puisque moi du moins je suis libre, puisque j'ai trouvé!
   Puisque moi du moins je suis dehors!
Puisque je n'ai plus ma place avec les choses créées, mais ma part
   avec ce qui les crée, l'esprit liquide et lascif.

                      (*L'Esprit et l'Eau.*)

The world which Claudel saw in Rimbaud's writings, lit up by the poor bull's-eye lantern of his imagination, would, I feel sure, have frightened the robust common sense of our honest convert but for the fact that in France, in America, and even, shall we say, in the small European world of Fou-Tcheou, French and English books declared that the sim-

---

[*]*Creative Evolution*, p. 284.

plest process of thought, when we put it into words,
is inadequate, unequal to real purpose of life, which
is to know Reality.

There would be no need to dwell on such points
were it not that M. Claudel has published his *Art
Poétique,* which is nothing but a metaphysical
treatise. In full reaction against romanticism, which
is a literature of woe, — he, the last child of romanticism! — wishes to testify to the livableness
of life, and, not content with writing wonderful
recitatives which he calls poems, he tries to reinforce their effect by a book written too often in an
emphatic key of expression. Joseph de Tonquedec
and other critics have reproached him with a want
of literary tact, and even with writing downright
nonsense. I wish sometimes he was quite honest
with his reader. For instance, he tells us he has
read Aristotle, Pascal, and we do not doubt his
word. But when he speaks of the Greek philosopher,
he has his tongue in his cheek. Bergson has been
sometimes too strong for him, and when we read
M. Rivière's clever analysis of this book, *l'Art Poétique,* we feel that, if Claudel is too big to slip into
a Bergsonian formula, he has at least read Bergson with enormous advantage. Claudel has much
of the temperament of the missionary in him, but
too often he bids the whole world stand and de-
liver with "Time and Free Will" in one hand, by
way of a pistol.

"Nous ne cherchons point à comprendre le mé-
canisme des choses de par-dessous, comme un chauf-
feur qui rampe sur le dos sous sa locomotive. Mais
nous nous placerons devant l'ensemble les cré-
atures, comme un critique devant le produit d'un
poéte, goûtant pleinement la chose, examinant par

quels moyens il a obtenu ses *effets,* comme un peintre clignant des yeux devant l'oeuvre d'un peintre . . .'' (pp. 13-14, *Art Poétique*).

And again. We realize "une relation constante entre certains motifs, comme d'une fleur à sa tige, du bras avec la main.'' And the whole of the first chapter tells us that the world ought to appear to us in its spontaneity, as Bergson preaches, that laws are means of simplification, useful processes "for finding out one's place in Nature's dictionary.'' "They have not in themselves any generating force nor necessary value.''

In order to understand the world one must have ever present to one's mind this idea that it is above all a harmony whose notes call up one another. "Nous ne pouvons définir une chose, elle n'existe en soi que par les traits en qui elle diffère de toutes les autres'' (*Art Poétique*).

Baudelaire had already written: "There is in nature neither line nor color'' (*L'Art Romantique*, page 17).

"Every object needs all the others in order to exist,'' Claudel adds later on. Once again we are plunged into that continual solidarity of all beings, that general correspondence demonstrated by Baudelaire and Bergson. And in order to underline as it were his adherence to the Bergson-Heraclitus idea, Claudel tells us that everything flows, ηάντα ρ'εî, and that it now flows unceasingly.

What, then, is Time if not the unrolling of the agreement of all things among themselves, the manifestation of their continued co-operation, the development of all the movements of beings? *Le Temps est le sens de la vie.*

Compare Bergson:

"This inner life may be compared to the unroll-

ing of a coil, for there is no living being who does
not feel himself coming gradually to the end of his
rôle; and to live is to grow old. But it may just
as well be compared to a continual rolling up, like
that of a thread on a ball, for our past follows us,
it swells incessantly with the present that it picks
up on its way; and consciousness means memory.''
(Page 10, *An Introduction to Metaphysics.* Transl.
by T. E. Hulme.)

And to remove all doubt Claudel adds: ''Underneath that which begins again, there is that which
continues. From that absolute duration our life
is, from birth until death, a division.'' The further
one reads in this *Art Poétique,* the more examples
one finds of ingenious poetical variations on Bergson's doctrine.

''All is movement and nothing but movement,
spirit as well as matter, and there is nothing inert
in the world. Material beings toil at this work
of progression by their perpetual efforts. As for
the animal, it no longer exists 'par une simple limi-
tation opposée du dehors il se fait du dedans lui-
même' '' (p. 70).

As for man, the supreme part is reserved for
him, — that of being the conscience of things.
Matter invokes the aid of spirit. ''Et voici que
la vie a tressailli dans son sein. Voici végéter le
visage.''

What, then, is Claudel's new contribution? He
has gone further than Bergson: he declares that
the world is making itself for a certain intention,
that it has an end, and that this end is willed by
God. For Claudel the very fact that the world
moves and passes away implies the other fact that
there is something which does *not* pass away. Berkeley had already suggested that the world is that

which is not. And thus Claudel: "Tout périt. L'univers n'est qu'une manière totale de ne pas être ce qui est" (*Art Poétique*). But this very instability of the world proves God. Alone the spirit of man does not pass away: that is the only thing which subsists, except God. The animal was created as a toy for some determinate leap, but man that he might grasp the connection between the world's flight and God's immobility. "Tout passe, et rien n'étant présent, tout doit être représenté" (p. 136).

M. Claudel will go further still. Having once set out in this direction, he will follow Pascal and declare that we are living in a state of disorder and that alone the Redemption, God-made man, has rescued us from sin.

Whatever opinion one may have of M. Claudel's theology as theology, it certainly reaches at times the greatness and beauty of the great mystics. The soul in God embraces the whole of creation and it is clear, as we have already said, that with Claudel this desire to feel everything, to spread and dilute oneself into everything, took a precise shape in the Catholic religion.

"Dans cette amère vie mortelle, les plus poignantes délices révélées à notre nature sont celles qui accompagnent la création d'une âme par la jonction de deux corps. Hélas! elles ne sont que l'image humiliée de cette étreinte substantielle ou l'âme, apprenant son nom et l'intention qu'elle satisfait, se proférera pour se livrer, s'aspirera, s'expirera tour à tour. O continuation de notre coeur! ô parole incommunicable! ô acte dans le ciel futur! O mon Dieu, tu nous as montré des choses dures, tu nous as abreuvés du vin de la pénitence! Quelle prise, d'un empire ou d'un corps de femme entre des bras impitoyables, comparable à ce saisissement de Dieu

par notre âme, comme la chaux saisit le sable!"
(Pages 181-182, *Art Poétique*.)

For some readers certain pages of *la Connaissance
de l'Est* are Claudel's masterpiece. *La Connaissance
de l'Est* is not a revelation of China, as might at
first appear, but an immediate Bergsonian view of
the things of the earth. The lesson of the book
lies in showing us that the world's beauty is all
around us in the tiny corner of it in which we happen to live, if only we have eyes to see it. The
infinite unfolds itself under a trained eye, in flat
ploughed fields over which the wind chases the
shadows of the clouds up to their boundary of blue
hills or in a cluster of thatched roofs by the shore,
or a clump of trees bent awry by the winds from
the open sea.

Claudel's eight dramas are musical prose poems
whose men and women are drawn certainly with
precise characterization, but they are most of all
men and women of all time, endowed with strong,
symbolic meaning. A large volume could be written to explain the religious and moral themes, the
leit-motiv of a philosophy which repeats its lesson
with infinite variations. *Tête d'Or* is a drama
played in every age. It is the story of every con-
queror whose effort "arrivé à une limite vaine se
défait comme un pli." It is the eternal story of
weakness putting its trust in strength, illustrated by
the touching friendship between *Cebès* and *Tête
d'Or*. *La Ville* is a story of strife and revolt, and
might just as well be laid in ancient Rome as in
France or England of to-day: it shows the power-
lessness of individualistic civilization to satisfy the
masses whom it merely tires, and it is one of the
most poignant criticisms that could be found of the
Victorian Era.

La Jeune fille Violaine and its second version *l'Annonce faite à Marie* are naïve mystic dramas animated with a religious fervor which makes twenty centuries of Christianity live under our eyes. *L'Otage,* a historical drama placed in the year 1815, is not only a picture of France after the Revolution, but shows also the conception of government as understood by feudality.

Georges de Coûfontaine:—Adieu donc O Roi que j'ai servi. . . .
Sygne:—Voici le Roi sur son trône.
Georges:—L'appelez-vous le Roi? Pour moi je ne vois qu'un Turelure
    couronné.
Un préfet en chef administrant pour la commodité générale, con-
    stitutionnel, assermenté,
Et que l'on congédie, le jour qu'on en est las.*

Le Repos du Septième Jour describes the visit of the Emperor of China to Hell and reminds one of a novel by Mrs. Oliphant. *L'Echange,* of which the scene is laid in America, and *le Partage du Midi* are dramas of passion recalling the Tristan and Yseult of mediæval story as well as of Wagnerian drama. These plays are truly poetic arsenals against the modern world. They are great because his characters are supported by long centuries of tradition: his lyricism carries us back, not so much to Shakespeare, as has been so often said, but to the Bible and Æschylus. In this he reminds us of that writer of genius who is even yet not widely enough known — Villiers de l'Isle Adam.

If we study these dramas we do not find in them that preoccupation of self-analysis, self-study, we see

Georges de Coûfontaine:—Farewell then, oh King whom I have
    served.
Sygne:—Behold the King upon his throne.
Georges:—Callest thou him the King? But I—I see only a
    crowned Turelure,
A chief prefect, administering the general good, constitutionally,
    on oath,
And one who will be dismissed on the day we are weary of him.

in the character of a Racine, a Marivaux, or a
Stendhal. They are more like some of Maeterlinck's
characters — in that they suggest rather than speak.
They might even be compared with Maupassant's
characters — so simple that they could be called
brutish, were it not for Claudel's constant vision
of the over-soul.

Art is working far ahead of language, and we do
realize that in M. Claudel's dramas he has recourse
to all manner of suggestions and exaggerations of
style —

> "Mais ap —
> — pelle L.
> — éon. Pourquoi ne parle-t-il pas?" —

to arrive at effects for which we have not yet a
direct name. Not that such effects do not enter into
the habits of everyday life, but Boileau and Victor
Hugo have taught us to consider everything vague
or obscure until we can formulate our thought in
precise analytical language.

Claudel, in introducing larger motives in the conception of character, had to contend against many
difficulties, the greatest of which was the French
language. French does not lend itself to the expression, I do not say of our complicated feelings
— (far from it!) — but of those imponderable
forces, such as the nature of a landscape, or the
atmosphere of a house, or the spirit of a *salon*, or
the action of God, which play such an important
part in our existence. And in the great stride M.
Claudel takes beyond his contemporaries, his seven-
league boots abandon him sometimes at the right
moment.

It is very interesting for this reason to observe
the success met with in England by *L'Annonce Faite*

à Marie, that play overflowing with the supernatural. It is clear that the English public discovered therein that spiritual life so carefully fostered by Anglicanism and by Quakerism.

It is still more interesting to see how Claudel has reconciled within himself two contradictory tendencies: the lyrical and the dramatic force, which, though they contest each other like two lawyers pleading against one another, finally come to an understanding. In this way one may say that his literary work is divided into two parts: the work of his youth, *Tête d'Or, la Ville,* and *la Jeune Fille Violaine,* and the work of his maturity, which is far from being finished (and no one knows what surprises it has in store for us), with *L'Otage* (1911), *L'Annonce Faite à Marie* (1912), *Le Pain Dur* (1918). One may look upon *L'Echange* (1894) and *Le Partage de Midi* (1906) as intermediary between the two manners.

When young, Claudel is frankly a symbolist. He has the intuition of universal life: that is to say, the intuition of the depth, the totality even, of the reality he intends to express by every means in his power. "Connâitre," he says, "c'est constituer cela sans quoi le reste ne saurait être." He will know, then, both the veil of the appearances of Maïa and also what is hidden behind the *Zaïmph.* If we take *Tête d'Or,* we are struck by the fact that the author would at all costs disconnect his drama with any particular country. The characters have strange, archaic, ancient or symbolic names: at one moment they speak the language of the Bible, and the next that of the Parisian *Voyou.* This mixture of exotism and antiquity, modernism and hellenism, is deliberate on the part of the author, who, not content with reading his Æschylus and translating the Agamemnon, has read his Shakespeare over and over again, perhaps also Webster, and probably the sturdy Spanish drama of the Sixteenth and Seventeenth Centuries. Once the first movement of surprise overcome — and the reader accustomed to the Elizabethan theatre easily enters the Claudelian stage, — the Anglo-Saxon reader readily understands that Simon Agnel and Cébès, the two characters in *Tête d'Or,* are the two sides of Claudel, or in fact of every human being inclining now towards good and now towards evil, with a general direction quite as much towards Hell as towards Heaven. The same reader, too, is not displeased at being brought up against certain mysterious passages which may be interpreted in different ways. For example, why does Simon Agnel bury a woman? (unless that woman represents all his past), why does he smear Cébès' hair with blood? (is it an allusion to certain ancient customs?). Finally, why is the princess changed into a thing of dread?

This brutal strangeness, this epic savageness, in Claudel is the proof of a genius which cannot contain itself, but which suddenly overflows in waves so rapid that the stream arrives in jerks, and frightens us. Admirers of the *Cinq Grandes Odes,* as well as of the *Art Poétique,* know that Claudel, while seeking to give a character of eternity to his conception, wishing to embrace the whole universe, accumulates image, metaphor, and picture, uniting the four corners of the world in a few lines. He is a veritable Rubens in poetry. Clearly such ardor carried on to the stage can only produce violent complicated dramas in the style of *Tête d'Or* and *la Ville,* plays calculated to exasperate devoted readers of the classic theatre. (Still, great as he is, Racine is not all humanity.) On reading Claudel one realizes that his sensual spirit, harassed and racked as it was by religious and metaphysical preoccupations, could but create hybrid characters: half-living beings and half-moral or philosophical personifications. Once again we are forced to remember Bunyan, and we realize how right Sainte-Beuve was in declaring there were families of minds.

M. Louis Richard-Mounet, in his pamphlet on Claudel, has declared that Claudel's work, though mystic in intention, is pagan in fact. We must be clear about the meaning of words. Claudel is no more a pagan than Bergson is a pantheist. The pagans, however intoxicated they may be with the beauties of the world, and the music of the heavenly spheres, have never conceived the universe other than as a block — universe. They have even imposed this conception upon us, teaching us at the same time a kind of voluptuous naturalism, or a selfish, arrogant stoicism. Claudel knows this better than anyone. But as he loves the wonderful force of the first of the great Greek tragedians, and the divine simplicity of the second, he endeavors to transport on to the French stage the vigor and simplicity of ancient drama, its epic value. And at once the question arises, How can a Baudelairean, or at least a reader of Rimbaud and Mallarmé, free himself from the yoke of these writers who are unbalanced by the modern antinomy between the faith of their country and their conception of Art?

If we study *l'Echange* and *le Partage de Midi* (leaving on one side *Le Repos du Septième Jour*), we become spectators of a conflict of passions expressed with such living lyricism that we are heart-wrung. *Le Partage de Midi* is so much a part of his innermost fibres that, as journalists tells us, M. Claudel has given orders for its destruction. It

has been said of Ysé, the heroine of this play, that her
character consists in having none, that she merely
displays "l'impulsivité morbide d'une détraquée."
But life itself gives the answer for M. Claudel. And
if we consult modern literature we find that the
brothers de Goncourt, whose passion for documentation was intense, studied and described the same
type of woman. Claudel is much truer than the
de Goncourts; he makes his woman fall, but brings
in the haunting sense of sin and of the presence
of God.

Pascal, one of Claudel's masters, wrote: "All that
is in the world is the lust of the flesh, or the lust
of the eyes, or the pride of life. Wretched is the
cursed land which these three rivers of fire inflame
rather than water." Claudel is profoundly convinced of the truth of that. He knows that such
is his malady and the malady of his age, but how
can it be cured?

Byron goes to die in Greece, Musset wears himself out by passion, Baudelaire tortures himself with
a thousand rare sensations and with Gautier pursues the infinite in his worship of Beauty. Sainte-
Beuve finds consolation in dissecting his own heart
and that of his contemporaries. After such predecessors Claudel himself tells us his own great
ambition:

"Moi qui aimais tant les choses visibles, oh!
j'aurais voulu voir tout, posséder avec appropria-
tion, non avec les yeux seulement, ou les sens, mais
avec l'intelligence de l'esprit, Et *tout connaître pour
être tout connu.*"

Thus we have the explanation of the profound
thought underlying Claudel's two greatest dramas,
L'Otage and *L'Annonce faite à Marie — the spirit
of sacrifice: Tout connaître pour être tout connu:* the

last stage of Réné's malady! *L'Annonce faite a Marie* and, above all, *L'Otage* are dramas not of a Christian, but of a frenzied Christian who deliberately looks for difficulties in the pursuit of self-improvement.

There is a kind of valetudinarian so-called healthfulness which is more sickly than sickness itself. True catholicism is not M. Claudel's catholicism. True health does not consist in exerting yourself and fagging. With all his love of life and sharpness of insight, Claudel (I am speaking of his dramas) lacks this geniality of our big, burly world heroes.

The spirit of sacrifice, the eagle that he is pursuing, will turn one day and tear his very entrails.*

.   .   .   .

Claudel's art, like Bergson's, is in a sense founded upon metaphor: "l'opération qui résulte de la seule existence conjointe et simultanée de deux choses différentes."† He is the hunter of images, the dragoman of the earth, since all is symbol and every metaphor pregnant with the universe. The magic silence of a summer night when the moon rises and "de temps en temps une pomme de l'arbre choit comme une pensée lourde et mûre"; splendid mornings of dazzling sunshine dancing on the sea; long lonely roads where friend rarely meets friend; moral crises as tempestuous as the equinoctial gales; the joy of worship; the lyricism of inspiration — all these things evoke intuitions which in their turn show us that life is made up of feelings which are interpenetrated with something like the musical reso-

*On Claudel's dramas consult two penetrating articles by P. Lasserre in *La Minerve Française* (1st and 15th August, 1919). We are glad to agree with the eminent French critic.

†"The operation that results from the simple existence, conjoined and simultaneous, of two different things."

lutions of Browning's *Galuppi Baldassaro*. The
whole universe is there crowding up against the door
of our consciousness, and it is the poet's part to
mingle the most imaginary things with the most
real (just as Goethe did with his Werther — who is
merely Goethe minus the suicide); to abandon himself, that is, to his fancy, taking care, however, to
bind the particular to the universal by the magic
of his art.

There is a passage in *La Connaissance de l'Est*
which must be studied carefully in order to understand Claudel's æsthetic theory. I mean the passage in which he compares European with Japanese
art and decides in favor of the latter:

"L'artiste européen *copie* la nature selon le sentiment qu'il en a;
le Japonais *l'imite* selon les moyens qu'il lui emprunte; l'un s'exprime et l'autre l'exprime; l'un ouvrage, l'autre mime: l'un peint,
l'autre compose; l'un est un *étudiant*, l'autre, dans un sens, un
maître; l'un reproduit dans son détail le spectacle qu'il envisage
d'un oeil probe et subtil, l'autre dégage d'un clignement de l'œil la
loi, et dans la liberté de sa fantaisie, l'applique avec une concision
scripturale."*

There is nothing surprising in such an attitude,
for we of the present day are tired of pure virtuosity and of that dexterity which the artist uses
only in order to display his own temperament.
Claudel is merely expressing in his turn the feeling of revolt against the French Academic School,
the feeling which in the great independent painters
of the latter Nineteenth Century produced so many
original masterpieces.

*"The European artist *copies* Nature according to the feeling
which he has of it; the Japanese *imitates* it according to the means
he borrows therefrom; the one expresses himself, the other nature;
the one works, the other mimics; the one paints, the other composes;
the one is a *student*, the other, in a sense, a master; the one repro-
duces in all its detail the spectacle envisaged by an astute and subtle
eye, the other, in a flash of insight, extracts from it its very law,
and in the freedom of his fantasy applies it with a rigorous precision."

There are moments when Claudel feels so tired
of Reason that he will only employ her as the
humblest of his servants. That is the explanation of
the passage in *la Connaissance de l'Est,* which
clearly shows Claudel's attitude towards earthly
things: "Aux heures vulgaires nous nous servons
des choses pour un usage, oubliant ceci de pur,
qu'elles soient; mais quand, après un long travail,
au travers des branches et des ronces, à midi, péné-
trant historiquement au sein de la clairière, je pose
ma main sur la croupe brûlante du lourd rocher,
l'entrée d'Alexandre à Jerusalem est comparable à
l'énormité de ma constatation."*

What does he mean exactly by *"l'énormité de ma
constatation"?* The same thing, I think, that Schopenhauer meant in the following passage: "If,
raised by the power of the mind, a man relinquishes
the common way of looking at things . . . ; if he
thus ceases to consider the where, the when, the
why and the whither of things and looks simply and
solely at the what; if, further, he does not allow
abstract thought, the concepts of the reason, to take
possession of his consciousness, but, instead of all
this, gives the whole power of his mind to perception; . . . if thus the object has to such an extent
passed out of all relation to something outside it
and the subject out of all relation to the will, then
that which is so known is no longer the particular
thing as such, but it is the Idea, the eternal form;
. . . and, therefore, he who is sunk in this perception
is no longer individual, for in such perception the
individual has lost himself; but he is pure, will-less,
painless, timeless *subject of knowledge."*†

This idealism necessarily led him to the concep-

La Connaissance de l'Est, page 164.

†*The World as Will and Idea.* Vol. I, page 231. Translated by
R. D. Haldane and T. Kemp. London: Trübner & Co.

tion of Time, which is the foundation of Bergsonian
philosophy. Five little words in Claudel, *"l'heure
sonne et je retentis,"* explain better than any long-
winded commentary what he means by saying that
"Le temps est le sens [direction] *de la vie."*
"L'heure sonne et je retentis" is only another way
of saying: What I know, I possess. I enjoy the
wonderful vision of the sea, but "alors que cette eau
deviendra noire, je posséderai la nuit toute entière
avec le nombre intégral des étoiles visibles et invisi-
bles." (*La Connaissance de l'Est,* p. 100.) *"L'heure
sonne et je retentis":* that is to say, "there is a pure
and uniform time, that which is written on our
clocks. . . . There is also a real qualitative time,
which is the progress of living beings and the continual modification of their relations; it is the artisan
of something real, which increases with every second." — *"L'heure sonne et je retentis."* Our mind
clings to the belief that there exists somewhere a
ready-made plan, a mechanism with pulleys, weights
and pendulum: a kind of grandfather's clock sur-
mounted by God the Father, with a flowing beard.
But the universe is always in the making. "Tout
mouvement est *d'*un point . . . et non *vers* un
point. L'origine du mouvement est dans ce fré-
missement qui saisit la matière en contact d'une
realité différente: l'esprit" (pp. 33-34, *La Connaissance de l'Est*). *"L'heure sonne et je retentis,"* because "man is a vibration, his spirit is movement."
So that we do not seek to understand "the mechanism of things from below, like an engine-driver crawl-
ing underneath his engine," but we stand "before
the sum total of creatures like a critic before a poet's
work, fully appreciating the thing, trying to see how
the effects were produced, like a painter half clos-
ing his eyes to look at the work of another painter,

like an engineer watching the working of a beaver."
"L'heure sonne et je retentis." In other words,
the world must appear to us in all its spontaneity.
Causes and laws are useful when we want to look
up something in Nature's Dictionary. It is for us
to create the present, clothe it in our own originality.

"Me voici,
  Imbécile, ignorant,
  Homme nouveau devant les choses inconnues,
  Et je tourne ma face vers l'année et l'arche pluvieuse, j'ai plein
    mon coeur d'ennui."*

This philosophy is a part of the intuitive psychology which makes Claudel hear only the grander
sentiments of the human heart and show us those
profound states of consciousness which are pure
quality. As his Fée Lala says: —

"Nul ne connaît le secret de ma joie, ni eux, ni les autres, ni vous-
    même.
  Coeuvre lui-même, bien qu'il soit le seul
  Homme qui ait eu de moi possession
  (Et tu es le fruit de notre union, ô roi)
  Ne m'a point connue tout entière.
  Car son esprit s'attache aux causes et il
  Les rassemble dans la profonde cavité de son esprit. . . .
  Mais le délice et ce saisissement
  Q'il y à sentir qu'on ne tient plus à rien est ce qu'il ne connâit pas
    encore.
  Le vol fixe de la pensée qui comme un nageur soulevé par le courant
  Le maintient dans la vibration de la lumière,
  Ces coups soudains, ces essors insaisissables, ces départs,
  Sont encore ce que tu sais mal, ô pontife."†

Here Claudel is expressing the feelings of a Saint
Francis of Assisi when he took Poverty as his bride,
or of any mystic, freed from corporal chains, as he
reaches his seventh heaven.

In the same way this philosophy is once more an
Art of Poetry which is Mallarmé's. Both men
try to recreate the poet's emotive state with words,

*Tête d'Or—
†La Ville, page 307.

and as many images as possible (Claudel's vocabulary is enormous — German critics, please note!), and above all with alliteration, strangeness of syntax, ambiguity of meaning (*le temps est le sens de la vie*), and with a rhythmic prose cut up into small paragraphs. Claudel wants to make us realize in all its fullness the intuition of emotion which has suddenly illuminated things for him. He knows that a word has the power of evoking numberless images, and he is not afraid of having recourse to the musical device of long pauses.

Music alone can render the privileged soul of the poet and the state of our more vulgar souls. Nevertheless, we must be grateful to Paul Claudel for having tried by means of every ingenuity of syntax, trick of rhythm and shade of language, to express the inexpressible.

"O Amie, je ne suis pas un dieu!
Et mon âme, je ne peux te la partager, et tu ne peux me prendre et me contenir et me posséder."

(Deuxième Ode.)

Side by side with Claudel there is a phalanx of Catholic writers and poets, of whom the most famous are Francis Jammes and Adrien Mithouard. M. Adrien Mithouard is now, I believe, Président of the Paris Municipal Council. He has written some truly wonderful meditations, of which *Le Pauvre Pécheur* is the masterpiece, and a *Traité de l'Occident* based, like Claudel's, on Bergson's idea of time. The dates rule out any question of imitation and the resemblance is the more striking. "L'heure sonne et je retentis"— so Claudel: and Mithouard: "Ce n'est pas la quantité qui crée le rythme, mais les coups que nous frappons." Not only does M. Mithouard, who is a distinguished musician, write on the study of music the very original pages noted by M. Tancrède de Visan in his *Attitude du Lyrisme Contemporain,* but he sees clearly — like Claudel once more — that this idea of Time is the same as our love of continuity and tradition. "C'est notre point d'honneur de persister tenaces, et tandis que nous doutons sans cesse si nous sommes bien aujourd'hui le même qui posa tel acte autrefois, c'est avec une ivresse infinie que nous retrouvons tout à coup dans l'autrefois ce quelqu'un qui est indubitablement nous-mêmes."

In a charming book, called *French Perspectives,* Miss Elizabeth Shepley Sergeant has shown this same admirable trait of the French race simply by recording conversations with French *ouvrières à domicile.*

"France is the country of unity," cries M. Mithouard: yes, but she is also the country of order and moderation, and her social preoccupations will never upset the working of her desire for order.

Francis Jammes, who stands in the front rank of modern poets, was long content with being the Theocritus of his native Béarn, and with proving once again that in order to give new life to old themes it is sufficient to be endowed with poetic genius. "J'ai fait des vers faux et j'ai laissé de côté, ou à peu près, toute forme et toute métrique. . . . Mon style balbutie, mais j'ai dit ma vérité" (Preface to his Poems).

The name of Theocritus comes naturally to mind when we read Jammes's ingenuous idyls laid round Orthez with their recurring note of such lines as : —

"Les chevrier trainards gonflant leurs joues aux flutes."

But he is often much more like the great Irish poet, A. E., and is even more than he in close communion with the beasts and lowly beings of the

earth.   Yet, whilst A. E. turned towards Buddhism,
Jammes never has recourse to the wonders of India.
For him the humblest life is full of mystery, and
the meanest of living creatures, by the very fact
that it is constantly in God's mind, is a perpetual
source of beauty.   Maeterlinck spoke to us of the
tragique quotidien, and the words are well fitted to
his conception of destiny.   For Jammes there is a
naturel quotidien, and it is all-sufficient.   "Toutes
choses sont bonnes à décrire, lorsqu'elles sont naturelles," he declares in his literary manifesto.   But:
"Les choses naturelles ne sont pas seulement le
pain, la viande, l'eau, le sel, les arbres et les mou-
tons, l'homme et la femme et la gaieté . . . ; il y
a aussi parmi elles des cygnes, des lis, des couronnes
et *la tristesse.*"   And it is probably on account of
that *tristesse* that he turned towards religion.

M. Charles le Goffic, who was a graceful poet in
the classic tradition before he became one of the
historians of the war, pointed out in the *Revue
Hebdomadaire** that Jammes was far from being
isolated in his attitude, reinforced as he was by such
men as Charles Guérin, Amédée Prouvost, Jean
Lionnet, Arsène Vermenouze, Adrien Mithouard and
Adolphe Rétté.   M. le Goffic shows in the same article
how things have changed since the day when Verlaine's Catholicism was accounted to him for
eccentricity, since neither Sully-Prudhomme, nor
Catulle Mendès, nor François Coppée, nor José
Maria de Hérédia, nor Léon Dieux, nor Mallarmé,
manifested any great affection for the Church.   But
the young writers, the men like Mauriac, Vallery
Radot, André Delacour, André Lafon, Maurice Bril-
lant, Louis Perroy, Charles Orsatti, are profoundly
religious poets.

*See *Révue Hebdomadaire,* 3 juin 1911.

JULES ROMAINS

JULES ROMAINS is the leader of the *Unani-miste* School. He is also a direct disciple of Claudel, and, although he differs essentially from his master from the religious point of view, it is clear that if Claudel had never written, Romains would be other than he is. Jules Romains himself makes no mystery about this influence. "De qui nous réclamons-nous?" he says. "De nous-mêmes d'abord et de la vie présente. Mais nous saluons des précurseurs: Whitman, Zola, Verhaeren, le Hugo de quelques poèmes, le Baudelaire des *Tableaux parisiens* et des *Poèmes en Prose.* Rimbaud et Paul Claudel ont pressenti la vertu de l'expression immédiate, Bergson en à donné la justification métaphysique."*

That is well said, and reminds us of the fact that Jules Romains is a professor of Philosophy. The study of his work only leads us further afield in the question of the influence of Bergson.

Two tendencies of Bergsonian philosophy appealed especially to Jules Romains: the theory of Intuition considered from a certain point of view, and the theory of the interaction and co-penetration of all beings.

M. Weber, in an article in the *Revue de la Métaphysique et de la Morale* (and M. Jules Romains

*Emile Henriot: *A quoi rèvent les jeunes gens?* page 35. Paris, 1913.

seems to me to share his opinion), showed that
M. Bergson's thesis on Time and Free-Will really
leads to this: life has no other law than itself. At
this date Bergson had not made his statements on
the importance of ethical values, and consequently
the reader was free, if he so willed, to construct
from the philosopher's writings an anarchist doctrine which delivered our instincts from all check
or control. M. Jules Romains, no doubt, would take
a certain amount of pleasure in proving to us, logically and mathematically, since he is a professor
of philosophy, that in reality the accomplished fact,
compelling as it does our admiration, becomes
thereby the basis of all ethics. In any case, the
poet-novelist side of him realized that this theory,
if cunningly mingled with others equally fashionable, could be made to produce new literary effects.

It is obvious, then, how different he is from Claudel; in fact, it is only the latter's literary process
which he imitates. But at the same time he does
not forget that our mind is not purely ours; it is
the product of race, *milieu*, the human groups in
which we live. Here clearly the influence of the
philosophies of Tarde, Durkheim, Le Bon reinforce
that of Bergson, so true it is that a period always
produces a number of thinkers who, without knowing one another, march in parallel lines towards the
same goal.

The master of whom he most often reminds me
is Verhaeren, who never ceased singing the praises
of will and power, who used to say: "L'homme est
un fragment de l'architecture mondiale. Il à la
conscience et l'intelligence de l'ensemble dont il fait
partie. Il se sent enveloppé et dominé, et en même
temps il enveloppe et domine."

Verhaeren was the first to express the poetry of

the age of machinery and crowds, that poetry which
the Vicomte Eugène Melchior de Vogüé felt when
he wrote of the Exhibition of 1889.   All Verhaeren's
work is devoted to the divinization of the "tumultu-
ous forces" which make of men first a plaything,
and then a "multiple splendeur," to borrow from
the titles of two of his books.   The beauty of many
of his poems is born of that anguish he feels in considering the "tentacled towns" which drag towards
them the toilers on the land, and of the emotion
he feels before a crowd, that unconscious worker
for beauty and peace.   Fervent idealist as he is,
he bequeaths to his disciples a creed of enthusiasm
and love such as neither Baudelaire nor Verlaine
had to offer.

This love of humanity is allied in Romains and
the younger poets with a conception of poetry as
far removed as could be from that which Malherbe
and Boileau imposed upon French letters.   Each
self is an enormous and new power in nature.   What,
then, is self?   Nothing, if you think of it as a brief
accident in duration.   Everything, if you think of
it as bound up in a host of other selves.   Thus
Jules Romains was led to conceive a new religious
emotion.   This soul which is no longer circumscribed
by a precarious self, but is lost in the great sea of
humanity, feels a really holy sensation. Jules
Romains is right in extolling man's altruistic side.
An act of charity is really an angelic thing, and
the good Samaritan experiences the same feeling
as those great saints who, as William James puts
it, "with their extravagance of human tenderness
are the great torch-bearers" in the belief in the
brotherhood of man.   But Romaines is wrong when
he wants to diminish our personalities, and when he

refuses to see that Will is ruler of the world. He cannot be unaware of the criminal instincts in the species man, nor of the importance of will and such factors as moral education which tend to suppress these instincts and make of us complete men.

In any case, Jules Romains realized that this idea of our self, if not new, had not hitherto received its full expression in literature. The subject of the highly original poems and novels which have compelled lovers of letters to study him is this human personality dwelling not in the understanding, but in a necessarily vague region, our subliminal self, and even in the masses around us. And in this way he appeals to a feeling which is older than man himself. He hymns the aggrandizement of human personality and consequently of all those tempestuous actions which bear our souls on into an unknown mysterious region. Once again we hear the Romantic cry: "Levez-vous vite, orages désirés qui devez emporter René dans les espaces d'une autre vie!"

So that this *Unanimisme* in Jules Romains is really the worship of the superman as he realizes himself in those nameless forces which everyone feels in an enthusiastic public meeting, or any great public demonstration. From this point of view his *Prise de Paris,* and in fact the whole of the volume called *Sur les Quais de la Villette,* is his masterpiece, and it realizes his dream of *unanimisme* at least in this, that all Frenchmen will be unanimous in praising. His volume of poems, *La Vie Unanime,* is the exposition of this new mystery, and I fear that in it Jules Romains is the victim of his own system. An idea cannot be drawn out indefinitely like a piece of gutta percha.

"L'espoir du paradis qui flambait autrefois,
 On eut beau le couvrir avec nos doigts, le vent a soufflé la chandelle;
Le vent a balayé l'eau-delà du zénith;
Mais pour nous consoler de la vie éternelle
Nous aurons la vie unanime."*

The same idea runs through the novel which perhaps made his name, and of which there exists an
admirable English translation, *la Mort de quelqu'un.*
It describes the utter disappearance of a being who
after death still exists in some small way in the
minds of those who knew him, but finally vanishes
entirely. Just before sinking into complete oblivion,
he appears once again in the mind of someone who
was present by chance at his funeral, but who no
longer remembers so much as the name of the man
who was buried.

"Dead man, dead man," he said, "you see that
I have not deserted you. True, you have no mouth
with which to complain and protest; but an hour
ago you had nothing at all. Am I not kind to you?
Will you say that I could not have done otherwise?
No, I consented; I made a choice, I picked you out
to love you, and for reasons tainted with nothing of mortality. I never saw you in the body, I
never loved your voice, your appearance, your way
of looking at things, the mere precarious husk of
your being. My desire was for your very essence,"
etc.†

And it is all really horribly sad. There is a religious feeling in our skeptic Jules Romains, a very
characteristic mixture of philosophic faith and human disillusionment.

Les Copains, which is generally voted the epithet
Rabelaisian, shows us very clearly the stuff of which

*La Vie Unanime, page 226.

†The Death of Nobody, translated by Desmond MacCarthy and
Sydney Waterloo.

Jules Romains's gaiety is made: no simplicity,
little abandon, but a great deal which is voluntary
and philosophically thought out. There is certainly
nothing spontaneous about the gaiety of this disciple of Bergson who sings the praises of spontaneity; his fun is strained, with a path well mapped
out in front of it, a true victory won over the sadness of intellect which was about to give way under the burden of life's sorrows. When the leader
of the Copains, at the close of the volume, looking
back on all the practical jokes played on the sober-
minded bourgeois, cries, "Vous avez instauré l'acte
pur. Depuis la création du monde. . . . il n'y à pas
eu d'acte pur. . . . Ce que les hommes ont de sé-
rieux et de sacré, vous en avez fait des objets de
plaisir . . . vous avez, sans ombre de raison, en-
châiné l'un à l'autre des actes gratuits. . . . A la
nature vous avez donné des lois et si provisoires!"
one recognizes the metaphysician in search of
amusement and the student who to get it laughs
at himself, and even at his master. But then, whom
are we to trust, the author of *Les Copains* or the
poet of *La Vie Unanime?* Doubtless he realized
that literature is after all a great game, and, because of that, much will be forgiven him. But as
we read over his poems we see that the man who
wrote *les Copains* is the same man who formerly
used to console himself by giving himself up to the
influence of the crowd and of the external world;
the man with a true child's heart amused by any
trifle:

> Tout de même, si j'étais
> En train de passer au pas
> Sur un pont dont j'ai mémoire
> Dans un noir quartier du Sud;
>
> Si je sentais maintenant
> Trembler sous mon corps en marche

Le trottoir du pont de fer
Qu' ébranlent des camions;

Une rumeur oublieuse
Emporterait toute peine;
Et je dormirais au bras
D'un rêve grand comme un dieu.

And this brings us to the question, What, then, is poetry according to Romains and his friends? By his friends I mean those he attaches to his ideas, but who distinctly intend to remain original: Georges Chennevière with *Le Printemps;* Pierre-Jean-Jouve with *les Ordres qui changent* and *les Aéroplanes;* René Arcos with *Ce qui naît;* Georges Duhamel with *l'Homme en tête* and Luc Durtain with *l'Etape nécessaire;* and Charles Vildrac with his *Livre d'Amour.*

According to this group of interesting writers, poetry is a spontaneous revelation, like the lightning tearing the clouds; it is the expression of all that is most secret, most mysterious — the poet's soul, the poet's soul in its relations with beings and things. But every poet worthy of the name knows this truth, which surely needs no underlining. As for spontaneity, there are two kinds — children's, which is amusing; old poets', which is profound: so that we are brought up against a kind of Irish bull — spontaneity is real only when it is deliberate. In any case what explains the attitude of this new school of poetry is that of the old school of poetry which was little else than eloquence in Alexandrines, and which certainly never tried to sound those depths of consciousness upon which Bergson loves to dwell.

The Anglo-Saxon reader, who has suffered under Racine, will sympathize with these young men (it was in England that Taine found his Racine criticism); therein is the enthronement of the conception held by most — though not all — English poets.

Classical tragedy aims at offering a series of faithful portraits of the human soul together with a good deal of very subtle dialectics; its achievement along those lines can never be destroyed. This idea of an eminently civilized art is the finest the human brain can conceive. Goethe came to it after his Romantic period and then wrote his masterpieces. The talented young poets we are now considering are refined, subtle barbarians cultivating for choice an essentially savage art. But then they are confronted with the supreme difficulty: when they are seized with a really intuitive inspiration one of two things must happen. Either their poem will be a song without words — in which case they must take refuge in music — or they will have recourse to words, and the resulting poem will be very like the poetry of — yes, Wordsworth; that is, of the most astonishingly prosaic of great poets.[*]

Charles Vildrac's little masterpiece, *Livre d'Amour,* is in a certain sense the demonstration of what I am trying to prove. The themes are Wordsworthian: two men drinking in an inn; an inn symbolical of woman's need of love; the description of nocturnal scenes (*Etre un homme*), a poor woman pushing a squeaky perambulator along the road, a sickly ill-clad landscape, the visit of a friend to his friends in spite of a snowstorm, a man drowning in the sea. . . . The great difference between the two poets is that the Lakist loses himself in Nature, while Vildrac dreams of a vast kingdom of brotherhood — as Wordsworth indeed did in his youth.

This humanitarian note is the great thing to remember about this French movement, and it is a

[*]Cf. The Chapter, "New Voices in French Poetry," in *French Perspectives,* E. S. Sergeant.

consoling note. In place of the sadness and melancholy of Romanticism, we find a love of life and love of man uplifting these young writers, and inspiring them with really human work which is as fine as that of their predecessors. These poets have come down from the "ivory tower" of thought, and, instead of passing in front of life without seeing it, they throw themselves into the thick of it. In this way, however different a man like Francis Jammes may seem from a man like Claudel, they are alike not only in their fluency, in the music of their poetry, not only in their search for simplicity, but in their love of humanity.

JEAN MOREAS

ALL the activities of intellectual life which form, as it were, the common atmosphere of an epoch, may start from different points, but they run on parallel lines and encourage one another, like groups of school-boys running through a playing field, each group bent on its own particular game, but catching zest and enthusiasm from the others. The man of letters, when he reaches a certain stage in philosophical research, cannot help discovering the eternal types of action and passion, and is moreover forced to ask himself 'what is their *raison d'être:* are the categories by which the intellect perceives phenomena, manifestations of a superior reality; and after all is not the artist's invention, which he himself believes to be conscious, rather the surrender of his being to the suggestions of some superior principle, be it called intuition, or abstract reason?

It may seem a far cry from the works of M. Bergson or of M. Ravaisson to the poems of Jean Moréas, and yet when we understand Ravaisson's or Bergson's philosophy as well as Moréas' stanzas we realize that at bottom we are dealing with the same hellenic, generous philosophy, the same striving to be independent of mere intellect, the same aspiring towards all the conditions of a musical art.

By Hellenism I do not mean that hellenism which is only a canon, a system of rules which the Greeks are supposed to have imposed upon their artists

and all those thereby inspired, a somewhat passion-
less range of effects which looks like a cold sensu-
alism without any inner ideals. On the contrary,
the great Greek philosophers and artists were the
first to see that a work of art is a living organism,
and genius an essence apart, anticipating, and even
creating, facts. The Bergsonian conception of reality brings us nearer this hellenism so well understood by Renaissance and Nineteenth-Century
humanists. Human thought, thus spiritualized and
refined by ages of aspiration and suffering, seeks
now only this unity, this solidarity of beings, which
the great philosophers of antiquity also sought.
The artist who seeks to limit himself to the concrete
— truly Greek therein — submits to what Bergson
calls the Immediate. For the desire to reproduce
the expression and individual character of. every
being and every thing, to write as it were the pri-
vate history of every soul, is to be essentially both
ancient and modern in character.

Fromentin called the Nineteenth-Century school
of painting the "sensation school." The name could
be applied to the more famous works of Nineteenth-
Century literature; Bergson or Moréas are the last
comers among the impersonations of their age: all
that was intense and original in it is crystallized
in them. The pedant will probably deny them the
title of pure hellenists, but they are both Renaissance
men, actuated by the same desire as the great men
of the Sixteenth Century to translate the movement
of life which is carried on in shaping itself, of the
eternal becoming which is ever new.

The symbolism of the French poets aims at expressing these efforts of the writer who tries, by
means of a perfect identification of form and matter,
to arrive not only at a reproduction of reality, but

to suggest something behind it, more distant, more
divine if possible. A perusal of Baudelaire's *l'Art
Romantique* will surely open the most prejudiced
eyes to this point of view. In order to give real
expression to what was in their hearts, and yet to
remain always hostile to all declamation and false
sentiment, the great Renaissance artists, and those
of our day, have recourse to a kind of incomplete
effect, something not quite finished which we see in
their sculptures and poems, something of that reluc-
tance to arrive at conclusions which Flaubert considered was an attribute of God. It is this infinite
suggestiveness that holds us in the statues of
Michelangelo and of Rodin, in the poems of Joachim
du Bellay or of Moréas.

But the art which, far more than sculpture, painting or literature, is a matter of pure perception is
the art of music. "De la musique avant toute
chose," cried Verlaine, echoing the dearest wish of
his age. We know what help music has lent to
Bergson's theories; on the other hand, after studying *les Syrtes* (1884), *les Cantilènes* (1886), *le Pélerin Passionné* (1891), *Eriphyle* (1894) and his
Stances (1899 and 1901), we realize that in spite
of his avatars, which we will presently consider,
Moréas was always an *intuitif* whose expression,
though very clear (for he has a holy horror of the
theatrical), was laden with the multiple meaning of
the most general feelings of the human mind. His
art might be defined by saying that his aim was
to sum up the most original or quintessential sensations of life in phrases often archaic in form, but
which were always original, but, and before all,
musical.

Anatole France, welcoming the *Pélerin passionné*
in 1892, certainly hits off the poet's real attitude of

mind when he says that Moréas would be acquainted with the Gods of ancient Greece only under the more slender form they wore on the banks of the Seine or the Loire, in the golden days of the Pléiade. M. France goes on to say that Moréas' real country is the north of France, with its blue slates and light gray skies, and which possesses those jewels of architecture decorated by the Renaissance with symbolic figure and subtle design.

The first number of the *Mercure de France* appeared in January, 1890, and the whole history of symbolism may be said without exaggeration to be closely connected with the history of this Review. The future historian of this great literary movement will be forced to go very carefully through every number of the *Mercure*.

The ruling æsthetician of the school was incontestably Rémy de Gourmont. Leaving on one side that part of his philosophy which only developed later — I mean his determinism which led him to declare, "L'esprit humain est si complexe et les choses sont si enchevêtrées les unes dans les autres que pour expliquer un brin de paille, il faudrait démonter tout l'univers" — it is clear that he devoted himself entirely to the exposition of that subjective or transcendental idealism according to which there is no reality save that which we imagine. The world is a representation made by our senses, and matter has no reality independently of the mind which perceives it. It was from Villiers de l'Isle Adam that Rémy de Gourmont learnt this principle, and he amused himself by looking for it in the works he studied with all the keenness of a collector.

Villiers de l'Isle Adam had taken his philosophy from the early Nineteenth-Century German philosophic school. It is interesting to see how careful young innovators are to provide themselves with predecessors, with ancestors for their support. Ronsard and the Pléiade chose the ancients; the Symbolists turned to the conquerors of 1870 who boasted that they were the leaders of the modern world and inventors of the very last word in culture!

Once again we see verified that law of which Tarde speaks in his book, *les Lois de l'Imitation:* progress is made by a man who invents and by others who imitate; only we must sometimes substitute the word *nation* for the word *man*. It would be easy to study and verify this law in its application to literature: here, in the case we are considering, Symbolism was the conversion of a large number of young minds to German mysticism; it is, as it were, the culminating point of that slow, sly operation of German penetration which was being accomplished throughout the Nineteenth Century. For close on a hundred years the French have been undergoing a philosophical and literary Germanization. Madame de Staël began the work which Wagner, Karl Marx, and Strauss were to finish.

The reaction was bound to come, and it came with a poet who had read Goethe, Winckelmann and Schopenhauer. Moréas was the poet with whom Frenchmen had most in common before 1914. This is easily seen by reading the studies made of him by two such different, not to say hostile, writers as Charles Maurras and René Gillouin.

In the first place, Moréas was of foreign extraction, like several other famous contemporary poets. His real name was the rather cumbersome one of Papadiamantopoulos, and he was born at Athens on April 15th, 1856. It is noteworthy that in the course of the last thirty years great French poets

have been born under other skies than those of the
Seine, or Loire, or Rhône. Moréas was a Greek,
Verhaeren a Fleming, Francis Stuart-Merrill and
Viélé-Griffin are, or were, American, Suarès is said
to be Portuguese, and Gustave Kahn of foreign de-
scent, Maeterlinck, Mockel and Van Lerberghe are
Belgian, Maria Krisinska was a Pole, Madame de
Noaîlles is a descendant on the paternal side of the
Wallachian Bibesco family, and her mother is of
Greek extraction. Many other examples will readily occur to the reader. There is something exciting
about reading these poets who have preferred
France to the land of their birth, for they make
us spectators of a dramatic contest. Which will
win with them — the Latin genius of which France
is the finest expression, or the genius of their own
land? Will French education, the influence of
salons and French society, in a word, will Paris melt
in her crucible all the precious metals these travellers bring her, and will she be able to make from
them a wondrous new alloy?

There is no doubt about the answer with Moréas
— and little with the others. "La contemplation
de la Seine," says Moréas, "et la lecture répétée du
24me chant de l'Iliade enseignent le mieux ce que
c'est que le sublime: je veux dire la mesure dans
la force. . . . L'ombre de Pallas erre dans sa ville
bien aimée, Athènes peut se contenter de l'ombre de
la déesse. Mais la fille de Zeus habite réellement
Paris."

After a certain amount of Ronsardizing and Symbolizing, Moréas in his later years was purely and
simply a classic poet. The reader remembers perhaps his words to Maurice Barrès on his deathbed:
"There is no such thing as Classic and Romantic,
that's all nonsense . . . if only I felt better I could

explain what I mean." We shall never know what arguments Moréas would have used: but we do know that after writing what seemed to many Frenchmen a somewhat tortured poetry, he finally produced the noblest and most classic. And in this he is symbolic of the evolution of the young school of 1890-1914. He is a representative man.

If we leave poetry for a moment and consider the novels of the younger men of the present day (I mean the men of about forty-five), we see a very curious thing. The influence of Jules Lemaître, Anatole France, or Maurice Barrès, or even Henri de Régnier, has served only to interest novelists in the eternal passions of the human heart, in man as the Seventeenth-Century writers saw him; and they pose him as a rule in a setting of centenarian trees. The younger writers, with some rare exceptions, are careful to compose in the classic manner, transfiguring reality into conformity with the desires of their hearts which are weary from much wandering. (Long past are the days of Dumas *père* and Victor Hugo and of Eugène Sue!) These young-old writers know that they do not invent existence; they receive it with a sad and contrite heart. They do not choose for subjects the physical abnormalities studied by Zola and his school. They love to study provincial life, but only in order that they may paint its old-world, humdrum, traditional side.

We have only to think of such men as René Boislère, or Henry Bordeaux, Charles de Pomairols, Alphonse de Châteaubriant, André Beaunier, and their numerous talented disciples. Charles Géniaux deserves a place to himself: his masterpiece, *Armelle Louannais,* — which has been "*couronnée*" by the French Academy, — a study of the Breton soul at the time of Lamennais, is a powerful work of lyrical realism with a picturesque style that evokes in us long, long thoughts. How different these writers are from Balzac! Their characters reck little of the struggle to make money — their creators attune them with infinite skill to the landscape which is their background, so that the pleasant land of old France, so dear to the romantic English heart, is reflected in themselves.

Of course it must not be forgotten that, on the other hand, free rein is given to temperament, and even Bergson's name claimed as authority for literary anarchy: —

> La raison, la raison ce n'est pas l'univers. . . .
> Je ne veux pas lancer devant moi des mirages,
> Créer des fruits abstraits dans un grand verger froid.*

cried a young poet who died before he had time to fulfil his promise. But, on the whole, Reason and old French tradition put up a gallant defense and brought such novelists as Louis Bertrand, Pierre Lasserre, Henry Bidou, or the brothers Tharaud, to that kind of asceticism which creates all things *sub specie aeternitatis*. Doubtless these novelists have read Constant's *Adolphe,* Fromentin's *Dominique,* and Feydan's *Fanny,* but they have grown tired of analysis, sick of hair-splitting.

Any serious study of Moréas leads us to exactly the same conclusion. Take an example from his famous book, *les Stances*. The poet has loved and has seen his love betrayed — he has suffered. See now how he has transfigured his sorrow, contenting himself with this invocation to Nature: —

> Ah! fuyez à présent, malheureuses pensées,
> O colère, ô remords,
> Souvenirs qui m'avez les deux tempes pressées
> De l'étreinte des morts!

*Henri Franck, *La Danse devant l'Arche.*

Sentiers de mousses pleins, vaporeuses fontaines,
  Grottes profondes, voix
Des oiseaux et du vent, lumières incertaines
  Des sauvages sous-bois;
Insectes, animaux, larves, beauté future,
  Grouillant et fourmillant,
Ne me repousse pas, ô divine Nature,
  Je suis ton suppliant.

This reads like a poem from the Greek Anthology
translated by a French classicist, whose art teaches
him to call to his aid all the beauties of Nature,
even the Beauty which is to come. The poem is
short, the divine afflatus is soon exhausted, if you
will. But the Tanagra statuettes are none the less
exquisite for being small.

Moréas began to write, or rather to publish, in
1884, when he was twenty-three. Vanier, the publisher of Verlaine and Mallarmé, published his *Les
Syrtes* about this time: then, in 1886, *Les Cantilènes*
appeared. The influence of Baudelaire — the sym-
bolistic Baudelaire — is very marked therein, and
also the influence of Verlaine. What is most striking in these compositions of a young writer is not
only the effort to note the mysterious, the fleeting
and sad, the reaction against the Parnassian poetry
and vulgar realism, but also the way in which the
old classic instinct is seeking for expression.

Towards 1890 those young American or English
artists who are always fond of lionizing French
poets were able to enjoy the spectacle of poor, sad
old Verlaine limping along in his bedraggled
trousers side by side with young Moréas, a perfect
dandy with his eyeglass in his eye, looking rather
like the *Ruffian* of his splendid poem.

Moréas's life was going to be a journey, not only
through the *cafés* of Paris and Europe, but through
French literature, starting from that of the Middle
Ages: and when he died in 1910 his poetry had

returned to the source of all true poetry, enriched by all that it had reflected, but calmed down into an ordered stoical nobility.

> Ne dites pas: la vie est un joyeux festin;
> Ou c'est d'un esprit sot ou c'est d'une âme basse.
> Surtout ne dites pas: elle est malheur sans fin;
> C'est d'un mauvais courage et qui trop tôt se lasse.
>
> Riez comme au printemps s'agitent les rameaux,
> Pleurez comme la bise ou le flot sur la grève,
> Goûtez tous les plaisirs et souffrez tous les maux;
> Et dites: C'est beaucoup et c'est l'ombre d'un rêve.
>
> Quelle bizarre Parque au cœur capricieux
> Veut que le sort me flatte au moment qu'il me brave?
> Les maux les plus ingrats me sont présents des Dieux,
> Je trouve dans ma cendre un goût de miel suave. . . .
>
> Triste jusqu'à la mort, en même temps joyeux,
> Tout m'est concours heureux et sinistre présage.
> Sans cause l'allégresse a fleuri dans mes yeux.
> Et le sombre destin sourit sur mon visage.

Such was the stoical equilibrium at which Moréas had arrived at the close of his life. But, in order to realize the roads he had trod, one should read his *Pélerin Passionné*, which scandalized the world of letters on its appearance in 1890.

Anyone who wants to know what the Parisian younger generation thought of the *Pélerin Passionné* must consult the newspapers and pamphlets of the day. In one of them, called *Fin de Siècle et Décadence*, I find the following judgment: — "Le titre emprunté à Shakespeare n'a aucun rapport avec les poésies contenues dans le volume: il n'y a ni pélerinage ni passion. Les vers sont libres; ils ont la rime, mais la mesure est absente . . . ; certains ont jusqu'à vingt et un pieds. . . .'"* And the hostile critic quoted among other lines the following, which are certainly rather bewildering to a scholar fresh from his Virgil: —

*Maurice Monteil, *Fin de Siècle et Décadence*, Tours, 1893.

On a marché sur les fleurs au bord de la route,
Et le vent d'automne les secoue si fort en outre.
La malle-poste a renversé la vieille croix au bord de la route,
Elle était vraiment si pourrie en outre.
L'idiot (tu sais) est mort au bord de la route,
Et personne ne le pleurera en outre.

It has been said that Moréas was lacking in emotion: such things are easy to say. It is not always those who are continually whimpering who have the most feeling. Ready tears are things of little count, like those rivulets which never run dry because they flow through chalky and infertile soil.

Moréas had discovered that our lives, like our speech, were encumbered with a great deal of unnecessary repetition, and he used the literary trick of piling Pelion upon Ossa in images, with no apparent logical connection. These three lines are the pattern of the style he most readily cultivated in his youth: —

Pire que bonne vous fûtes, et je fus sage.
Vous aviez un bouquet de cassie au corsage,
Et votre cou cerclé d'un collier de ducats.

That was his manner. He exaggerated a trick of which Verlaine, Rimbaud and Tristan Corbière had set the fashion, and which can be discovered by the careful seeker in most great poetry. But it was the originality of the latter Nineteenth Century to emphasize the process. There were painters with the same way of working, arranging splashes of color one beside the other, without any preconceived agreement of design, and leaving the public to compose the harmony of the picture with a mosaic of colors and shades. The hearer of Debussy's works is in the same manner confronted with a whirlwind of dancing musical atoms, — painter and composer toy, the one with every bar, the other with every tint, progressing slowly, seeking rare sonori-

ties or minute subtleties of color; and often they succeed in obtaining penetrating effects which rival
those of Nature. Such work is the image of our
own souls, which are like those great rooms in old
châteaux whose echoes are so memory-laden that
they repeat the cries of joy and pain of all humanity. To produce that effect there have striven,
each in his own way, poets so different as Francis
Viélé-Griffin, Henri de Régnier, Paul Fort, Camille
Mauclair, and Charles Guérin.

Next, still in pursuit of his Renaissance ideal,
Moréas took to studying old French, adapted *Au-
cassin et Nicolette*, translated the *History of Jean
de Paris, King of France*. It was at this period,
when he was under the influence of the old French
poets, and of Ronsard and du Bellay, that he wrote
his *Eriphyle*, which for every Romanist is a pure
masterpiece. Moréas's *Eriphyle* is the same suffering soul whom Æneas meets in Hades.

> Maestamque Eriphylen,
> crudelis nati monstrantem vulnera, cernit.

> Essence pareille au vent léger
>   J'erre
> Depuis que la vie a quitté
>   Mon corps.
> Mais les souillures et les maux du corps,
>   La mort ne les efface.

The appearance of the *Pélerin Passionné* in 1891
had given rise to a manifestation which was soon followed by the foundation of the *Ecole Romane*. The
members of this new Pléiade were Raymond de la
Tailhède, Maurice du Plessys, Charles Maurras,
Ernest Raynaud, and Hugues Rebell. Moréas was
the acknowledged leader. But it was a constitu-
tional monarchy, and the prime minister was a
young man of subtle and penetrating mind whose
hour of fame had just struck; for had not the great

Taine climbed up the six flights of stairs leading
to the young man's flat and all because of an article
which this same young man had written? This
prime minister was Charles Maurras. Since those
days he has attained a certain amount of fame.
M. Faguet, in his *Histoire de la Littérature Française,* boldly declares: "The masters of French literature at the present day are Messieurs Bergson,
Barrès, and Maurras." Maurras at twenty was the
same firm, complete character he is at fifty, and
there is little doubt that it was he who pointed out
to Moréas whither his excessive decadence and
so-called symbolism were leading him. Moréas
realized himself, thanks in great part to Maurras,
and in this way, after his somewhat disturbed linguistic revolution, his verbal punctiliousness, and
his turgid lucubrations, he returned little by little
to classic order.

As he grew older he came to appreciate Malherbe,
since in a sense Malherbe is the continuation of Ronsard and his art essentially an intellectual reasoning art. Moréas renounced his *vers libre* and the
other novelties which had amused him in his youth.
He saw, as Malherbe had seen, that the great
beauty of the French language is that it is analytic; he realized that it is unwise to strain
one's talent; further, he became convinced that
the only true art is hellenic art and its pupil French
art.

The soul of Moréas is revealed to us in *Les Stances,*
a kind of breviary for stoic unbelievers. Moréas,
like his friend Charles Maurras, believed only in
Reason, and Reason in the Greek sense, or as the
French classicists of the Sixteenth and Seventeenth
Centuries understood it. The perfection of art is
the approach of the divine.

Me voici seul enfin, tel que je devais l'être:
  Les jours sont révolus.
Ces dévouements couverts que tu faisais paraître
  Ne me surprendront plus.
Le mal que tu m'as fait et ton affreux délire
  Et ses pièges maudits,
Depuis longtemps déjà les cordes de la lyre
  Me les avaient prédits.
Au vent de ton malheur tu n'es en quelque sorte
  Qu'un fétu ballotté.
Mais j'accuse surtout celui qui se comporte
  Contre sa volonté.

Of a different order from that of Alfred de Musset is this poetry, with its conciseness, its bitterness against the woman who betrays, its loftiness of tone and its perfection. Here a thoroughly disillusioned heart took refuge in poetry, seeking a cure for the malady of life. There is a passage where Moréas speaks of Goethe and La Fontaine which reads like a confession applied to himself: —

"La vie artistique de Goethe, telle que Nietzsche la dépeint, est un exemple, une raison de désespérer et une consolation à la fois. Sa fameuse sérénité a quelque rapport avec le prétendu égoïsme de la Fontaine. Les conclusions morales, si dures parfois, du fabuliste ne sont qu'une sensibilité violente, mais éclairée, qui se tourne en dérision elle-même et se met à philosopher. Quant à Goethe, faites attention que s'il fixe sur le monde un regard calme, c'est avec l'expression la plus triste et la plus passionnée."

Yes, it is certainly thus that I see Moréas with his sorrowful yet severe temperament. M. Barrès in his funeral oration spoke of a kind of Oriental acceptance of life, but I think there was much more of profound and learned love of French poetry which consoled him in his life, together with a resignation more Olympian even than that of Alfred de Vigny.

Moréas came at an equivocal moment, as he himself said. None of the themes dear to the heart of the symbolists corresponded with his real temperament. He was too Græco-French to be a pantheist in the German manner, too Greek to have any real Christian faith. There is nothing of a Villon or a Hugo in him, nor of a Byron or a Swinburne. So that the only way open to him was to sing the poems of his destiny and to take refuge in the theatre. The *Iphigénie* of Moréas calls for comparison with that of Racine. Racine's is much more French, Moréas' much closer to the Greek text; yet both may fitly be cited as examples of that classic art whose aim is to paint the universal and attain the eternal beauty of which Greece has given imperishable models.

That is the great lesson Moréas teaches us. He is a Platonist in the same sense as Charles Maurras. In the eyes of these two writers the human being, be he poet or statesman, so long as he has not grasped the eternal reason which lies behind the ephemeral aspect of things, can only have fevered visions of reality. It is impossible to understand Moréas without having read Maurras's masterpiece, *Anthinea*. For many a young Frenchman *les Stances* and *Anthinea* are the *vade mecum* which enables them to see themselves and their destiny according to the eternal laws which the Greeks discovered.

A sincere examination of the hellenism of many Frenchmen (an exceedingly powerful factor in the intellectual formation of the Nineteenth Century) discloses the fact that we have here a phenomenon precisely similar to the anglomania of Taine and Bourget. The hellenism of Maurice de Guérin, or of Louis Bouilhet, or of Leconte de Lisle, and above all that of Louis Ménard, is a reaction against the surroundings in which these men live. One must be something of a globe-trotter to appreciate properly the Vicar of Wakefield's little garden; one must have suffered from one's *milieu* before dreaming of a truly ideal land. Tacitus, with the corruption of

Rome under his eyes, imagined Germania as the
home of virtue; which merely means that our greatest certainties are really sentimental. Jules de
Gaultier gave the name of Bovarysme to that faculty we possess of seeing ourselves other than as we
are: the name remains to be found for its near relative, the faculty of seeing the Golden Age in the
land we do not ourselves inhabit. So that we are
always deceiving ourselves and others: but ignorance
is truly bliss, when it helps on progress.

The French hellenizing poets are many. François
Viélé-Griffin deserves careful study. This wonderful poet with all his intuitive originality is of the
same family as Moréas. He began by being a fero-
cious individualist, and is now a traditionalist; and
being an utterly disillusioned idealist, he mixes a
very subtle irony with his stoicism. In any case, from
la Cueille d'Avril to *Swanhilde*, from *la Chevauchée
d'Yeldis* to *l'Amour Sacré*, from *l'Amour Sacré*
to *Phocas le Jardinier*, we are watching the drama
played in the poet's soul between lyric passion and
philosophic reason. M. Henri de Régnier is the
Andrea del Sarto of poetry. Albert Samain is also
at times a ''perfect poet'' in the style of André
Chénier, but they are both lacking in the lyric intoxication which is the magic quality of the poems
of Madame de Noailles. Their vehemence is so voluntary that it nips our emotion in the bud. The
art of Madame de Noaîlles, on the contrary, is a part
of her nature. We feel that the senses of sight,
hearing, touch, smell and taste have been given her
to use on the numberless fruits and perfumes of
the earth. Further, she adds to them, and we are
her accomplices. The land she lives in is the land
of the Arabian Nights, where love is brother and
sister to death: the Muse of *Cœur innombrable*,

L'Ombre des jours, Eblouissements, Les Vivants et les Morts, is closely connected with the Muse of Walt Whitman, who laughs at our set ideas of morality. But it must be admitted that she is superior to the American. "I think I could turn and live with animals, they are so placid and self-contained." Doubtless, but if we substitute for animals the fatalistic Orientals with their land of wondrous dreams, which have given birth to so many religions; their landscapes, which set us musing upon countless story and symbol; their towns, wherein sleep ages of forgotten greatness; their gardens, with marvellous cool and luscious fruits — life immediately becomes the paradise of our childhood, a land of delight.

Of course, the art of Madame de Noaîlles is romantic art, and has incurred thereby the wrath of Charles Maurras; a fate shared by the works of other poetesses, such as Madame de Régnier, Madame Delarue-Madrus, Madame Renée Vivien. Who loveth well chastizeth well: that is probably why M. Maurras calls them Mænads. He might have waited for the saraband and dance to finish — then the lights are put out and in that unbecoming moment before dawn we are cold, we shiver.

One day Madame de Noaîlles saw standing in her path the dread spectre of Death, and in her terror she turned towards God.

> Mais je ne vous vois pas, ô mon Dieu, et je chante
> A cause du vide infini. . . .

Madame de Noaîlles reminds one of Sygne de Coûfontaine, the heroine of Claudel's play *l'Otage,* when she cries: "Les choses grandes et inouïes, notre cœur est tel qu'il ne peut y résister." Adventures are to the adventurous: Eve proved that very clearly.

CHARLES PEGUY

I PURPOSE to study Péguy here from only one point of view:* as the pupil of Bergson who applied the master's doctrine to his own life. Studies have already been written of Péguy, but all that I have seen consider him from the outside, seeing in him only the Socialist, the politician, pamphleteer and patriot, except perhaps Suarès's little work, with all its sympathy and delicate insight, where grief speaks words dictated by friendship.

To say, for example, that Orléans and its Cathedral throw their vast shadow over Péguy's soul and explain his love for Joan of Arc is to consider Péguy in one attitude; a very favorite attitude if you

*This chapter was already written when M. Doumic, on the day he received M. Bergson into the French Academy (Jan. 24, 1918), said in his reply to M. Bergson's speech:

"Dans la foule de vos auditeurs, il est un groupe que je tiens à distinguer tout particulièrement: celui des jeunes gens. C'est parmi eux que vous avez trouvé vos plus fervents admirateurs. . . . Pas un de vos cours où l'on n'aperçût, dans son éternel capuchon de ratine bleue, qui lui donnait l'air d'un écolier de la rue du Fouarre, ce généreux Charles Péguy, qui lui-même était un des guides suivis par la meilleure jeunesse."

In treating of the influence of Bergson upon Péguy, I am of course deliberately leaving on one side a whole host of facts which are the woof of a man's life, and which in themselves are by no means negligible. It is impossible to exhaust the whole reality of facts in order to arrive at absolute and entire truth; one is lucky if one can arrive at a part of truth. Clearly, over and above the feelings and ideas which Péguy had — if one trusts his writings and personal testimony — there must have been many others acting upon him from time to time. It may always be said of any study of a writer, that it does not contain the whole man. If Péguy is studied here as falling under the Bergsonian sway, it is because that appears to me to be the real Péguy, the Péguy who influences his contemporaries. After all — influence — that is the whole of the question.

212

will, but still a single attitude. To explain his so-called socialism, or his patriotism, by his ancestors, the Orléanais vine-growers and peasants, is to be the dupe of so-called scientific formulas. For, after all, not every Orléanais is an admirer of Joan of Arc, nor is every descendant of peasants necessarily a socialist or a patriot.

The foundation of Péguy's character seems to have been an indomitable will. A son of the people, — of a mother who recaned the chairs of Orléans Cathedral, and for whom he had always the most filial respect and love, — he taught himself because he so willed it; entered the Ecole Normale Supérieure because he so willed it; left it for the same reason; founded, at the age of twenty-five, his Review, *Les Cahiers de la Quinzaine,* by his own force of will; and never rested from the struggle of opposing his will to other men's throughout a life of ceaseless contest.

Barrès, in the article* he devoted to Péguy on the news of his heroic death on the battlefield of the Marne, speaks of the wondrous radiance emanating from his personality. V. Boudon, one of the soldiers of his regiment, who has published an account of the marches and countermarches in the first weeks of the campaign — all too brief, alas! for Péguy — has tried to tell us of the impression produced on his soldiers by their heroic officer.† Clearly, with such a writer the least detail is of importance. But once the nobility, saintliness, or greatness of a hero acknowledged, there always comes a moment when we must try to enter into our subject, and find out on what food the writer's soul was nourished.

*Echo de Paris, 17 Sept., 1914.

†V. Boudon. *Avec Charles Péguy. De la Lorraine à la Marne.* Paris, 1916.

Now, from the day when he first met with it, Bergson's philosophy never ceased to inspire Péguy. Péguy is Bergson's most brilliant pupil; not his most brilliant university, scholastic pupil, but his most brilliant free-lance pupil. The greater part of his Cahiers are the best, the liveliest, existing commentary on the philosophy of Bergson.

Péguy's criticism is Bergsonian, his theology is Bergsonian, his style is Bergsonian. I do not mean that Péguy is a pale imitation of Bergson, or a servile copyist; on the contrary he is a highly original thinker who applies the Bergsonian ideas to criticism, history, religion and life itself, and makes of them the inspiration of his writing.

"Lotte* was saved from materialism by the Bergsonian philosophy, of which Péguy made him an enthusiastic neophyte. This liberation of Lotte is attested to by a study published by him in 1907, and which is a succinct exposition of Bergsonism in connection with Creative Evolution."†

But even if we had not Mgr. Battifol's testimony, we have the texts of Péguy's writings, which are a thousand times more instructive than any outside information. We have not only the pages in which he honors his master, but also those inspired by that master's ideas; finally, we have the fact of his evolution.

M. Maurras explains Péguy's "volte-face" by what he calls the "*coup de Tanger.*" "Du jour où les effets de ces actes anciens se prononcèrent contre la force de la patrie, c.a.d. si je ne me trompe, au lendemain du coup de Tanger, Charles Péguy se

---

*Lotte became Péguy's intimate friend from the day they met at the Lycée St. Barbe. On the news of Péguy's death he enlisted in a fighting regiment and was soon killed. For further details of this touching story of a friendship, see J. Pacary's book on Lotte.

†P. XIII of Mgr. Battifol's Preface.

révolta. . . . Il se déclara patriote ardent, militariste passioné, serviteur de la tradition nationale jusqu'à la mort.'' (*Action Française,* September 18, 1914.)

Between the *Jeanne d'Arc* of 1897 which Péguy signed with the name Beaudouin, and the *Mystère de la Charité de Jeanne d'Arc* which burst upon Paris in 1910 and aroused so much polemic, thirteen years intervened, thirteen years of incessant combat, first for Dreyfus, then for the ideas Péguy held dear. But if anyone will take the trouble to read the first *Jeanne d'Arc* after the second, he will find the explanation of Péguy's so-called volte-face.

There is a deepening of thought, a progression, in the Bergsonian sense of the word, a steady broadening of personality. Péguy grew always on the sentiment side, and the impulse in this direction came from Bergson; he dug deeper and deeper with the spade his master handed him.

It would, of course, be ridiculous to deny the influence of national and international political events upon each one of us in his daily life, more especially in youth when the mind is forming. Péguy, by very reason of his education which had taught him all that men owe to the past, was bound to feel an affront to his country more deeply than an ordinary man. The year 1905 was a decisive date in Péguy's life, when France was threatened with German invasion, and when ''the immanence of this invasion was a reality.'' Many another Frenchman, after passing through the same anxious hours, had henceforward but one idea, the strengthening of his country. But Péguy did not have to wait for the Tangier affair to learn the lesson of patriotism — for that it is quite enough to be born on the banks of the Loire.

On the other hand, when one remembers all Péguy's quarrels with the Sorbonne (which occurred at the same time as those of M. Pierre Lasserre, with whom, however, he has so little in common), one sees that it is the humanist in Péguy, the good pupil of those good humanists of the University of France, the "normalian" fresh from his classics, as well as the patriot which brought the whole-hearted Drey-fusard of 1899, all these led him not to the renuncia-tion of his past, but to the perception of certain realities, to the realization of the fact that all the fine phrasing of political programmes only served for the advancement of plotters and climbers and trimmers, and did little or nothing for the happi-ness of a great nation.

From the moment when Péguy really entered into Bergson's realm, — having realized that our feel-ings, far from being contemptible, have their source in the depths of reality; having understood that the great spiritual currents which carry us out of our-selves make us create the only true reality — from that moment he went forward upon his journey to Damascus, though it must be admitted that he had long discovered which way that journey lay. The perfect understanding between Bergson and Péguy — that is to say, between a man of Jewish descent and an Orléanais — is not an extraordinary phe-nomenon when we remember that the Christian reli-gion is founded upon the Old Testament, and that Bergson was nourished on all that is most purely French and is the disciple of Maine de Biran and of Ravaisson.*

*Maine de Biran and Ravaisson based their doctrine firmly upon the theory that the development of our knowledge was comprehensible only if we believed that the spirit was above and before all a mysteri-ous force reacting upon matter. Ravaisson declared that in its asso-ciation with the brain the mind drank the waters of Lethe. And Bergson was to say in his turn that cerebral activity was only an infinitely small part of mental activity. The brain contented itself

Péguy's protest — so instinctive and so sincere — against *sabotage* springs from all that is deepest in him and in France. "L'ouvrier qui endommage son outil est un fou qui se mutile lui-même." Péguy speaks here in the name of all great workmen. And Bergson who wrote so finely of man's tools, and of *l'Homo faber,* could not have expressed the truth better. "J'ai vu dans mon enfance rempailler des chaises, du même esprit et du même coeur et de la même main que ce même peuple avait taillé des Cathédrales." There speaks the son of that admirable Orléanaise. But it needs no great perspicacity to see that this deep filial love is animated by Bergson's doctrine of art and human work; the doctrine that everything holds together in a system of metaphysics, in a religion.

It might then be said that it was his innate honesty, his instinctive generosity, and the natural uprightness he inherited from his forefathers, which prevented Péguy's accepting any subversive doctrines; but it must also be added that his master's philosophy brought to him each year a very precious element of encouragement and emulation. In this connection there is one of Péguy's numerous Cahiers which one would like to quote in its entirety: that of February 3, 1907, in which, after giving us the little masterpiece of the brothers Tharaud, *Bar-Cochebas,* he continues his meditating "on the present situation in the modern world of history, sociology and

with translating into terms of motion a small part of what was happening in our consciousness; there was infinitely more in a human consciousness than in the corresponding brain. If, then, to these ideas we add the theory that the instinctive knowledge one species possesses about another on a particular point has its root in the unity of life, we easily realize the dignity of spiritual life, and can place this spiritual life not only in deeply poetic dreams as Maeterlinck did, but in religious meditation as Péguy does, and above all in the respect of everything which is the outcome of the Spirit.

the intellectual party.'' It seems as if Péguy, with his ears still full of Bergson's doctrines, wanted to clarify them by applying them to the surrounding world and reality; and in particular to destroy the modern theory that man and humanity may be known and understood ''by means of a system of properly arranged documentary slips.'' And he does it so amusingly, and in such Bergsonian fashion, and in truth in so many fashions, and with so many parentheses, that the first effect is rather bewildering.

There is no idea upon which Péguy loves more to dwell than this distinction between theory and practice, because metaphysics, as he understands the word, is for him the only direct way of research for knowledge, physics being only an attempt at indirect knowledge administered by the intermediate ministry of the senses.

Analysis, which is so necessary for the discovery of the secret of things when these things are machinery, is exactly the factor which blinds us and prevents our seeing a living thing from the inside. The locks of nature are not the locks of industry. Science can only arrive at a knowledge of phenomena which repeat themselves, but the phenomena of the soul, which so seldom repeat themselves, escape it. So that we always come back to that article of the Bergsonian faith: genius is not talent carried to a very high degree; ''genius is something given, like life itself.''

This view of Bergson's made a deep impression upon Péguy; on a mind, that is, which of itself had already recognized intuitively the abyss which separates immortal and living work from ephemeral literary production. These words of Bergson's explained to him the presentiments he had had while reading certain books or studying certain pictures in the Louvre.

Péguy gave his most vigorous expression of this view in his Cahier of 1906: *De la situation faite à l'histoire et à la sociologie dans les temps modernes* (November 4, 1906). Later on, when he returned to the faith of his childhood, he transported the distinction into the domain of religion: by substituting the word "grace" for the word "genius," as Pascal seems to me to have done also, and making this transposition of the Bergsonian doctrine perfectly natural. The world of metaphysics is smaller than might first appear. This Cahier could have been written only by a man convinced of the truth in the Bergsonian doctrine that there is an invincible internal opposition between works of genius and works of intellect.

There are within us obscure regions: our subliminal self is so mysterious, so complex and forever changing, that it can really express itself only in the harmony of numbers. Music is the idealized expression of our invisible continuous subconscious life, *"arithmetica nescientis se numerare animi,"* as Leibnitz puts it. We may be able to understand our purely material actions, our animal automatism, and to grasp the meaning of the workings of our *ego,* but we are brought to a standstill on the threshold of that far off land, where we sometimes listen for news of the unknown. Now there is one thing which gives us an eloquent glimpse of that region which, for mystics, is nothing but the mind of God, and for sensualists nothing but vibrations of matter. It is genius.

The Puritans, who had so high an idea of the omnipotence of God and of the impotence of man, were much nearer Reality than our hedonist communities.

There is profound truth behind their *credo,* only it is much deeper even than they thought. Genius, like the grace of God, is that irreducible, inexplicable driving power which is merged into life itself.

In 1904 in his Cahier *Israel Zangwill* (*Chad Gadya,* translated by Mathilde Salomon) Péguy had made his examination of conscience, still under the influence of Bergson, and had asked himself what Taine or Renan had given to the modern world. He said rightly or wrongly (this is not the point here) that their method was far from faultless and that, there as everywhere, the great debating ground of modern thought is nothing other than the old one of Science and Art. I have not the space to analyze Péguy's Preface, which takes up some ninety pages; but never was he more true to himself, never more inspired in his criticism of the Taine method.

Lovers of Bergson, however, may be glad to meet again with some of Bergson's favorite axioms, as Péguy brandishes them against his foes. Among others he uses the idea that the "forces de connaissance ne sont rien auprès de nos forces de vie et de nos ressources ignorées, nos forces de connaissance étant d'ailleurs nous, et nos forces de vie au contraire étant plus que nous"; for "nos connaissances ne sont rien auprès de la réalité connaissable, et d'autant plus, peutêtre, auprès de la réalité inconnaissable," etc., etc. (pp. LXXXIV à LXXXV, *Zangwill*).

Thus, as early as 1904, Péguy, socialist and freethinker, believed in the perpetual openness of our soul to new influx of light: a theory which is proved by the ever increasing idealism of English and French literature. Show me the men who will make history, and after that we will talk of scientific methods.

In this way Bergson had come to his help, drawn
him out of his pride ("orgueil enfantin des doctes
et des avertis") and encouraged him to combat those
conceptions of history which make progress depend
upon purely material conditions. And then, as we
know, the great figure of Joan of Arc had long been
taking shape in his mind. For not only have the
martyrs of all causes been characterized by their
indifference to material pleasures, and to economic
life, but they are the agents of that life which, in
its marvellous spontaneity and inner richness, is
irreducible to thought. The great vital impulse
transcends our experience and our consciousness,
and the result is that side by side with the truths of
reasoning there are truths of action and truths of
intuition.

Bergson declares that the spiritual impulse which
reaches its perfection only in the mind of man is
the greatest of all realities. Henceforward the consequences are clear. There are in the universe other
relationships than the mechanical relationships of
impenetrable atoms. There are intimate, inner relationships, so deep that they transcend Reason and
make of her their servant. In any deeply religious
or patriotic enterprise one realizes that man dies
for an ideal cause. The World War was waged by
us for a truth, for a faith. And the realm of the
Spirit must be very powerful indeed to force some
peoples to renounce their prejudices and make themselves the soldiers of Justice. But Péguy did not
wait for the World War to realize these great truths.
A nation never seemed to him a heap of stones, an
aggregate of gravel from which a few silexes may
be removed without changing anything. A man's
native land did not appear to him merely as a collection of acres of soil, but a living body, the body

which the Spirit — or, let us say, the vital impulse — had given to Justice.

With a man of such double or triple foundation as Péguy, account must needs be taken of his interest in the Jewish question. No other Frenchmen went into the "anti-Semite" question with so much force and passion for a persecuted race. George Eliot seems lukewarm beside him. Let it be said to the eternal honor of a soul thirsting after justice that he spoke with truth on this matter, *sine ira et studio*. The result was curious, in that the study of the Jewish question plunged Péguy deeper still into Catholicism. Here one must quote Péguy himself:

"Israël nous a donné le Dieu même. Rome nous a donné le seule répartition du monde où ce Dieu pouvait mouler son nouvel empire. Plusieurs fois et notamment dans *l'Argent Suite* Péguy* avait entrepris de nous représenter ce qu'il nomme la légation du monde temporel à Jésus. Nulle part autant que dans Eve, on ne sentira cette immense préparation poétique, philosophique, militaire et gouvernmentale qui se disposait dans le même temps qu'Israël poursuivant la longue préparation de race et de peuple."† Péguy is like Bergson, a believer in the divine truth of things, but he goes farther than his master. But the one is a philosopher, the other almost a priest.

Bergsonian philosophy, and sympathy with the Jews: such are the great currents flowing into Péguy's religion, feeding it, and leading him to write his three *Mystères de Jeanne d'Arc*, and his great poems. Perhaps one should also add the profound

---

*A friend is supposed to speak in Péguy's name.

†This article, although signed by Lotte, seems to me to be by Péguy. Jean Pascary tells us, in this connection, "Cette étude sur Eve représente un type particulier de collaboration entre Lotte et Péguy."

feeling of human solidarity, which is merged with Péguy — as with Claudel and many other writers — into the love of Fame, the desire to survive. (The last feature is still more striking when one studies Claudel.) André Suarès has a very good passage about this in his study of Péguy (Preface to the fourth volume of Péguy's *Œuvres Complètes*).

"Passion de la gloire dans le coeur d'un enfant ingénu et dans l'âme d'un adolescent qui vole vers son rêve! C'est un feu pour toute la vie. On a beau l'étouffer: il est toujours là qui veille. On l'épure. On mue la chaleur en lumière. On s'élève même à la sainteté. Mais en ceux qui ont bu de ce sang héroïque à guise de lait, ce premier amour est le foyer qui ne s'éteint qu'avec l'existence; et dans leur mort même, je gage, si l'on savait chercher, qu'il y a ce tison de soleil, au fond du coeur: la gloire."

That is all true. But, enamored as Péguy may have been of glory, he was still more passionately attached to the idea he believed to be essential, that of human solidarity. It is that spirit which animates his socialistic sketch *Marcel* (1898), a work of the highest optimism which shows us the City of the Future as a reign of perfect happiness, marvellous harmony and absolute justice.

The generosity of his nature, which made him, when he was quite young, embrace socialism as the doctrine best satisfying his conscience, and which later led to his revolt against politics as certain men understand them; the violent rancor and bitter disgust which seizes him when he sees what certain so-called statesmen have made of his dream — all this is important for the reader who seeks to understand the real Péguy. Tired with the contest, heart-wrung at what he has seen, he turns away to knock at the door of the City of God. The would-be reformer reforms himself. Denied the splendor of a statesman, he longs for the halo of a saint.

Thus Bergson helped Péguy to see clearly that the roots of his thoughts, striking down into an eternal past, gave him his holiest and most solid support. "Such a doctrine," as Bergson himself says, "does not only facilitate speculation, it gives us also more power to act and to live. For with it we feel ourselves no longer isolated in humanity, humanity no longer seems isolated in the nature that it dominates."

Ever since his earliest studies in classical and French literature, Péguy had felt the working of this strong current of deep-seated sympathy which forced him to recognize that "life is not contained in the category of the many nor in that of the one," that mechanical causality cannot give a sufficient interpretation of the vital process, that our consciousness by expanding more and more introduces us into life's own domain, which is reciprocal interpenetration and creation.

If Péguy never wavered from that conviction, it is because his instinct, his upbringing, the influence of classical antiquity and of his master, Bergson, all united to plunge him deeper and deeper into the way of life he had chosen — with its aim of making classical culture supreme in the cause of true liberty. That is the explanation of the profound feeling animating the pages of *Notre Patrie*, or his splendid hymn to the Virgin Hypatia (*Bar Cochebas*), of that ardent humanism we admire in so many of his *Cahiers,* and finally of his conception of history not only as a great art broadening our outlook, but as the narrative of the divine on earth. It is quite easy to sneer at the "Bible of History" idea, and to laugh at the suggestion that all human affairs are but a misty revelation of the divine: the new French history school indeed shows us how that may be done. But Péguy will not allow history to escape from the domain of literature. In his edition of *Chad Gadya*, he had remarked how history can never be more than imperfect readings of reality, and that he alone is worthy of the name of historian who, having weighed all the evidence obtainable from the best sources, has the warmest human sympathy, the highest human imagination.

The unity of the posthumous work *Clio* lies in this idea that history is not and cannot be a science, because history is not a scientific deduction but a literary description of fact, an intelligent sympathetic narrative of events, and at times a more or less successful guess at the most human causes and effects. Therein, according to Péguy, lies the importance of literature: the pages of the classics are facts which deceive no one and which teach us most about human nature. Therein also lies the importance of memoirs, and chronicles, and of every document which can throw light upon the mechanism of our faculties and passions. This man, then, who was never tired of studying Homer and Virgil in the text, who wrote such wonderfully acute pages on Corneille, Racine, Beaumarchais, Victor Hugo, had realized that no man of talent has ever cut away his roots, the roots of his race; and here the importance he attaches to ethnography comes to him from Renan as well as from Bergson.

Clio is a long commentary on this truth, that a line of Homer, a chorus of Sophocles, a few words of Hesiod, reveal to us in a wonderful way "les augustes profondeurs du monde antique." Such a conception of the artistic method in history — in spite of a momentary distrust of the views and ways of the mind — is imposed upon Péguy by the Bergsonian idea of *duration*. That is made quite clear in *Clio*. It is because Duration admits of no distinction between past, present and future, because the past exists in the present, that history can be written, thanks to memory, which is an inner searching of one's self, a spiritual resurrection.

The philosopher most akin to Péguy on this point is the modern Italian, Benedetto Croce — who declares that history comprises all literature. Péguy may very possibly have read Benedetto Croce. In any case he was soaked in Michelet, who knew his Vico by heart, and Vico had great influence upon Benedetto Croce.*

The mere fact of conceiving the mind as an ever-working, essentially dynamic activity explains how it is that writers, differing so widely on many points, have reached the same conclusion, in order to prove as far as they can the dynamic aspect of reality. This conclusion is essentially favorable to religion, for it emphasizes the undivided continuity of conscience and, by thus bringing all beings into closer connection, cannot evade the idea that a great spiritual force directs the universe. This realization of the solidarity of all beings, and consequently of God and man, was bound to bring Péguy back to the religion of his ancestors, to a community of ideas with all his people.

The essential aim of *Clio* is to show us that history, real history, is not what we read, not the records of an uncertain past, wave-worn wrecks on the ocean of the ages, but that it is what we are, what

---

*The reader should consult Professor Wildon-Carr's brilliant lecture, "Time and History in Contemporary Philosophy, with special reference to Bergson and Croce" (*Proceedings of British Academy*, Vol. VIII).

we have been, what we cannot prevent ourselves becoming. The idea, as George Eliot expressed it, that "our life is determined for us, and it makes the mind very free when we give up wishing and only think of bearing what is laid upon us and doing what is given us to do" is complicated in Péguy by the other idea that France has a definite mission to accomplish in the world. So that — as moralist, or as disciple of Michelet, or of Hugo, or, as he would have liked to say, as disciple of Joinville — he adapts the Bergsonian theory that we must install ourselves within the movement. *Gesta Dei per Francos*. Convinced as he is that nations do not march to the slaughter house guided by blind forces or by the mere action and reaction of cause and effect, artificial divisions of duration, he desires to see in the efforts of Athens, Rome and Paris one and the same continuative gesture, which is an overcoming of matter, a triumph of mind.

That sentence of Bergson's, "Duration is a material and not merely a formal element of the world," which is so mysterious for the uninitiated, has a very clear meaning in Péguy's *Clio,* and it also explains Péguy's theory, which has scandalized many of his readers, that humanitarian Europe and France of 1848, revolutionary Europe and France of 1789, humanistic Europe and France of the Sixteenth Century, are all sisters of the Europe and France of the Middle Ages adoring their God-made Man. His anthropomorphism is Bergsonism. Who will may laugh — but his greatness is not to be denied. Péguy has only one aim: to render humanity greater, graver, more human, more humane, more humanistic, more careful of mind, of culture, of goodness and of the solidarity uniting all created beings. That is the explanation of this hatred of our mechanical age with its so-called conquest of matter and of the mechanizing of French Thought by those "scientific" methods which make of Frenchmen the Pomeranian grenadiers of a proud but futile learning.

We must come back to the Cahier *Bar-Cochebas* to understand his point of view. "We are witnessing a kind of explosion of scientific industry. Man has subdued matter, but has at the same time submitted to it. Science has become theorized industry. Our thought has become mechanical, at once the image and slave of our machines. We must make war upon matter and for that purpose have recourse to metaphysics. Metaphysics alone can give us a direct knowledge of reality.

"Great metaphysical systems are like great races, nothing other than the languages of Creation. Each new great philosopher is a man who has discovered some new aspect in Reality. He is a man taking part, in his turn and with his own voice, in the eternal concert. There are some airs that have never been played twice to humanity. Practice and technique may advance in continued progress, but not metaphysics. Metaphysics belong to the order of *time;* they are *une réussite,* they might or might not have happened." And since everything is deeply bound up together, Péguy sees in the Frenchman's power of invention, in his faculty for throwing off a yoke and of falling to rise higher, the real source of the greatness of his race.

More than that, the Frenchman is the man who best understands instinctively and intuitively what Duration really is. He contributes towards making the world of history an ever fresh reality. Everyone knows those famous, and so very Bergsonian, pages where Carlyle proves that Cromwell was never a hypocrite. Even so the Frenchman has never his career mapped out, nor is his world ever a precontrived puppet show moved by wood and wire.

Everything, once more, combined: the Greek and Roman idea of civilization, and the Christian idea of a God-made Man, and the revolutionary idea of human progress, to fix Péguy the more firmly in his own theories.

"Et l'arbre de la race est lui-même éternel."*

* * * *

Such is the explanation of the *Mystères de Jeanne d'Arc,* and all those works written in the last four or five years of his life, when Péguy, after making political and mystic acquaintance with the natural and supernatural world, aspires only to participation in the solidarity of Christendom — one might almost say longs to merge himself into Joan of Arc.

The Jeanne d'Arc of 1897 is a drama inspired by Michelet. It is a story of the Maid — a story cut up into a series of tableaux — in which his passion for liberty shines forth in all its glory. *Le Mystère de la Charité de Jeanne d'Arc* is a meditation upon the Passion of Christ, and upon the problem of evil and suffering. But between 1897 and 1910 a great deal has happened, and not a little blood has been shed. Péguy's aim now is to translate into the plane of theology not only what Bergson says in the plane of metaphysics, but also what he has led his pupils to believe. Anyone reflecting upon certain consequences of the Bergsonian teaching upon Time and God is led quite naturally to the conflict which exists

---

*Students of this vast question of History as Art or Science should consult M. Henri Berr's valuable book, *La synthèse en histoire,* and Mr. Trevelyan's *Clio, a Muse.*

in every religious soul between the idea of God's
goodness and the reality of evil.*

This is a book of literary criticism, and it would
therefore be out of place to enter into the heart of
theological debate in the midst of what Montaigne
calls "this coile and hurly-burly of so many Philosophical wits." Besides, the question of Péguy's
religion is far from being decided, and probably
never will be. Charles Maurras judged it as "capable de désordres immenses." Pascary declares
Péguy to be "un catholique trop incomplet." Suarès
boldly affirms that Péguy was a born heretic and
was heretical in all his creeds. Even Monsignor
Battifol admits that Péguy's religion was ruled by
a mysticism which, like all mysticisms, is exposed to
the temptation of becoming "libertaire" and agnostic. We may leave them to their debate and merely
study how the idea of the divinity presents itself to
Péguy.

Here Péguy seems to me to be a pure pragmatist.
(For there is a close relationship between William
James's teaching and that of Bergson and Professor
Schiller.) We must not forget that Bergson's God
is not identical with nature. God expresses Himself — or tries to express Himself — by conquering
the conditions which oppose His freedom. He lives
in duration. He is really a living God, because in
this way His creation is full of surprises, and He
never dwells upon the cold and abstract heights of
the Absolute. "The prince of darkness may be a
gentleman as we are told he is, but whatever the
God of earth and heaven is, He can surely be no
gentleman. His menial services are needed in the

---

*The reader may refer to a fine poem by Mr. Cloudesley Brereton,
Contemporary Review, June, 1914, in which he will see a sincere
admirer of Bergson asking himself the same question as Péguy did.

dust of our human trials, even more than His dignity is needed in the empyrean.''* God can only act in and through matter, and matter, though separable from His being, is inseparable from his actions. Péguy, after his ''conversion,'' will naturally be orthodox, but this conception of Bergson's is always at the back of his mind. For most English readers an excellent introduction to Péguy's *Mystères* would be Professor Schiller's *Riddles of the Sphinx*. The chapter which Professor Schiller devotes to the relations between man and God, his assertion of ''the finiteness of God'' which ''is primarily the assertion of the knowableness of the world, of the commensurateness of the Deity with our intelligence'' enables one to understand many of Péguy's bold sayings. This for example: ''Les calculs de Dieu par nous peuvent ne tomber pas juste; Dieu, par le mystère de la liberté, s'est mis dans les mains de sa créature. Littéralement les saints commandent la volonté de Dieu et la dirigent.''†

Another passage from Professor Schiller expresses in more precise form than Péguy's words what Péguy felt in his heart: ''God cannot be happy while there is misery in the world. God cannot be perfect while evil endures, nor eternal, nor changeless, while the aim of the world process is unrealized. If we suffer, He must suffer; if we sin, He must expiate our Sin.''‡

Péguy's attitude, with which many reproach him because it may seem to be lowering God, making Him speak like a venerable graybeard who sent His son upon earth, has naturally occasioned much criticism. ''Mais moi qui ne suis pas vertueux, dit Dieu,

*William James, *Pragmatism*, p. 72.
†*Entretiens avec J. Lotte*, p. 340.
‡*Riddles of the Sphinx*, p. 431.

Je ne pousse pas des cris et je ne suis pas scandal-
isé,'' etc.*

This passage only needs for commentary Professor Schiller's words:

"The conception of a Deity absorbed in perfect,
unchanging and eternal bliss is a blasphemy upon
the Divine energy which might be permitted to the
heathen ignorance of Aristotle, but which should
be abhorred by all who have learnt the lesson of the
Crucifixion. A theology which denies that the im-
perfection of the world must be reflected in the sorrows of the Deity simply shows itself blind to the
deepest and truest meaning of the figure of Him
that was 'a man of sorrows and acquainted with
grief' and deaf to the gospel of divine sympathy
with the world. Thus the world-process is the process of the redemption alike of God, of the world,
and of our own selves.''†

And again to those words I would add these of
Péguy:

"Toute la faiblesse, et peut-être faut-il dire la
faiblesse croissante, de l'Eglise dans le monde moderne vient non pas, comme on le croit, de ce que la
Science aurait monté contre la Religion des systèmes soi-disant invincibles, non pas de ce que la
Science aurait découvert, aurait trouvé contre la
Religion des arguments, des raisonnements censé-
ment victorieux, mais de ce que ce qui reste du monde
chrétien socialement manque aujourd'hui profondé-
ment de charité. Ce n'est point du tout le raisonne-
ment qui manque. C'est la charité. Tous ces raisonnements, tous ces systèmes, tous ces arguments
pseudo-scientifiques ne seraient rien, ne pèseraient

*Mystère des Saints Innocents, p. 80.
†Riddles of the Sphinx, p. 431.

pas lourd, s'il y avait une once de charité.''*

If I had to choose one from among Péguy's greater works, I think it would be the poem he called *Le Porche du Mystère de la Deuxième Vertu* and in which he sings of Hope. Into it he put the purest part of his heart and faith. It is a spiritualisation of Bergson's doctrine: "Il n'y a que ce qui change qui dure": the becoming and the permanent are not two contraries; they are one and the same thing. By a real touch of genius, Péguy shows that man's *becoming* guarantees the permanence of the word of God:

"O misère, ô bonheur, c'est de nous qu'il (Dieu)
    dépend. . . .

   .   .   .   .

Nous qui ne sommes rien, qui ne durons pas, . . .

   .   .   .   .

. . . C'est encore nous qui sommes chargées de con-
    server et de nourrir éternelles
Sur terre
Les paroles dites, les paroles de Dieu . . .'' etc.,
    etc.†

One is almost tempted into saying that what Bergson calls Time, Péguy calls Hope. The whole poem must be read in order to understand Péguy's temperament. One of the most beautiful passages is that where he describes a wood-cutter working all alone in a forest on a mid-winter's day: his teeth chatter, for the wind chills him to the bone; he is miserably cold. Suddenly he bethinks himself of his wife, who is such a good housekeeper, and of his children who are playing by the fireside. And

*Charles Péguy—*Notre jeunesse*, p. 136.

†Pp. 108, 109, 110, 111—*Le porche du mystère de la deuxième vertu*.

this mirage of the warm cosy cottage cheers the woodman's loving paternal heart. Passages such as this make us think of the pictures on old manuscripts, for Péguy is at one with those illuminators who paint the work of the fields with their ingenuous brushes: so also the Passion of Christ in the *Mystère de la Charité de Jeanne d'Arc* recalls the Crucifixions in mediæval missals. The wood-cutter is symbolical not only of Jesus, "the man who hoped," as Péguy puts it, but of God who centers all his hopes in man, while man concentrates all his hopes in God; and in this wonderful relation between the Deity and mankind, man tyrannizes over God even as God tyrannizes over man, and both continue creating heroes and saints for ever. Faith plays, Charity loves, but Hope leads the Eternal Power to Creation.

It is in this way that Péguy's art is the outcome of his deepest feeling. His charity which, like his wood-cutter's thought, is the absolute opposite of the Lucretian *Suave mari magno,* is closely connected with his theology — God, acting ceaselessly upon the world, is the comfort of Péguy the sinner. And he is always calling upon us to love God.

Lovers of Milton and his virile language (and there are still some such in these days) will plunge with real delight into these writings of Péguy. The present pages are written with the aim of inviting them to do so.

Again, in the *Mystère de la Charité de Jeanne d'Arc* and in *Les Saints Innocents,* we find once more the same doctrine of freedom, and the same conception of God, or rather of divine love.

And in *Eve,* the idea of Christ coming to bring a new law, to superimpose the order of grace upon the order of nature, though without lowering the order of nature, the idea that creation had prepared salvation, — all that is worthy of Milton.

But there is little good in a skeleton summary of these poems.

Of course we must not exaggerate, and above all we must never lose sight of, Péguy's eminently pragmatic attitude, when he speaks with merry familiarity of God or his saints.

We are a long way from Kant and his Categorical Imperative! But on this point Péguy has expressed himself very clearly. "Le Kantisme a les mains pures, mais il n'a pas *de mains*. Et nous, nos mains calleuses, nos mains noueuses, nos mains pécheresses, nous avons quelquefois les mains pleines. . . ."*

Péguy gave free rein to all his intuitive lyricism in treating the extraordinary story of Jeanne d'Arc, about whom men will never cease writing, and all the more so because he saw therein additional evidence in favor of Bergson's theory of intuition. Hanoteaux felt the same thing when he wrote his *Jeanne d'Arc.* Very wisely, Péguy has left the facts on one side, for a poem in its very definition cannot be the exposition of an historical inquiry; above all, a poem which aims at being a meditation upon Christian mysteries. And, like all religious writers, Péguy leaves a clear road for his critics. Obviously those who see only a series of irritating subtleties in Milton's *Paradise Lost* would do better not to read such books. This brings us naturally to the study of Péguy as an artist.

Péguy, as an artist, will always stand out from his contemporaries by reason of his style, which he wished to render as Bergsonian as possible.

*François Marie, *Comte Hugo*, pp. 496-7. *Œuvres complètes*, Tome IV.

There are a great many readers who share Péguy's ideas, but detest his style, while there are others — a man like M. Paul Souday, for example — who declare the style to be peculiarly attractive.*

Péguy himself knew perfectly well what he wanted to do, and he had his defense carefully written by his friend Lotte:

"Un lecteur dira: 'Péguy a peut-être beaucoup de génie mais il semble dénué de talent. De grâce priez-le donc d'écrire comme tout le monde et de rendre ainsi son oeuvre accessible. Je serais pour ma part fort désireux d'y pénétrer. Encore faudrait-il qu'il en dégageât les avenues, au lieu de les barricader avec les ronces et les épines de son style hérissé.' "†

Obviously the abundance of words, the repetitions, reiterations, discourage the reader; and, to be frank, I fear that Péguy, who loved the people so well, will never be popular. It is true that the French peasant seizes upon a word and brings it into his talk over and over again, but he is not likely to love the man who imitates this habit. Péguy had certainly a wonderful mastery of his language (Jules Lemaître spoke in his defense on this point in the Academy), he was very sure of his syntax, but he gave himself up too much to his game of *leit-motif* and *da capo*. His aim was to establish "the continuity of life in the discontinuity of Words," to express life "dans son écoulement," to attain such fluidity that it would be impossible to cite the shortest sentence without being thereby obliged to quote a whole page or even several pages. It is true that he was successful in that, but perhaps he paid too dearly for what he considered a great merit.

*Paul Souday, *Les Livres du Temps*, p. 218.
†*Joseph Lotte*, p. 268.

In order to make his reader absolutely at one with him, Péguy has recourse to a kind of flux of words, or continuous Bergsonian current of phrase, so that our vocables appear less stable, less material, less prosaic, and express his spiritual impulse, the fluidity and mobility of reality.

Like every great conscious artist he feels that words are quasi-incapable of rendering great passions. That is why he tries to express the ever flowing stream of life. Sometimes he plays with words like a cat with a mouse; he leaves his idea, then goes back to it, tosses it into the air to catch it as it falls, and plays with it again. Those who read a book "for the story," to see what happens, had better not open Péguy's books or poems. They will find them dreadfully tiresome. A rather amusing point is that some of Péguy's critics are speechless with admiration before Rabelais. Well, Péguy is another Rabelais in verbal invention, and is really far less intoxicated than Rabelais by the clatter of words. Rabelais when he "gets going" is like a child who shakes a policeman's rattle till the household is distracted. He has whole chapters which are nothing but a succession of vocables. It would be vain to seek in Péguy those passages which abound in Rabelais and in which he lets loose a torrent of words, alliterations, assonances which become at last positively deafening.

* * * *

When men speak of Péguy they never forget that he fell on the field of battle, but they too often forget that he was still young. True, his was a hero's death, but that is insufficient consolation for his premature end. When he fell, facing the enemy in 1914, Péguy was far from having said his last word. When, under the direction of Bergson, he began to exploit the riches of his mind, and to give to his latent pessimism the broadening acquired by religious thought, he knew very well what he was doing. André Suarès likens him to "un frère prêcheur, un petit capucin." That is good. Péguy the idealist was worthy to number among the first companions of Saint Francis of Assisi: for he was one of the great confessors of poverty, and for our modern hedonic democracies there is no more necessary, salutary teaching. There was profound truth behind André Chénier's line:

"Qui ne sait être pauvre est né pour l'esclavage."

I may be wrong, but I seem to find above all in Péguy the same qualities which exist in the best men of his generation, in all those whose education was too dialectical and founded upon too many books, in writers as different from him as André Gide and Jules Romains — a strained desire for spontaneity, and a very deliberate love of lyricism; and then, right at the back of his mind, that other idea, that men are illogical beings and often need a Reformer.

* * * *

Any study of Péguy would be incomplete if no mention were made of the literary group among which he moved. M. Doumic has spoken of the very considerable influence exercised by Péguy. To tell the truth his influence is mixed up with that of Bergson. It was exercised upon young schoolmen for whom "his words were half-battles" and to whom he taught respect of their own country and of the classics and the love of things spiritual. Here we have to deal with the imponderable. A literary clique creates for itself, and lives in, a certain atmosphere, and the critic who has not lived in that atmosphere can realize what it must have been only by looking through library catalogues, or hearing the talk of survivors.

When we look through a complete collection of the *Cahiers de le Quinzaine* (which, we may add for the benefit of the bibliophile, commands a very high price at the present day), we are struck first of all by the want of unity and direction in the young writers who published in this way their first works — and very often masterpieces at that.

For example, there is not the slightest resemblance between the classic, or neo-classic, art of the brothers Tharaud or of Jean Schlumberger, and the romantic art of Romain Rolland. The former follow in the tradition of the French analysts; sometimes they remind one of Benjamin Constant, and sometimes of Stendhal: they want above all to see realities, and for this end they accumulate small facts. A certain amount of bitter pessimism seems to them to be the condiment necessary to the swallowing of life. Romain Rolland, on the contrary, offers us his Jean Christophe, a great clown of a German, a kind of clock ornament in the Romantic fashion — hair ruffled by the wind, hurling defiance at the tempest.

In the same way the criticism of André Suarès with its fine shades of meaning, its depth too, has nothing in common with Péguy's criticism, which is much simpler, with its savor of hearth and pot and pan. Nor is there in the irony and realistic art of Emile Moselly anything faintly resembling the deliberate moralization and tactful discrimination of Daniel Halévy. And it is equally obvious that many other contributors to the *Cahiers* are brought together only by sharing the same political ideas.

Their aims may be expressed in the exceedingly

simple rule — so exceedingly hard to keep: above all
be honest! M. François Porché, the poet, brought this
out well in his very interesting, though rather too
short, study of Péguy in the *Mercure de France*.[*]

One may also quote in this connection the powerful words of André Suarès in which he delivers a
kind of funeral oration upon his own youth and
that of his companions in arms:

"On n'a jamais vécu pour l'art avec plus d'abandon, plus de foi, ni plus de sincérité. Et certes, si
tout se renouvelle en France d'ici à trente ans, et
de là en Europe, c'est en nous qu'il faudra chercher
l'origine de toute rénovation et les premiers mod-
èles de chaque nouveauté. Le poème en prose, le
vers libre, la poésie toujours prise de plus près à
la source musicale; le roman tournant aux mémoires
ou au rêve de la conscience; la musique infiniment
étendue dans le plan de l'harmonie; la peinture et
la statuaire qui tendent à un poème logique de la
couleur et des volumes: en tout nous avons trouvé
la sensation et le fragment, ou le document sec et
l'importune rhétorique; en tout nous avons voulu
garder plus amoureusement le trésor de la nature et
la régler par le style. Un ou deux même se sont
élevés jusqu'à la rêver ainsi: rêver la nature et lui
donner le style, l'art n'a rien de plus grand."

André Suarès attributes to a single literary group
what was really the work of several, but his attitude
is very pardonable. Besides, what we are trying to
find out here is whether there was not some profound connecting link animating all this ardent
youth. Indeed, among all the remarkable works published in the *Cahiers,* there is one which is indeed
the true reflection of the modern spirit, with all its

---

[*]See in the *Mercure de France*, March 1, 1914, a very interesting
article by M. François Porché.

subtlety and complexity, its preoccupation with the affective forces of the soul, and its respect of the inner life, and that is Albert Thierry's wonderful little book, *l'Homme en proie aux enfants.** *L'Homme en proie aux enfants* is the young schoolmaster who is intrusted with the care of young souls, and who is obliged to take a class of boys who have just reached "the awkward age." This book, with its theory of life as a perpetual birth, is full of Bergsonism, and ought to be in the hands of every schoolteacher. It shows that in order to be a teacher worthy of the name, it is necessary first and foremost to realize that children are not machines, and that to understand them one must use sympathy, and again sympathy, and still more sympathy. Everyone should read his chapter called Silence. (Ch. XXIV.)

After reading this wonderful *Cahier,* and the works of Péguy, the poems of François Porché, André Spire, René Salomé, and the novels of the brothers Tharaud, one realizes that for them literature was, or was meant to be, the spontaneous outflow of a soul; that reality for them was, or tried to be, a hold on immediate consciousness, that is, without the intermediary of logic. And it may well be that, without perhaps appearing to do so, Albert Thierry came nearest this ideal. Alas, that he too should have fallen in the World War!

In any case all honor and glory to Bergson for having given its metaphysical justification to such an attitude, and to Péguy for having given a new significance to the words and symbols we use, for having shown, indeed, that "the only way into nature is to enact our best insight."†

Troisième Cahier de la onzième série, November 7, 1909.
†Emerson.

EMILE CLERMONT

M. EMILE CLERMONT, who fell on the battlefield at Maison-de-Champagne on March 5th, 1916, was certainly the most highly gifted novelist of the young school. M. René Gillouin in a very interesting article in the *Revue de Paris* has told us how Clermont excelled in all subjects at the Lycée Henri IV, showing a special predilection for philosophy, which he studied first under Henri Bergson and later under Victor Delbos. M. René Gillouin is himself one of the most remarkable of Bergson's disciples and naturally lays stress upon Bergson's teaching as being more than an illumination, rather an enfranchisement, a liberation, of Clermont's mind. But even without this testimony from a co-disciple, to read Clermont's novels is to realize the truth of M. Gillouin's statement.

It remains then to be seen to what extent Clermont was influenced by the Bergsonian philosophy, and in what measure his conception of art is attuned thereto. His output was unhappily all too short, since, if we except a historical study written when he was at the Ecole Normale Supérieure, it consists of only three novels. But as these three novels treat the same themes, and show the same moral preoccupation, it is clear that Clermont's thought varied little. To put it briefly, these three novels might be looked upon as three chapters in the William James manner on the Varieties of Religious Experience.

The whole depth of Bergsonian philosophy is contained in his theory that reality cannot be enclosed in a formula. The first corollary of this theory is the idea that we may communicate with this reality without necessarily seeking to understand it; and the second corollary is the idea that ethical or æsthetic feelings are the best means of harmonizing with this same reality. In this way we are plunged into the uttermost depths of self wherein two feelings are perpetually present: egoism and altruism, those two primitive forces of the human mind. Altruism, more commonly called charity, is only another name for that deep-rooted instinct which is the religious instinct and which ever since man was created has manifested itself in so many different forms, but which in spite of all obstacles always manages to come to light. Taine used to tell us that "we sleep and eat and seek to make a little money or gain a certain amount of men's esteem; and our way of life is simply petty when it is not animal." But when Taine wrote like this he saw things only from the outside, he simply did not care about discovering the powerful forces of the mind, the religious forces, — such as Puritanism, for example, — which have played so important a part in the history of nations.

When one looks back upon the Nineteenth Century it seems to be the history of efforts to create a new religion or restore the old one. That is its pathos. In reality no one can understand Clermont's attitude of mind who has not also read the work of other young writers of his day. "Agathon's" book, *les Jeunes Gens d'aujourd'hui*, shows us a whole generation of lovers of ethics and action, who seek in the religion most generally professed in their country, that is to say in

Catholicism, not so much a body of metaphysical doctrines all more or less subject to theological dispute, but rather a kind of decalogue such as is alone capable of endowing social life with strength, health and happiness. Together with this book of Agathon's which is so full of information upon the mentality of the young Frenchmen of pre-war days, should be read Romain Rolland's *la Nouvelle Journée*. There you have two authors who differ widely in religious thought, but who describe the same tendencies in a generation which might be called pragmatico-bergsonian, to coin a not very neat phrase, a generation which loved health, sport and physical contests yet at the same time realized that sentiment had its importance too. Georges Jeannin, the young man studied by Romain Rolland, is tired "of Tolstoi's nihilistic pity, of Ibsen's somber distinctive pride, of Nietzsche's frenzy and of Wagner's heroic, sensual pessimism." So are "Agathon's" correspondents. There is not a shadow of doubt that the state of mind of these young men was in part produced by Germany's attitude towards France from 1887 to 1914. But there is another, deeper cause which explains their mentality, their utilitarian mysticism, their rational ethics, and we see it working in America and also in England — I mean their lassitude, not of reason, as Romain Rolland believes, but of that reasoning kind of reason which creates numberless philosophical systems, but leads to nothing. This skepticism on the subject of Truth with a capital T has never been better expressed than by Professor Schiller, in a page written since the outbreak of the World War, and which renders admirably the feelings in the heart of hearts of a host of young Frenchmen:

"If only philosophers could be got to face the facts of actual life, could any of them fail to observe the enormous object-lesson in the truth of pragmatism which the world has been exhibiting in the present crisis? Everywhere the 'truths' believed in are relative to the nationality and sympathies of their believers. It is, indeed, lamentable that such an orgy of the will to believe should have been needed to illustrate the pragmatic nature of truth, but who will dispute that for months say 999 persons out of 1,000 have been believing what they please, and consciously or unconsciously making it 'true' with a fervor rarely bestowed even by the most ardent philosophers on the most self-evident truths? No improbability, no absurdity, no atrocity, has been too great to win credence and the uniformity of human nature has been signally attested by the way in which the same stories (mutatis mutandis) have been credited on both sides."[*]

Young Frenchmen had not waited for the war of 1914, any more than Professor Schiller had, to become humanists, — humanists, that is, in practice after the French fashion, — neo-classicists, or simply ardent patriots. A great country, which has deserved so well of humanity as France, has every right to a life and development according to her own genius. Even though she appears to waste her strength in seemingly futile efforts, even if she makes mistakes in her endeavors to find a faith, it is not for the skeptic in his study to criticize.

Emile Clermont stands out among the group of remarkable young men by the fact that he seems still more strongly imbued with that Bergsonian doctrine which made Péguy's friend, Josephe Lotte,

[*] *Mind.* Year 1915. *Realism, Pragmatism, William James.* 1915.

say: "Je n'oublierai jamais l'émotion dont me transporta *l'Evolution créatrice*. J'y sentais Dieu à chaque page."

Now bring this philosophy into contact with a naturally highly strung temperament, a deeply cultured mind fresh from all the best French authors of the Nineteenth Century, and see what lessons this young writer will have retained. He finds himself faced with the two hostile forces which are necessarily maintained by Bergson's doctrine, since the one is engendered by the other, — on the one hand our self, with its cortège of more or less conscious mystic phenomena; on the other, a spirit of analysis and self-examination (what the French call *dédoublement*) which brings into play the forces of intellect. It cannot be denied that a part of Bergson's doctrine exalts the importance of feeling — but a century ago Rousseau and the Romantics gave "sensibility" the predominant place over reason. Romanticism is at bottom a mystic movement; and its mystic fervor a good dose of quinine for those whom the cult of Reason had rendered anæmic. "We were drunken with poetry," said Gérard de Nerval — "with mysticism" would have been more accurate. And this European movement is the same everywhere: Wagner, Tolstoï, Nietzsche, Ibsen, are all descendants of Rousseau, whether they acknowledge it or no.

But in France, the land of men who always want to see things clearly, the struggle between the intellect, always busy in plucking out of duration moments that interest us, and intuition, leading us always to the very inwardness of life, created a state of mind which, as it developed, turned against itself and exaggerated itself still further. Thus was hypertrophied that faculty for dividing one's

personality into two halves of which the one
watches the other act, that spirit of morbid analysis
of which Benjamin Constant's *Adolphe** is the type,
but which type is repeated in all the psychological
novels of the Nineteenth Century, in Stendhal's
masterpieces, in Baudelaire's prose poems, and in
certain of Bourget's and Barrès' writings. All that
part of Bergson's doctrine relating to the *becoming*
is meaningless to the intellect. It does not experience anything like the sensations described by M.
Le Roy in his study of Bergsonian philosophy: "Ne
vous est-il pas arrivé parfois, entraînés à travers
mille détours dans une course imprudente d'une
extrême vitesse, de vous abandonner sans pré-
vision au charme étrange du changement, à l'ivresse
délicieuse du devenir? Et n'avez-vous pas alors
observé que vous perdiez le sentiment ordinaire de
l'écoulement régulier du temps pour ne ressentir
qu'une vive impression de rythme et qu'une émotion
d'attente sans cesse renouvelée?" Clearly, the
description of such sensations can make no appeal
to the novelist, whose tendency is to follow the
cinematographical method, and whose logical efforts
are, in his eyes, the most positive of all his spiritual
efforts.

The novelist is ruled in the first place by the complex and subtle laws of his own sensibility, then by
those no less subtle of the art he practises. The
analytic method is forced upon him by his very
intellectualism, which gives him a wonderful delicacy of touch in dealing with the niceties of conscience and all the twistings and turnings of our
moral being. When he is a great artist, he gives
himself up to his own innumerable emotions and

---

*The reader may consult with profit Professor Rudler's: *la Jeu-
nesse de Benjamin Constant*."

through them he unveils to us the mysterious working of a human soul.

Then he is forced by the laws of his art to describe life and set human beings in motion more or less *more geometrico*. He must needs have a method, according to which facts and feelings will be docketed and pigeon-holed. He feeds on logic and "fine language." But very soon he realizes that all the living, moving, throbbing side of humanity escapes him, that he is like a child trying to hold water in his hand, that his so-called method is an arbitrary one and his labels too often imaginary, and finally that mere words cannot keep pace with thought. If he can meditate on states of consciousness, he cannot meditate on his own meditation. He can only describe his actions when they are accomplished; but when he lives them, his one resource is silence.

Emile Clermont found a device to satisfy both his need for analysis and his fidelity to the Bergsonian doctrine, by studying what Bergson himself calls "the ultimate reason of human life"; and in this way he also satisfied the innermost cravings of his own heart and of his contemporaries.

Emile Clermont's three books, *Amour promis, Laure,* and *l'Histoire d' Isabelle,* are all works of intense spirituality. His heroines are those middle class French girls, who have what M. de Pomairols calls "la faculté de voir mentalement l'invisible et de percevoir la présence du surnaturel." They have a kind of sixth sense which authoritatively declares to them the existence of the beyond.

With Laure and Isabelle we are a long way from Diderot's *Religieuse!* Indeed such heroines have that very faculty of meditation and introspection so distasteful to many of our women of to-day; they

are even incomprehensible to the mind of a world
which has lost the habit of thinking for itself.

Emile Clermont's first novel, *Amour Promis,* will
take its place with *René,* and *Adolphe* and *Volupté*
and *Dominique.* It should be read with the works
of a talented young writer, who died in 1909, when he
was hardly twenty-five years old, Charles Demange.
M. Demange was a nephew of Maurice Barrès, and
the uncle's influence is perceptible on every page of
le Livre du Désir. He was still trying to find a way
out of the terrible Nihilism in which he was struggling when he died. Dilettantism is a dangerous
thing in a human being who, after dabbling in various forms of civilization, goes on to demand of life
and love impressions with which neither life nor love
can furnish him, but it is a still more dangerous thing
in the exaggerated temperament of an artist who
attempts to build the world anew with the materials
discovered by a distorted vision. The angel with
whom Jacob wrestled was probably called Discipline. *Amour Promis* is a far truer book than
Bourget's *Disciple.* Bourget wanted to make his
philosopher Adrien Sixte responsible for the crime
committed by his pupil Robert Greslon, while really
the poor old determinist philosopher is no more
responsible than Spinoza for the low instincts of an
ill-bred young man. Emile Clermont shows us the
psychological drama played in the inner mind of a
young dilettante. No sooner has André won Hélène
than he is seized with disgust. But his is not merely
the despair of a moral being who in a moment of
forgetfulness betrays the trust of the girl who loves
him; it is also the despair of the voluptuary who
sees that his fleeting pleasure has not made him
master of the soul, nor of the love, nor of the beauty,

of his mistress; it is the despair of the egoist who realizes that his soul can never know any other land than the melancholy deserts of egoism; it is the despair of the *littérateur* tired of his own thoughts and his own actions and who then declares that all is Vanity. "Tu le connais, lecteur, ce monstre délicat!" said Baudelaire of *Ennui*.

Laure, Clermont's second book, is an eminently spiritual drama foreshadowed in certain pages of *Amour Promis*. It is the story of a girl, Laure, who is preoccupied by the great moral and religious questions. She believes herself to be loved by a young man who is paying her attention and gives herself up to this tender feeling. But when her sister Louise appears upon the scene the young man transfers his attention from Laure to Louise. Not a very complicated story, and the writer's art consists in showing us Laure's evolution, how she rises through sorrow to purest renunciation. She goes into a convent, leaves it after some years and devotes herself to charitable work. She comes home to her sister to rest, but her very presence upsets the peace of the household, so that she is obliged to return to her life of good works, though still anxious and henceforward disillusioned.

There are very many pages in this book which sound the Bergsonian note: for example, the influence of the part of the world in which the scene is laid and which has left its mark upon the minds of those who live there (p. 3)*, the difference in the

---

*For it must not be forgotten that Bergson is or has been a pure nominalist. According to him the faculty of thought is merged into the faculty of imagination, which amounts to saying that our mind is merely a series of memories and imaginations, desires and fulfilments (for a long time M. Bergson did not admit the existence oï any substance in the background, though he now accepts the immortality of the soul); his theory was fundamentally the same as that of the sensualists and Taine.

character of the two sisters, and the conception of Laure's character as a soul in whom the spiritual aspirations have burst into spontaneous bloom like some unknown flower almost without any assistance or revelation from outside, and have freely developed (pp. 21-22), and also in the very definition of her mind which was ill at ease in the exact sciences, but which moved freely in the domain of delicate sentiments and ethical values.

There is something of Madame Bovary in Laure, as in all of us; Madame Bovary dreamed of a vague and wonderful universe. In truth, the failure to make life equal to our dreams (that failure which made torment of Baudelaire's existence*) is the subject of all Flaubert's books,† and of Clermont's novels: it is the great 19th century theme, and rightly so.

In *Laure* the descriptions of landscape are as important as those in *Madame Bovary,* for Clermont sees in landscape a means of showing us the workings of his heroine's temperament, and in this way of illuminating the interior world by means of the external world. That is why he has given us that admirable scene on a summer's night, "lorsque'à la voûte du ciel s'éploie la clarté de la lune et qu'on entrevoit par delà cette nappe de lumière des abîmes bleus avec une douceur particulière des étoiles," when Laure talks with Marc of the landscape as of intimate objects which affect her personally, bringing with them the vision of the Infinite (p. 79 et seq.). In the same way when Laure, having realized

---

*Je suis venu trop tard dans un monde trop vieux
D'un siècle sans espoir naît un siècle sans crainte;
Les comètes du nôtre ont dépeuplé les cieux.

†M. Louis Bertrand in his most interesting book on Flaubert endows Flaubert with a conception of life very like Bergson's. But *sub judice lis est.*

that Marc loves her sister, resolves to bring the two together and to give up her own dream of happiness, Clermont puts her in a landscape which is a fit setting for renunciation, and makes her distribute her jewelry to a band of beggars at a monastery gate. Again, when Laure comes back from the convent, and the past, which has lain buried for so many years, reappears between the two sisters, the scenes of analysis, subtle as they are, are laid in the open air, and the actors call to witness now the clear azure sky and the peace of evening as it descends upon this sunlit corner (p. 301), now the scenery of the banks of the river they know so well (p. 303). Nature is closely linked with human feelings and accompanies them as an obligato throughout the book, but the drama is made by human feelings. It is Laure's conflict with love which sends her into the path of spiritual life, first making her sympathize with all suffering and thereby leading her to a comprehension of the Man of Sorrows. Clermont in all these pages is merely describing those states of mind well known to mystics, when the soul in its desperate need utters a cry which it cannot afterwards repeat and realizes that it has loved sorrow too well.

The different states of Laure's soul which, in its passion for the ideal and the Beyond, could not suit itself to ordinary life, nor to convent life, show that she considered the religious life as being eminently an inner experience of an overweening individualism. Here Clermont is on that solid ground wherein the founders of all religious orders have always stood, restraining by severe discipline the impulses of a mystic soul. So that Laure's mysticism is merely the sign of a desire to ally with God the proud ambition of expanding her own being, by taking up the religious life. The same desire and the same pride are to be found in every artistic temperament. When Marc, the husband of Laure's sister, says to Laure, "Pour ceux qui n'ont qu'une vie simple et commune cela seul est déjà une grande chose de savoir que vous existez," it is Clermont's final view he is expressing.

Emile Clermont has left us a third book, *Histoire d'Isabelle* which has appeared in fragments in the *Revue de Paris* in 1912 under the separate titles *Un petit Monde,* and *le Recit d'Isabelle,* but the two tales were really only one. The author's premature death prevented him from leaving things in his ideal state of achievement. The publisher, in the note at the beginning of the book, tells us that this novel was meant to be one of a series of several, in which, as in Balzac's *Human Comedy,* the same characters would be met with again, each in his turn in the foreground. In *l'Histoire d'Isabelle,* as we now have it, we see under different names the same souls we already know. Geneviève Arlet in *Un petit Monde* goes into a convent just as Laure does, but Geneviève does it to expiate the sin of her brother, who has seduced and finally abandoned a young girl, and also to expiate universal evil. This last idea was never so much in fashion (for it is a veritable fashion) as at the end of the Nineteenth Century. Formerly if anyone went into a convent it was for her own salvation.* But the grand idea of the Communion of Saints had great hold over Clermont, and one may remark in passing that this

---

*"The Catholicism of the sixteenth century paid little heed to social righteousness; and to leave the world to the devil whilst savings one's own soul was then accounted no discreditable scheme." —WILLIAM JAMES, *The Varieties of Religious Experience,* p. 354.

This point is well brought out by M. Strowski in his *Tableau de la littérature française au dix neuvième siècle.*

idea of the union of the dead with the living is fully
in harmony with Bergsonian philosophy. If life is
the pursuit of happiness, whatever form it may take,
Emile Clermont has always conceived happiness as
an ideal aspiration. In this he is a Romantic and
a Christian too.

He would have made of the French novel a kind
of Lives of the Saints, not for the edification, but
for the instruction, of all those who are interested in
problems of mysticism as manifestations of human
activity in its most extraordinary, and at the same
time most efficacious, actions. The idea of God
directing humanity lies behind all Clermont's novels just as it lies behind Bergson's philosophy. The
writer- and thinker-side of Clermont sought an
ethical equilibrium which always eluded him, as is
shown by the end of *Laure;* the moralist in him
sought the realization of God, as was proved once
more by the books and papers he was studying just
before his death.

And now if we turn to the book just published
by Mademoiselle Louise Clermont in memory of her
brother, in which she gives the public some of the
papers left by the young soldier, we realize still
better that here was a writer who from his early
youth had felt intellectual passion "like the pressure
outward of wings from within." He seemed born
to have that knowledge of things from within "that
can grasp facts in their springing forth instead of
taking them already sprung" (Bergson), one of
those souls who hunger for the Absolute. Nature
for him is but a symbol of his inner life. His greatest love, one of his friends tells us, was for springs,
running waters, because he could see in this bright,
crystalline element the purity, changeful light, and
endless flow of his own consciousness. He reminds

us at times of Richard Feverel, who felt "those wand-like touches of I know not what, before which our grosser being melts, and we, much as we hope to be in the Awaking, stand etherealized, trembling with new joy."

But at the same time this young *normalien* is the product of a very old and very subtle civilization: analytic and sensual too. It would be well if our sensuous intuitions really were, as Bergson claims, in continuity with our supra-intellectual intuitions. Clermont reveals to us the secret drama of a soul who feels and realizes that knowledge is not entirely resolvable into terms of intelligence, and yet has not always the strength to establish himself in the extra-intellectual matter of knowledge by a higher effort of intuition. And here we must pause and ask ourselves, Was he likely to succeed? Our mind is the product of cosmic evolution, but will the Vital Impetus ever be able to make us change all its constitutive elemental parts?

When M. Bergson bids us turn homeward and strive to gain contact with the living principle whence we emanate, do we not feel — in the very effort we are making to be in communion with the flux of matter, with the sleepy life of the plants or of the infusoria, with the unconscious knowledge of the new-born babe, with the consciousness of men — the Divine will always in need of creation, do we not feel that we go against the grain of our intellect?

And now picture a young man wanting to live a spiritual life amid the thousand and one emotions and sensations of Parisian life: is the intensive culture gained by his education calculated to set him on his real way? On the contrary, when human mind is thus dispersed amid swarming troops of dishevelled ideas, it is far less likely to have those wonderful intuitions, when we see into the life of things—

"... with an eye made quiet by the power
Of harmony and the deep power of joy."

Numerous are the pages where we find utterances of a mind ill at ease with itself — where we can see *René, Adolphe,* or *Volupté* warring with *Creative Evolution.* Such pages help us to understand why Bergson has been variously understood by the majority of Frenchmen and the majority of Anglo-Saxons. For the latter he is the creator of some fine sayings which reveal — by the vistas they open or by their depth of sound — the vast, unseen, magnificent future of our becoming. "The gates of the future are wide open," is a phrase rich in suggestion to men who want to re-create the universe according to their needs and will, and who, far from thinking that the universe is wound up once for all, would fain make new keys, new lever, new pulleys, to lift it onwards.

Frenchmen — or rather, Parisians, either because the romantic malady has strained their intellect, or because they are, on the contrary, robust and react against all that savors of indulgence in "sensibility" — can see in Bergson only the apostle of a certain morbidity, a moral sexlessness, or the supporter of a *dolce far niente,* mother of all vices.

In the same way, the reader of these fragments published by Mademoiselle Clermont will see that too often Clermont read his Bergson through his favorite analytical authors. He even went so far as saying that Sainte-Beuve's *Volupté* gave him the best idea of the Bergsonian Time — viz., of a voluptuous state of the soul, with innumerable sensations following one another closely, and, if so, of a being neutralized by the play of circumstances and off-spring of Chance.

It would be unfair to Clermont to say that the adulterated atmosphere of Parisian life assimilated him entirely to itself: here and there he has flashes of intuitive truth, recurring moments in which he acknowledges that Bergson is a real master.

And it is the contact of his thoughts with those of Bergson, as well as his intense susceptibility, the bold feeling of a spirit of life in outward things, which constitutes the attraction of some of the pages of this young writer and give to his all-too-short work a unity of lyrical effect.

．　　．　　．　　．　　．　　．　　．

In this way Clermont stands at the head of a whole group of French novelists. The best known among them in England is probably Ernest Psichari, the grandson of Renan, who was killed in action near Neufchateau, at the end of August, 1914. His *Voyage du Centurion* was translated into English in 1917, and the wide interest it excited is in itself significant of modern taste. It is the story of a young French officer who leads his native troops through the Sahara and finds faith for himself in the desert. The French edition of the book gained the honor of a Preface by Paul Bourget, to which there would be nothing to add if M. Bourget had really shown that Psichari's ancestral beliefs had been reawakened by reaction against Mussulman faith. If Psichari turns to Rome, "la plus forte organisation de l'Inconnu," like Charles Demange, it is for other reasons.

Such literature is not composed of sleep and sloth, as certain critics have assured us. Psichari was overflowing with energy and knew by experience that the hero would make the event his obedient servant.

Another writer with mystical tendencies, though not of the same group, who is less well known in England, but a far more powerful writer than Psichari, is Charles Louis Philippe. He has been compared with Dickens and with Dostoïevski, on account of his sympathy with the sufferings of those unfortunate and apparently unimportant small souls who fall into baseness, one hardly knows why. *Bubu de Montparnasse, le Père Perdrix, Marie Donadieu, Croquignole, Charles Blanchard,* are the works in which he develops to the utmost this Russian feeling. But the striking thing about him, and the trait which links him with Clermont, is his intense care for moral life.

The books of François Mauriac (*L'Enfant chargé de Chaînes*), Robert Vallery Radot (*l'Homme du Désir*), Jean Variot (*les Hasards de la Guerre*), above all those of M. André Beaunier (*l'Homme qui a perdu son moi*), most of those of M. André Gide (*la Porte étroite, l'Immoraliste, les Caves du Vatican*) and the writings of M. André Suarès, treat in their turn the same problems, dressing in the fashion of to-day the questions which Pascal, Tolstoï or Nietzsche racked their brains to solve.

Pascal encouraged no one to sound the depths of the Copernican theory, and Tolstoï echoed him when he rallied those who busied themselves with such questions as the origin of species. But those who know, as William James puts it so well, that our moral and practical attitude at any given time is always a resultant of two sets of forces within us, — impulses pushing us one way, and obstructions and inhibitions holding us back, — believe that the struggle will always continue with varying fortune, and victory now on one side and now on the other.

The charm, and at the same time the value, of

writers such as Suarès or André Gide lies in the fundamental sincerity with which they study the eternal problems which have never ceased to agitate humanity, and at the same time in the taste and moderation which characterize their truly French productions.

It is obvious that the ideas accepted between 1850-1880 by men of letters and science upon the nature of reason, the influence of a certain kind of science and on the insignificance of our sentimental life, are no longer current. Bergson, Barrès, as well as Suarès or Gide, may sometimes seem to be carried away too far by the reaction against their predecessors' work. But their work is never in bad taste. We can smile to-day at the ultra-positive, ultra-Gradgrinding spirits who flattered themselves they had discovered the real agents of the universe by a diligent study of astronomy, or of the microbes disclosed by a microscope, for, after all, facts will never be anything more than the results of analysis made by the human mind, of abstractions into which the abstractor is forced to put a good deal of himself. It is the eternal story of the grocer who weights his scales to his own advantage. In any case, science will always be science, — that is to say, an essential condition of human progress.

From time to time, then, Bergsonism, in its own efforts to catch the elusive source of life, came very near to a German kind of pantheism which makes of the human soul a very tiny thing quivering in the claws of deified nature. But it soon corrected itself, because it had been brought up in the traditions of a race possessing to the highest degree the taste for the precise and the definite.

Then came the great war, wreaking irreparable havoc as it mowed down so many brilliant songwriters. Yet the war will have served to show us, even if we admitted, with the pure intellectual, that action or thought are due only to an automatism acquired by centuries of adaptation or of education, that strength of soul and delicacy of heart, ardent force of patriotism, rapid intuitions of a Being which is superior to the world, heroic acts of sacrifice, are the most perfect product of our civilization; and, since this is so, even the intellectuals will realize their importance and counsel their cultivation with most jealous care.

CONTEMPORARY FRENCH THOUGHT

WORKS OF REFERENCE

Blondel, Maurice. L'Action. Paris, 1893. Histoire et Dogme (La Chapelle — Montligeon, 1904).

Brochard, V. Etudes de philosophie ancienne et de philosophie moderne — Recueillies et précédées d'une introduction par V. Delbos. Paris, 1912.

Brunschvicg, Léon. Les Etapes de la philosophie mathématique. Paris, 1912. Introduction à la vie de l'esprit. Paris, 1900. La Moralité du Jugement. Paris, 1897.

Berth, Edouard. La Politique anticléricale et le socialisme. (Cahiers de la quinzaine, sér. IV, No. 11.) 1903. Les Méfaits des Intellectuels. (Préface de Georges Sorel.) 1914. Dialogues socialistes. Paris, 1901.

Cresson, André. Le Malaise de la Pensée Philosophique. Paris, 1905.

Durkheim, Emile. Director of l'Année Sociologique, 1898. De la division du travail social. 2nd ed. Paris, 1902. Les Formes élémentaires de la vie religieuse. Paris, 1912.

Dauriac, Lionel. Essai sur l'esprit musical. Paris, 1904. Croyance et Réalité. Des Notions de matière et de force dans les Sciences de la nature (épuisé).

Delbos, Victor. Figures et doctrines de philosophes, Socrate, Lucrèce, Marc Aurèle, Descartes, Spinoza, Kant, Maine de Biran. Paris, 1918. Le Spinozisme. Paris, 1916. L'esprit philosophique de l'Allemagne et la Pensée française. No. 40 of Pages actuelles. Paris, 1915.

Hamelin, Octave. Le Système de Descartes. Paris, 1911.

Lasserre, Pierre. Le Romantisme français. Paris, 1907. La Doctrine officielle de l'Université. Paris, 1912. La Morale de Nietzsche. Paris, 1902.

Le Bon, Gustave. Les opinions et les Croyances. Paris, 1911. La Vie des Vérités. Paris, 1914. Psychologie du Socialisme. 1899.

Pillon, F. La Philosophie de Charles Secrétan. 1898.

Penjon, A. Etude sur la vie et les œuvres philosophiques de G. Berkeley, Evêque de Cloyne. Paris, 1878.

Milhaud, Gaston. Essai sur les conditions et les limites de la certitude logique. 2nd ed., 1898.

Sorel, Georges. De l'Eglise et de l'Etat. 1901. (Cahiers de la Quinzaine, sér. III, No. 3.) Les Illusions du Progrès. 1911. (Etudes sur le devenir social.) Le Système historique de Renan. 1905-1906.

Sangnier, Marc. L'Esprit Démocratique. 7th ed., 1906. La Lutte pour la Démocratie. 1908, 2nd ed. La Jeune République. 2 vols. 1913.

Tarde, J. G. Underground Man (Fragment d'histoire future) — trans. by Cloudesley Brereton — Préface, H. G. Wells. Pages choisies par ses fils. Introduction par H. Bergson. 1910.

Schiller, Professor F. C. S. Humanism. 2nd ed., 1912. Formal Logic. A scientific and social problem. 1912. Riddles of the Sphinx. 2nd

ed., 1910. Scientific Discovery and Logical
Proof. 1917.

Tharaud, Jean et Jérôme. Bar-cochebas, Cahiers
de la quinzaine, sér. VIII, No. 11. 1907. La
Fête arabe. 3rd ed., 1912. Dingley, l'illus-
tre écrivain II ed. 1906. 1st part. Cahiers
de la quinzaine. Sér. III, No. 13. Les frères
ennemis. 1906. (Cahiers de la quinzaine. Sér.
VII, No. 10.) Les Hobereaux. 1904. (Cahiers
de la quinzaine. Sér. V, No. 19.) L'Ombre de
la croix. 1917. La Maîtresse Servante. 1911.
La Tragédie de Ravaillac. 1913. La Ville et
les Champs. (1870-1871.) 1906. Paul Déroulède. 1914.

Wilbois, Joseph. Devoir et Durée. Essai de morale sociale. 1912.

Le Roy, Edouard. Dogme et Critique. 1907. Une
Philosophie Nouvelle. Henri Bergson. 1912.

De Voguë, E. M. de. Le Roman russe.

Richard, L. R. F. Brunetière. 1905. (Bibliogs.)

Roz, Firmin. Edouard Rod. 1906. (Bibliogs.)

Sansot-Orland, E. Jules Lemaître, 1903. (Bibliogs.)

Séché, Alphonse. Emile Faguet. 1904. (Bibliogs.)

Fullerton, W. M. French Idealism and the War.
(Quarterly Rev.) Oct., 1915.

Fisher, H. A. L. French Nationalism. (Hibbert
Journal.) Jan., 1917.

Gosse, Edmund. Some Literary Portraits of France
in the War. (Fort. Rev.) March, 1919.

HENRI BERGSON

WORKS OF REFERENCE

Brunschvig, L. Les étapes de la philosophie mathématique. 1913.

Brockdorff, C. von. Die Wahrheit über Bergson.
1914.

Carr, H. Wildon. Henri Bergson: the Philosophy
of Change. New Ed. 1919.

Chiapelli, A. Idée et figure moderne. 1912.

Chide, A. Le mobilisme moderne. 1908.

Coignet, G. De Kant à Bergson. 1911. Vie de
Henri Bergson. 1910.

Dwelshauvers, G. La Synthèse mentale. 1908.

Elliott, H. S. R. Modern Science and the Illusions
of Professor Bergson. 1914.

Fouillée, A. Le mouvement idéaliste et la réaction
contre la science positive. 1896. La pensée et
les nouvelles écoles anti-intellectualistes. 1912.

Gerrard, T. Bergson, au Exposition and Criticism.
1914.

Gillouin, R. La philos. de Bergson. 1912.

Grandjean, H. Une Revolution dans la Philos, la
doctrine de M. Bergson. 1913.

Guyan, Augustin. Le philosophie et la sociologie
d'Alfred Fouillée. 1913.

Hellmann, H. H. Bergson's Philosophie. 1911.

Hermann, E. Eucken and Bergson. 1912.

Hoeffling, H. Henri Bergson's Filosofi. 1914.
Modern Philosophers. 1915.

Hoogveld, J. E. H. J. De Niewe Wijsbegeerte (trans. A. C. Mason). 1915.

Jacobson, M. Henri Bergson's Intuitions filosofi. 1911.

Kallen, H. M. K. William James and Henri Bergson. 1914.

Kitchen, D. B. Bergson for Beginners. 1914.

Le Roy, E. Une philos. nouvelle. 1913.

Lindsay, A. D. The Philos. of Bergson. 1911.

Maritain, J. La philosophie bergsonienne. 1914.

Miller, L. H. Bergson and Religion. 1916.

Peguy, Charles. Note sur M. Bergson. 1914.

Penido, M. T. L. La Méthode Intuitive de M. Bergson. 1918.

Olgiati. La filosofia di Bergson. 1914.

Osty, E. Lucidité et Intuition. 1914.

Rageot, G. Les Savants et la Philosophie. 1908.

Ribot, Th. Essai sur l'imagination créatrice. 1914.

Ruhe, A., and Paul, N. M. Henri Bergson. 1914.

Russell, Bertrand. The Philos. of Bergson. 1914.

Solomon, Joseph. Bergson. 1912.

Stewart, J. M. A Critical Exposition of Bergson's Philosophy. 1914.

Tonquédec, de J. La notion de la verité dans la Philos. nouvelle. 1908. Dieu dans l'Evolution créatrice avec deux lettres de M. Bergson. 1912.

Wilbois, J. Devoir et durée. 1912.

Wundt, W. Die Nationeu und ihre Philosophie. 1916.

Aimel, G. Individualisme et Phil. bergsonienne. (Reo. de Philosophie. June, 1908.)

Alexander, H. B. Socratic Bergson. (Mid West Quarterly. New York, Oct., 1913.)

Altmann, B. Bergson's Welterfolg. (Die Aehre. 1914-15.)

Antal, I. Jahrbuch der Schopenhauer-Gesellschaft. 1914.

Antonelli, E. Bergson et le mouvement Social contemporain. (Wissen and Leben. 1912.)

Armstrong. Bergson, Berkeley and Philosophical Intuition. (Philosophical Rev. 1914. 4.)

Babbit, J. Bergson et Rousseau. (Rev. Polit. et Litter. Rev. Bleue II. 1912.)

Baeumker, Cl. Bergson's Philosophie. Phil. Jb. d. Görres-Ges. Vol. 25. 1912. Anschanuung und Denken. 1913.

Balsillie, D. Bergson: on Time and Free Will. *Mind,* Vol. 20. 1911. An Examination of Bergson's Philosophy. 1912.

Barr, C. The Dualism of Bergson. Phil. Rev., XXII. 1914.

Bazaillas, A. La vie personnelle. 1915. Musique et Inconscience. 1908. Bergson (Renaissance 21 Feb.). 1914.

Beaumier, A. Nouveaux Acadamiciens. (Figaro 13 feb.) 1914.

Belot. Un nouveau spiritualisme. (Rev. philos. Vol. 44.) 1897.

Benda, J. Réponse aux défenseurs du Bergsonisme. (Mercure de France. Vol. 104.) 1913. Une méprise sur l'intuition bergsonienne. (Rev. du mois. May.) 1912.

Bennett, C. A. Bergson's Doctrine of Intuition. (Phil. Rev. Jan.) 1916.

Benrubi, I. Henri Bergson. (Zukunft. Vol. 71.) 1910.

Bernhard, E. Bergson's Lebensgriff und die moderne Umschau. (Tat. 4.) 1912.

Berrod, P. La philos. de l'intuition. (Rev. phil. T. 74.) 1912.

Beyer, P. Bergson's Rückkehr zum wildentum. Türmer 107. 1914.

Biach, R. Bergson's Entwicklungstheorie. (Kosmos. 49.) 1914.

Biegeleisen, B. Der Einfluss von H. Bergson's Philosophie auf die französische Literatur. Sphinx. 1912.

Blacklock, W. Bergson's Creative Evolution. Westminster Rev. Vol. 177. 1912.

Bonhoff, K. Aus Bergson's Hamptwerke. (Protèstant. Monatshefte.) 1913.

Bonijas, H. Catholicisme et Bergsonisme. (Foi et Victoire 16 Nov.) 1914.

Bonus, A. Bergson muss es wissen März. 5 Sept. 1914.

Botté, L. Bergson è messo all Indice. (Rasseg. Nazionale. Vol. 198.) 1914.

Bouché, J. La philos. de Bergson. (Questions Eccles. Feb.) 1913.

Bourdeau, J. Esmétique de Bergson. (Journ. des Débats. 24 feb.) 1914.

(*Brockdorff, C. von.* Die Wahrheit über Bergson. 1916.)

Buraud, G. L'origine scolastique de la théorie de la perception exterieure de Bergson. (Entretiens Israélites I.) 1914.

Bush, W. T. Bergson Lectures. (Col. Univ. Quarterly. Vol. 15.) 1913.

Columbia Univ. Press. Contrib. to Bibliog. of Bergson. 1912.

Corrance. Bergson's philosophy and the idea of God. (Hibbert Journal. Vol. XII. 2.) 1914.

Cory, C. B. Bergson's Intellect and Matter. (Phil. Rev. Vol. XXII. 5.) 1914.

Cantecor, G. La philos. nouvelle et la vie de l'esprit. (Rev. Phil. T. 55.) 1903.

Carr, H. Wildon. Bergson's Theory of Knowledge. (*Proc. Arist. Soc.* IX.) 1909. The Philos. of Bergson. (*Hibbert Journ.* VIII. July.) 1910. Time & History in Contemp. Philos. (Proc. Brit. Acad. Vol. VIII.) 1918. What does Bergson mean by Pure Perception? (*Mind.* July.) 1918.

Calcagno, A. Bergson et la cultura contemporanea. (Rev. d'filos. Vol. IV.) 1913.

Calkins, M. W. Bergson Personalist. (Phil. Rev. Vol. XXI. No. 6.) 1912.

Carns. The Anti-Intellectual of Today. (Monist. Vol. XXII. No. 3.) 1913.

Catta. A propos d'une réfutation de Bergson. (Univers. 19 Nov.) 1913.

Céli, G. de. Philosophie à la mode. (Gazette de France. Feb. 2nd.) 1914. Sorcier d'Israël. (*Ibid.* 22 Feb.) 1914.

Christiani, Abbé L. M. Bergson et le matérialisme. (Univers. 25 July.) 1913.

Colonna, L. Bergson et son Enseignenement. (Rev. des Cours et des Conférences. 5 March.) 1914.

Coly, R. Bergson's Intellect and Matter. (Phil. Rev. T. 22.) 1913.

Costelloe, K. Philos. of Bergson. (Monist. Vol. 22.) 1914. What Bergson means by interpenetration. (Pro. Ar. Soc., p. XIII.) 1913.

Couchond, P. L. La métaphysique nouvelle. (Rev. de met et de mor.) 1902.

Couturat, L. La théorie du temps de Bergson. (Rev. de met et de mor.) 1902.

Crespi, A. I. Le spirito nella filosofia del Bergson. II. La metafisica Bergsoniana. (Cultura contemp. Vol. VI. Fasc. 4-5.) 1912.

Croce, B. Bergson e Taine. (Critica. X. 6.)
1912.

Cunningham. Bergson's conception of Duration.
(Phil. Rev. XXII. 5.) 1914. Bergson's conception of finality. (*Ibid.* Vol. XXIII. 6.)
1914.

Dauriac, L. Réflexions sur la phil. de Bergson.
(Année phil. Vol. 22.) 1912. Mouvement
Bergsonien. (Rev. phil. de la France et de
l'étranger. Vol. 75.) 1913.

Dawid, J. Bergson et son Evolution créatrice.
(Ksiazka Warsaw. 15 May.) 1913.

Delisle-Burns, C. Bergson. (N. American Rev.
Vol. 197.) 1913.

Delmont, T. Philosophie à la Mode. (Univers. 14
Feb.) 1914.

Desaymard, J. La pensée d'Henri Bergson. (Mercure de France.) 1913. Bergson à Clermont-
Ferrand. (Bull. hist. et scient. de l'Auvergne.)
1911.

Dwelshauvers, G. La philos. de M. Bergson. (Rev.
des courset conférences.) 1906-1907. Bergson
et la méthode intuitive. (Rev. du mois. Sept.)
1907. Evolution et durée des la philos. de Bergson. (Rev. de l'université de Bruxelles.) 1912.

Evans, S. Bergson et Schopenhauer. (Renaiss.
Contemp. 10 June.) 1913. La vie et l'intelligence. (*Ibid.* 24 June.) 1913.

Ewald, O. Henri Bergson. (Lit. Echo. XV.) 1913.

Farges, A. Cosmologie Bergsonienne. (Rev. d'Clergé
Francais. 15 March.) 1913.

Fawcett, E. D. Matter and Memory. (*Mind.* Vol.
21. Jan.) 1912.

Feuling, D. H. Bergson und der Thomismus.
(Jaheb. f. Phil. und spin. Theologie. XXVII.)
1912.

Frank, S. L. Die Philosophie der Intuition von Bergson. (Russkaja Mysl. III.) 1912.

Garrigou-Lagrange, R. P. R. Chronique du métaphysique: autour du Blondelisme et du Bergsonisme. (Rev. thom. May-June.) 1913.

Gemelli. H. Bergson und die italiensche Neuscholastik. (Philos. jahrb. d. Görres-Ges. Vol. 27. St. 4.) 1915.

Gerrard, Th. H. Bergson and finalism. (Cath. World. June.) 1913. Bergson and Freedom. (*Ibid.* May.) 1913. Bergson's Philos. of Change. (*Ibid.* Jan., Feb.) 1913. Bergson and the Divine fecundity. (*Ibid.* Aug.) 1913. Bergson, Newman and Aquinas. (Ibid. March.) 1913.

Gillouin, R. Philos. de Bergson. (Rev. de Paris. V. Jan.-Aug.) 1911. Philos. de M. Bergson. (l'Olivier. I.) 1914.

Goldstein, Julius. H. Bergson and die Sozial wissenschaft. (Archid. f. Sozialwies n Sozialpolitik. Vol. 31.) 1910. H. Bergson und die Zeitlosigkeitsidealismus. (Frank. Ztg. supplement.) 1909.

Gramsow, O. Bergson. Westermann's Monatshefte. Aug.) 1915.

Granberry, J. Bergson and his philosophy. (Method. Rev. I.) 1913.

Gundolf, E. H. Bergson's Philosophie. (Jahrb. f. geist. Bewegg. III.) 1912.

Harward, J. What does Bergson mean by Pure Perception? (*Mind.* April.) 1918. Second article, October, 1919.

Hébert, M. Bergson et son affirmation de l'existence de Dieu. (Rev. de l'univ. de Bruxelles. 17.) 1912.

Heymans, G. De philosophie van H. Bergson. (Tijdschr. wijsbeg.) 1912. Deux Memoires de Bergson. (Labor d. psychol. psysiol. d l. Sorbonne, Hautes Etudes, l'Annee psychologique. 19.) 1913.

Hocking, W. E. Significance of Bergson. (Yale Review, New Series III.) 1914.

Hoeffding, H. Philosophische Probleme. 1903.

Hüboner, G. Husserl, Bergson, George. (Die Güldenkammer. 111.) 1913.

Jacob, B. La philosophie d'hier et celle d'aujourd'hui. (Rev. de Meta. et de Morale. Vol. 6.) 1898.

Jacoby, G. Henri Bergson's pragmatism und Schopenhauer. (Arch. f. Hydrobiologie. IX.) 1914.

James, W. The philosophy of Bergson. (Hibbert Journal. Vol. 7.) 1908.

Johnstone, J. Bergson's philosophy of organism. (Proc. of Liverpool biolog. soc. Vol. 26.) 1913.

Jordan. Kant and Bergson. (Monist. XXII. No. 3.) 1913.

Jourdain, E. B. Bergson and H. G. Wells. (Hibbert Journ. X.) 1913.

Joussain, A. L'Expansion de Bergsonisme et la Psychologie musicale. (Rev. Bleue. I.) 1912.

Kallen, H. M. James, Bergson and Traditional Metaphysics. (*Mind.* Jan.) 1914.

Keeffe, D. O. Bergson's Critical Philosophy. (Irish Theol. Stud. April.) 1913.

Kehr, T. Bergson und das Problem von Zeit und Dauer. (Arch. f. d. gesamte Psych. Vol. XXVI, Parts 1-2.) 1913.

Keyserling, H. Bergson. (Beil 2. Allg. Ztg. No. 35.) 1908.

Kiefer, O. Ueber Bergson's Philosophie. (Märs. 23 May.) 1914.

Klimke, Fr. Henri Bergson der Philos. d. Lebens. (Stimmen der Zeit. Vol. 89.) 1915.

Kohler, J. Bergson und die Rechts philosophie. (Ardi f. Rechts—und Wirtsch—Phil. VII.) 1913.

Kronenberg, M. Henri Bergson und Hegel. (Lit. Echo. 16.) 1914.

Lalande. Philosophy in France. (Phil. Rev. XXII.) 1914.

Lautsheere, de. Les caractères de la philosophie moderne. (Rev. neo-scolastique. XX, No. 77.) 1913.

Larges, A. Philosophie bergsonienne. (La Croix. Dec 2nd.) 1913.

Larsson, Hans. Intuitions problemet. 1912.

Lasserre, P. Que nous vent Bergson? (Act Fr. 21 June.) 1913. Une critique de Bergson. (Act Fr. 29 June.) 1913.

Latour, P. C. de. La Vogue de trois Philosophes. (Gaulois du dimanche. 15 March.) 1914.

Le Roy, E. Le positivisme nouveau. (Rev. de Met. et de Mor.) 1901. Science et philosophie. (*Ibid.*) 1900.

Lewis, C. J. Bergson and contemporary thought. (Univ. of California chron. Vol. 15.) 1914.

Licorish, R. F. Bergson's Creative Evolution. (Lancet. Vol. 182.)

Lodge, Sir O. Balfour and Bergson. (Hibb. Journ. X.) 1913.

Lovejoy. Some Antecedents of the Philos. of Bergson. (*Mind.* Oct.) 1913. Practical Tendencies of Bergsonism. (*Internat. Journ. Ethics.*) 1913. Bergsonism and Romantic Evolutionism. (*Univ. California Chron.* XV.) 1914.

Macintosh, D. C. Bergson and religion. (Biblical World. Vol. 41.) 1913.

Maire, G. Bergsoniens contre Bergson. (La Revue. Vol. 106.) 1914.

Maritain, J. Les deux bergsonismes. (Rev. thomiste. XX. 4.) 1912. L'esprit de la philosophie moderne. (Rev. de Philos.) 1914. L'evolutionisme de Bergson. (Rev. de Philos. Vol. 18.) 1911.

Marot, J. Le cours de Bergson. (Renaissance. Jan.) 1914.

Mason, J. W. T. Bergson's method confirmed. (N. American Rev.) 1913.

Meredith, J. C. Critical side of Bergson's Philosophy. (Westminster Rev. Vol. 177.) 1912.

Messer, A. Bergson's intuitive philosophie. (2tschr. f. christ Erziehungswissch. VIII.) 1914. Geschichte der Philosophie. III. 1918.

Mitchel, A. Studies in Bergson's philosophy. (Bull. of Univ. of Kansas.) 1915.

Montagne, R. P. Bergson et ses plus recents commentateurs. (Questions Actuelles. 17 May.) 1913.

Mories, A. Bergson and Mysticism. (Westminster Rev. Vol. 177.) 1912.

Moore, A. W. Bergson and Pragmatism. (Philos. Rev. XXI.) 1912.

Müller, E. H. Bergson. (Arch. f. syst. Phil. Vol. 18.) 1912.

Nève, P. Le pragmatisme et la philos. de Bergson. (Ann. de l'Inst. sup. de Philos. I.) 1912.

Ostertag, H. H. Bergson. (Nene Kirchl. Ztschr.) 1913.

Perry, R. B. Philos. of Bergson. (Journ. of phil. and psych. Vols. 8-9.) 1911.

Picard, G. Enquête sur Henri Bergson et son influence sur la sensibilité contemporaine. (Grande Revue. Feb.-March.) 1914.

Pitkin, W. B. James and Bergson. (Journ. of Philos. Psych. and Scientific Methods. VII. April.) 1910.

Procházko, R. Bergson's intuitiver Naturalismus. (Cestea Mysl. XIV.) 1913.

Quick, Rev. O. Bergson's Creative Evolution and the Individual. (*Mind.* Jan.) 1913.

Rauh, F. La conscience du devenir. (Rev. de Met. et de Morale.) 1897.

Radharkrishnan, S. Is Bergson's Philosophy Monistic? (*Mind.* July.) 1917. Bergson and Absolute Idealism. (*Mind.* Jan. and July.) 1919.

Reymond, A. Phil. de Bergson et problème de la raison. (Rev. de theol. et de phil. Hav. ser. I.) 1913. Bergsonisme. (*Ibid.*) 1914.

Ribot, Th. Le problème de la pensée sans image et sans mots. (Rev. philos. An XXXVIII. 7.) 1913.

Russell, Bertrand. The Philos. of Bergson. (Monist. Vol. 22. No. 3.) 1913.

Salomon, J. Philos. of Bergson. (*Mind.*) 1911.

Schäfke, F. Bergson's evol. créatrice in den Hauptpunkten dargestellt und beurteilt. (Thesis.) 1914.

Scott, T. W. The Pessimism of Bergson. (Hibbert Journ. XI. I.) 1913. The Pessimism of Creative Evolution. (*Mind.* April.) 1913.

Segond, J. Les antithèses de Bergson. (Ann. de Phil. Chretienne. XIV.) 1913. Bergson. (La chronique. 22 Feb.) 1914.

Ségur, N. Bergson en het Bergsonisme. (Wetensch. bladen.) 1913. Bergson et Bergsonisme. (La Revue. Vol. 98.) 1912. L'intellectualisme et la philos. bergsonienne. (Rev. phil. July.) 1917.

Seillière, E. Schätzung und Wirkung der Phil. Bergsons un hentigen Frantireich. (Internat. Monatsschr. f. Wissch. Kunst u. Technik. Vol. 7.) 1913.

Seydl, E. H. Bergson's Intuitive Philosophie. (Allg. Littlatt. No. 3.) 1916.

Shinner, H. W. Bergson's view of organic evolution. (Pop. Sc. Monthly. Vol. 82.) 1913.

Shotwell, J. T. Bergson's Philosophy. (Pol. Sc. Cl. Vol. 27.) 1913.

Solomon, J. Phil. of Bergson. (Fort. Rev. Vol. 96.) 1912.

Stebbing, L. S. The notion of truth in Bergson's theory of knowledge. (Proc. Artist Soc. Vol. 12.) 1912.

Stork, T. B. Bergson and his Philosophy. (Luther. Quest. 2.) 1913.

Strange. Bergson's theory of Intuition. (Monist. Vol. 25. 3.) 1913.

Schrecker, P. H. Bergsön's Philos. der Personlichkeit. 1912.

Schultze, Martin. Das Problem der Wahrheitserkenntnis bei W. James und H. Bergson. 1913.

Segond, J. L'intuition bergsonienne. 1913.

Shastri, P. The conception of freedom in Hegd. Bergson, Indian Philosophy. 1915.

Stebbing, L. S. Pragmatism and French Voluntarism. 1915.

Teodorescu, C. A. Die Erkenntnislehre Bergson's. (Thesis. 56 pp.) 1914.

Sujot, A. Le nouveau spiritisme de M. H. Bergson. (Protestant. 9 Nov.) 1913.

Taylor, R. H. Bergson. (Quest. No. 1.) 1912.

Tilgher, A. L'Esteticia di Bergson. (La Nuova Cultura.) 1913.

Tonquedec, J. de. Bergsonisme et scholast. (Rev. crit. d. idees et d. lines. Vol. 23.) 1914.

Townsend, J. G. Bergson and Religion. (Monist. Vol. 22.) 1913.

Tronche, H. L'évolution créatrice. (Rev. de phil.) 1908.

Visan, T. de. Ce que nous devons à Bergson. (Le Temps Présent. 2 Feb.) 1914.

Waterlow, S. Philos. of Bergson. (Quarterly Rev. Vol. 216.) 1912.

White, E. M. Bergson and Education. (Ed. Rev. Vol. 47.) 1914.

Willcox, L. C. Some implications of Bergson's philosophy. (N. Am. Rev. Vol. 199.) 1914.

Williams. Syndicalism in France and its relation to the Philos. of Bergson. (Hibb. Journ. Vol. XII. 2.) 1914.

Wilm, E. C. Bergson and the philos. of Religion. (Bibl. World. New ser. Vol. 41.) 1913.

MAURICE BARRES

WORKS OF REFERENCE

Gillouin, R. *Maurice Barrès*, 1907 (bibliogs.) A full bibliography is appended by M. Ad Van Bever to *la Pensée de Maurice Barrès*, by Henri Massis, 1909.

Jary, Jacques. *Essai sur l'Art et la psychologie de M. Barrès*, 1912.

The latest works of M. Barrès are:
La Colline Inspirée, 1913.
La Grande Pitié des Eglises de France, 1914.
Les Traits Eternels de la France, 1916.

JULES ROMAINS

WORKS OF REFERENCE

Jean Moréas. Par Jean de Gourmont, 1905. (Contains good bibliography.)

Maurras, Charles. Anthinea. D'Athènes à Florence. 7ᵐᵉ édition. Paris, 1912. 8vo.

Henriot, Emile. A quoi rêvent les jeunes gens? 1913.

Sergeant, E. S. French Perspectives. 1917.

Bersancourt, A. de. Francis Jammes, poète chrétien. 1910.

Braun, T. Des poètes simples, Francis Jammes. 1900.

Lowell, Amy. Six French Poets. 1915.

Duhamel, G., et Vildrac, C. Notes sur la technique poétique. 1910.

Rivière, Jacques. Etudes (Baudelaire, Claudel, etc.) (Bibliogs.) 1911.

J. de Tonquédec. L'œuvre de Paul Claudel. 1917.

Richard-Mounet, Louis. Paul Claudel. 1918.

CHARLES PEGUY

WORKS OF REFERENCE

Lotte, E. J. Un Compagnon de Péguy; Joseph Lotte, 1875-1914. Préface par Mgr. Battifol. 1917.

Suarès, André. Charles Péguy. 1915.

Boudon, V. Avec Charles Péguy de la Lorraine à la Marne. 1916.

Johannet, René. Péguy et ses Cahiers. 1914.

Halévy, Daniel. Charles Péguy. 1918.

This book was published after the foregoing pages were written.

CONTENTS OF
CAHIERS DE LA QUINZAINE
PREMIERE SERIE.

Vol.	No.	
1900.		
I. 5 janvier.	1.	Charles Péguy. *Lettre du Provincial; Réponse au Provincial;* le *"Triomphe de la République."* L'affaire Liebknecht. Avant la première quinzaine.
I. 20 janvier.	2.	Du second Provincial. Réponse provisoire. La préparation du congrès socialiste national. Travail des enfants. Quinzaine.
I. 5 février.	3.	Pour et contre le socialisme. La préparation du congrès socialiste national. Travail des enfants.
I. 20 février.	4.	Charles Péguy. *De la grippe.* La préparation du congrès socialiste national. Travail des enfants.
I. 5 mars.	5.	*La consultation internationale* ouverte à *la Petite* République sur *l'affaire Dreyfus et le cas Millerand.*

I. 20 mars.	6.	Charles Péguy. *De la grippe. La même* Consultation internationale.
I. 5 avril.	7.	Charles Péguy. *Annonce au Provincial; Toujours de la grippe.* La dernière préparation et la tenue du congrès socialiste national — Jérôme et Jean Tharaud, *la lumière.*
I. 20 avril.	8.	Première annonce; Deuxième annonce. *La même* consultation internationale — Jérôme et Jean Tharaud, *la lumière.*
I. 5 mai.	9.	Charles Péguy. *Entre deux trains* — Rectifications: — Paul Lafargue. *Le Socialisme et les Intellectuels.* Jérôme et Jean Tharaud, *la lumière.*
I. 20 mai.	10.	Communications. *Les Petits Teigneux.* — Annonce. — Emile Vandervelde. *Socialisme et Collectivisme.*
I. 4 juillet.	11.	Charles Péguy. *Réponse brève à Jaurès.* Le Socialisme et les Intellectuels. Comparaison. *La même* consultation international.
I. 16 novembre.	12.	Charles Péguy. *Deuxième série au Provincial; Administration; Nouvelles communications;* Demi — réponse à M. Cyprien Lantier.

DEUXIEME SERIE.
1900-1901.

1900. II. 29 novembre.	1.	Ajournement. Nouvelles Communications. *Ecole des Hautes Etudes Sociales,* discours de MM. Boutroux et Duclaux.
II. 17 décembre.	2.	René Salomé. *Vers l'action.*
II. 21 décembre.	3.	Pour ma maison; administration; pages libres. *Rectifications:* Matinée — Conférence, *Parti Socialiste.* Comité général, dimanche 22 juillet 1900, etc. Conférence donnée ce jour par Jean Jaurès, *le théâtre social.*
1901. II.	4.	Hubert Lagardelle. *Les Intellectuels devant*

18 janvier

le Socialisme, causerie faite au groupe des étudiants collectivistes de Paris, le 14 décembre 1900. L'amnistie et les socialistes.

II.
28 janvier.

5. Où il y a des renseignements et des avis de l'administration; pour moi; contribution aux *Preuves*, etc. (Différents articles sur l'Affaire Dréyfus, Lionel Landry, courrier de Chine.)

II.
7 février.

6. Romain Rolland. *Danton*. Trois actes.

II.
2 mars.

7. Administration; Cassecou; librairie des Cahiers *Pour et Contre Diderot*, confrontation; Dans la *Petite République*, datée du mardi 31 juillet 1900, discours prononcé par Anatole France, etc.

II.
2 mars.

8. Lionel Landry. Bacchus, drame en trois actes.

II.
19 mars.

9. *Intellectuels et Socialisme:* une contribution de M. Paul Mantoux, etc.; une contribution de M. Charles Guyesse. *Intellectuels et Socialisme* André Bourgeois. *Quatre jours à Montceau.*

II.
4 avril.

10. Cahiers d'annonces, etc.

II.
25 avril.

11. La révolution sociale sera morale ou elle ne sera pas, etc. Charles Péguy. Compte-rendu de mandat.

II.
13 juin.

12. Antonin Lavergne. *Jean Coste ou l'Instituteur de Village*. Octobre 1894-juin 1895, Evreux.

II.
22 juin.

13. Librairie des cahiers. Jean Coste. Georges Sorel, *Quelques mots sur Proudhon*, etc. Couverture: Immense victoire socialiste.

II.
6 juillet.

14. Couverture: Emouvant débat socialiste. — *Expulsion de Nicolas Paouli*. Lionel Landry. *Courrier de Chine*. Léon Deshairs, *Boecklin chez les Français*. Louise Lévi, *Congrès de Lyon*, 26-28 mai 1901, etc.

II.

15. Mémoires et Dossiers pour les libertés du

23 juillet.		personnel enseignant en France; Préface du gérant: Interpellation Lavertujon. Le cas Jaurès. Daniel Delafarge. *M. Brunetière historien.* Attentats dans l'Yonne.
II. 13 aôut.	16.	Compte-rendu sténographique du Cinquième Congrès Socialiste international, tenu à Paris du 23 au 27 septembre 1900.

TROISIEME SERIE.

1901. III. 1 octobre.	1.	Compte-rendu de congrès; bilan; *Attentats dans l'Yonne,* suite; l'affaire du *Pioupiou de l'Yonne,* etc.
III. 17 octobre.	2.	Charles Guyesse. Les Universités Populaires et le mouvement ouvrier.
III. 26 octobre.	3.	Georges Sorel. De l'Eglise et de l'Etat.
III. 5 décembre.	4.	Jean Jaurès. *Etudes Socialistes.*
III. 19 décembre.	5.	Georges Delahache. *Juifs.*
III. 28 décembre.	6.	Jean Hugues. La Greve, — trois actes.
1902. III. 16 janvier.	7.	M. Gustave Téry, Polémiques et dossiers. Lettre de F. Challaye sur l'Indo-Chine.
III. 13 février.	8.	Bernard Lazare. *Les Juifs en Roumanie.*
III. 25 février.	9.	Tolstoï. Une lettre inédite, adressée, à Romain Rolland, datée du 4 octobre 1887.
III. Début de Mars.	10.	*Les Universités Populaires* 1900-1901. Paris et banlieue.
III. 20 mars.	11.	Romain Rolland. Le Quatorze Juillet. Trois actes.
III. 5 avril.	12.	Monographies. *Personnalités.*
III. 15 avril.	13.	Jérôme et Jean Tharaud. Dingley. L'illustre écrivain.
III.	14.	Georges Sorel, Socialismes nationaux, daté

22 avril.		novembre 1901. Félicien Challaye. La Russie vue de Vladivostok, journal d'un expulsé.
III. 29 avril.	15.	Anatole France. *Cahiers de la Quinzaine.*
III. 24 mai.	16.	Les élections; emprunt des cahiers.
III. 3 juin.	17.	Félicien Challaye, *impressions sur la vie japonaise.* Edmond Bernus, *la Russie vue de la Vistule.* Jean Deck — *Courrier de Finlande.*
III. 10 juin.	18.	Personnalités. *Monographies.* René Salomé, courrier de Belgique.
III 26 juin.	19.	Pierre Quillard. *Pour l'Arménie.* Cahier de Courriers. Impressions sur la vie Japonaise de Félicien Challaye.
III. 22 juillet.	20.	Les Universités populaires. Départements. La Russie vue de la Vistule. (Anonyme.) Courrier de Finlande. (Anonyme.)
III. 16 aôut.	21.	Jean Deck. *Pour la Finlande.*

QUATRIEME SERIE.
1902-1903.

IV. 9 octobre.	1.	Anatole France. *L'Affaire Crinquebille.*
IV. 23 octobre.	2.	Moselly. *L'Aube fraternelle.*
IV. 4 novembre.	3.	Charles Péguy. De Jean Coste; conclusion.
IV. 20 novembre.	4.	Antonin Lavergne. *La Médaille. La lettre de convocation.*
IV. 4 décembre.	5.	Textes et commentaires. Emile Zola. (Funérailles d'Emile Zola. Gabriel Trarieux; Emile Zola.) Les récentes œuvres de Zola. (Essai de Péguy.) Lettre de Zola à M. Félix Faure, président de la République.

IV. 18 décembre.	6.	Cahier de Courrier. Courrier de Paris. Inventaire des Cahiers.
IV. 23 décembre.	7.	*Cahier de Nöel.* Quelques vers de Villon. Trois lettres de Tolstoï; Jérôme et Jean Tharaud — la légende de la Vierge. Louis Gillet, *la tour d'Armor.*
IV. 30 décembre.	8.	René Salomé. Monsieur Matou et les circonstances de sa vie, écrit à Bruxelles en 1902.
1903. IV. 13 janvier.	9.	Almanack des cahiers pour l'an 1903. Félicien Challaye, second courrier d'Indo-Chine.
IV. 27 janvier.	10.	Romain Rolland. *Vie des hommes illustres. Beethoven.*
IV. 3 février.	11.	Edouard Berth. *La politique anticléricale et le socialisme.*
IV. 17 février.	12.	Vient de paraître. Henri Bergson. Introduction à la Métaphysique. Conclusion.
IV. 24 février.	13.	Cahiers de Courriers. Félicien Challaye. Impressions sur Java. François Dagen. Courrier d'Algérie.
IV. 12 mars.	14.	Romain Rolland. Le Temps viendra. Trois actes.
IV. 1 avril.	15.	Pierre Baudouin (Charles Péguy). La chanson du roi Dagobert.
IV. 9 avril.	16.	Gabriel Trarieux. Les Vaincus. Joseph d'Arimathée (trois actes).
IV. 28 avril.	17.	Affaire Dreyfus. *Débats parlementaires.* Intervention Jaurès.
IV. 12 mai.	18.	Affaire Dreyfus. *Cahiers de la Quinzaine.* Débats parlementaires.
IV. 26 mai.	19.	Gaston Raphaël. *Le Rhin allemand.*
IV. 16 juin.	20.	Affaire Dreyfus. *Cahiers de la Quinzaine.* Reprise politique parlementaire.
IV. 21 juillet.	21.	*Edgar Quinet.*

IV.
25 aôut.

22. Maurice Kahn. Courriers de Macédoine.

CINQUIEME SERIE.
1903-1904.

V.
13 octobre.

1. Henri Dagan. *Les massacres de Kichinef* et la situation des prolétaires juifs en Russie.

V.
27 octobre.

2. Paul Dupuy. *La vie d'Evariste Gallois.*

V.
10 novembre.

3. Cahier de l'inauguration *du monument de Renan* à Tréguier, le dimanche, treize septembre 1903.

V.
24 novembre.

4. Romain Rolland. *Le Théâtre du Peuple.*

V.
8 décembre.

5. Georges Clémenceau. *Discours pour la liberté.*

V.
24 décembre.

6. Daniel Halévy. Histoire de quatre ans 1997-2001.

1904.
V.
5 janvier.

7. Cahier de Courriers. Henri Michel. Notes sur la Hollande et sur l'Intimité — Lebeau et Tharaud. Moines de l'Athos — Bulletin de l'office du Travail. La grève des Tisseurs d'Armentières — Charles Péguy. Cahiers de la Quinzaine.

V.
19 janvier.

8. Dr. Karl Brunnemann. Maximilien Robespierre.

V.
4 février.

9. Romain Rolland. *Jean Christophe. L'aube.*

V.
18 février.

10. Romain Rolland. *Jean Christophe. Le matin.*

V.
1 mars.

11. M. M. Mangasarian. Le Monde sans Dieu. Avertissement de Péguy.

V.
15 mars.

12. Petites Garnisons. Laval. Orléans. Paris. Charles Péguy. Avertissement.

V.
29 mars.

13. Gabriel Trarieux. Les vaincus. Hypatie.

V.
11 avril.

14. Joseph Bédier. Gaston Paris.

V. 26 avril.	15.	Emile Moselly. *Jean des Brebis* ou le livre de la Misère.
V. 24 mai.	16.	Gaston Raphaël. Le Congrès de Dresde. Septembre. 1903.
V. 9 juin.	17.	François Porché. A chaque jour. Poemes.
V. 28 juin.	18.	Louis Ménard. Prologue d'une Révolution.
V. 16 juillet.	19.	Jérôme et Jean Tharaud. *Les Hobereaux.* Histoire vraie.
V. 13 septembre.	20.	Congrès des U. P. Mai 1904.

SIXIEME SERIE.
1904-1905.

VI. 27 septembre.	1.	Charles Péguy. Texte sans commentaires. *Catalogue analytique sommaire. 1900-1904.*
VI. 11 octobre.	2.	Alexis Bertrand. *L'égalité devant l'instruction.*
VI. 27 octobre.	3.	Israël Zangwill. Chad Gadya: traduit de l'anglais par Mathilde Solomon.
VI. 8 novembre.	4.	Raoul Allier. *L'enseignement primaire des indigènes à Madagascar.*
VI. 22 novembre.	5.	*Le Testament politique de Waldeck Rousseau.*
VI. 6 décembre.	6.	Elie Eberlin; Georges Delahache. *Juifs russes — Le bund et le Sionisme; un voyage d'études.*
VI. 22 décembre.	7.	Cahier de Noël. François Porché. A ma grand'mère. *Les primitifs français.* Louis Gillet. — Nos maîtres d'autrefois — *Les Primitifs.* Jérôme et Jean Tharaud. *Contes de la Vierge.*
1905. VI. 12 janvier.	8.	Romain Rolland. Jean Christophe III. *L'adolescent.*
VI. 24 janvier.	9.	*La délation aux Droits de l'homme.*

VI.
7 février.

10. Brenn. *Yves Madic*, professeur de collège.

VI.
21 février.

11. Suarès. *La tragédie d'Elektre et Oreste.*

VI.
7 mars.

12. Urbain Gohier. Spartacus — cinq actes.

VI.
21 mars.

13. Tolstoï — *L'Eglise et l'Etat; les événements. actuels en Russie.*

VI.
4 avril.

14. Une campagne du *Siècle:* — Raoul Allier, — *la séparation des Eglises et de l'Etat; l'enquête du Siècle: résultats et conclusions de cette enquête par de Lanessan.*

VI.
20 avril.

15. Eddy Marix. La tragédie de Tristan et Iseut. Cinq actes.

VI.
9 mai.

16. Robert Dreyfus. *La vie et les prophéties du comte de Gobineau.*

VI.
23 mai.

17. Paul Desjardins. *Catholicisme et critique.* Réflexions d'un profane sur l'affaire Loisy.

SEPTIEME SERIE.

VII.
26 septembre.

1. Charles Péguy. Petit index alphabétique du catalogue analytique sommaire, et table analytique très sommaire de la sixième série.

VII.
3 octobre.

2. Charles Richet. *La paix et la guerre.*

VII.
17 octobre.

3. Charles Péguy. *Notre patrie.*

VII.
26 octobre.

4. Raoul Allard. La Séparation des Eglises et de l'Etat; *la séparation au Sénat.*

VII.
14 novembre.

5. Charles Péguy. Courrier de Russie. Etienne Avenard. *Le 22 janvier nouveau style.*

VII.
21 novembre.

6. Pierre Mille. *L'enfer du Congo léopoldien.* E. D. Morel. *Préface;* post-scripturn.

VII.
12 décembre.

7. Charles Péguy. *Les suppliants parallèles.* François Porché. *Les Suppliants.*

VII. 26 décembre.	8.	Charles Péguy. Louis de Gonzague. André Spire: *Et vous riez,* — poèmes.
VII. 9 janvier 1906.	9.	Ferdinand Lot. *De la situation faite à l'enseignement supérieur en France.*
VII. 25 janvier.	10.	Jérôme et Jean Tharaud. *Les frères ennemis.*
VII. 6 février.	11.	Ferdinand Lot. *De la situation faite à l'enseignement supérieur en France.*
VII. 20 février.	12.	Félicien Challaye. *Le Congo français.* Les derniers jours de M. de Brazza.
VII. 6 mars.	13.	Georges Picquart, lieutenant-colonel en réforme. *De la situation faite à la défense militaire de la France.*
VII. 20 mars.	14.	Gabriel Trarieux. Les vaincus. *Savonarole*
VII. 3 avril.	15.	Gabriel Trarieux. *Arnold Schérer.*
VII. 17 avril.	16.	Pierre Mille. *Les deux Congos devant la République et devant la France.* Félicien Challaye. La réorganisation du Congo Français.
VII. 29 mai.	17.	Jean Schlumberger. *Heureux qui comme Ulysse.* . . .
VII. 26 juin.	18.	Romain Rolland. *La vie de Michel Ange.* I. la lutte.
VII. 24 juillet.	19.	Emile Moselly — *les Retours* — *les haleurs* — *le soldat.*

HUITIEME SERIE.

VIII.	1.	Charles Péguy. *Petit index alphabétique* de nos éditions antérieures et de nos sept premières séries (1900-1906). *Table analytique* très sommaire de notre septième série (1905-1906).
VIII.	2.	Romain Rolland. Vie des hommes illustres. *La vie de Michel Ange.* II. L'abdication.
VIII. 4 novembre.	3.	Charles Péguy. *De la situation faite à l'histoire et à la Sociologie dans les temps modernes.*

VIII.	4.	Romain Rolland. Jean Christophe. IV. *La révolte*. 1. Sables mouvants.
VIII. 2 décembre.	5.	Charles Péguy. *De la situation faite au parti intellectuel dans le monde moderne*.
VIII. 16 décembre.	6.	Romain Rolland. *Jean Christophe*. IV. *La révolte*. 2. L'Enlisement.
VIII. 23 décembre.	7.	Charles-Marie Garnier. *Les sonnets de Shakespeare*. Essais d'une interprétation en vers français.
VIII. 30 décembre.	8.	Jean Bonnerot. *Le livre des livres*. Fragments.
1907. VIII. 6 janvier.	9.	Romain Rolland. Jean Christophe. IV. *La Révolte*.
VIII.	10.	Edmond Bernus. Polonais et Prussiens. I. La Délivrance.
VIII. 3 février.	11.	Jérôme et Jean Tharaud. *Bar-Cochebas*.
VIII.	12.	Edmond Bernus. *Polonais et Prussiens*. II.
VIII. 3 mars.	13.	Henriette Cordelet. Swift.
VIII. Mars.	14.	Edmond Bernus. Polonais et Prussiens. III.
VIII. 31 mars.	15.	Charles-Marie Garnier. *Les Sonnets de Shakespeare*. Essai d'une interprétation en vers français. II.
VIII. 14 avril.	16.	Georges Sorel. *Les préoccupations métaphysiques des physiciens modernes*. Avant-propos de Julien Benda.

NEUVIEME SERIE.

IX. 6 octobre.	1.	Charles Péguy. De la situation faite au parti intellectuel dans le monde moderne *devant les accidents de la gloire temporelle*.
IX. 20 octobre.	2.	Robert Dreyfus. *Quarante-Huit*. Essais d'histoire contemporaine.

IX. 3 novembre.	**3.**	Etienne Buisson. Le parti socialiste et les Syndicats.
IX. 17 novembre.	**4.**	Emile Moselly. *Le rouet d'ivoire.* (Enfances lorraines.)
IX 1 décembre.	**5.**	Jean Deck et G. von Wendt. *La représentation proportionnelle et la récente loi électorale du Grand-duché de Finlande.*
IX. 15 décembre.	**6.**	Daniel Halévy. Un Episode.
IX. 29 décembre.	**7.**	René Salomé. Par le Chemin des Souvenances. (Poèmes.)
IX. Décembre 1907 or Janvier 1908 ?	**8.**	Gaston Raphaël. *Der Professor ist die deutsche National Krankheit.*
1908. IX. 26 janvier.	**9.**	Robert Dreyfus. Alexandre Weill, ou le prophète du faubourg Saint Honoré, 1811-1899.
IX.	**10.**	Maxime Vuillaume. Mes cahiers rouges. I. *Une journée à la cour martiale du Luxembourg. Avant-propos* de Lucien Descaves.
IX.	**11.**	Maxime Vuillaume. Mes cahiers rouges. II. *Un peu de vérité sur la mort des otages*, 24 et 26 mai 1871.
IX.	**12.**	Maxime Vuillaume. Mes cahiers rouges. III. *Quand nous faisions le "Père Duchêne."* Mars, avril, mai, 1871.
IX. 22 mars.	**13.**	Romain Rolland. Jean Christophe. La Foire sur la Place. I.
IX. 29 mars.	**14.**	Romain Rolland. Jean Christophe. La Foire sur la Place. II.
IX. 5 avril.	**15.**	Romain Rolland. Jean Christophe à Paris. *Antoinette.*
IX. 5 juillet.	**16.**	Pierre Mille. *Quand Panurge Ressuscita.*

DIXIEME SERIE.

X. 18 octobre.	1.	Pierre Mille. *L'Enfant et la Reine Morte.*
X. 1 novembre.	2.	Pierre Hamp. *Dix Contes écrits dans le Nord.*
X.	3.	Pierre Hamp. La Peine des Hommes. I. *La Marée fraiche.*
X. 28 novembre.	4.	Pierre Hamp. La Peine des Hommes. II. *Vin de Champagne.*
X. 13 décembre.	5.	A. Suarès. Le Portrait d'Ibsen.
X. 27 décembre.	6.	René Salomé. Plus près des choses.
1909. X.	7.	Maxime Vuillaume. Mes cahiers rouges. IV. *Quelques-uns de la Commune.*
X.	8.	Maxime Vuillaume. Mes cahiers rouges. V. *Par la Ville Révoltée.*
X. 16 février.	9.	Romain Rolland. Jean Christophe à Paris. Dans la maison. I.
X. 23 février.	10.	Romain Rolland. Jean Christophe à Paris. Dans la maison. II.
X.	11.	Maxime Vuillaume. *Mes cahiers rouges.* VI. *Au large.*
X. 25 avril.	12.	Daniel Halévy. Le travail de Zarathoustra (a criticism of Friedrich Nietzsche).
XI. 10 octobre.	1.	A. Suarès. *Visite à Pascal.*
XI. 24 octobre.	2.	Gabriel Trarieux. *Le Portique.*
XI. 7 novembre.	3.	Albert Thierry. *L'Homme en proie aux enfants.*
XI. 5 décembre.	4.	Georges Delahache. La carte au liséré vert.
XI. 19 décembre.	5.	André Spire. Israël Zangwill.

XII. 30 avril.	9.	Julien Benda. L'ordination.
XII. 25 juin.	10.	Les Milliet. VII. Adrien de Tucé. Cinq ans au Mexique 1862-1867. Charles Péguy. *Œuvres choises de Charles Péguy.*

TREIZIEME SERIE.

XIII. 6 aôut.	1.	Les Milliet. VIII. Voyage d'études en Italie 1868-1869.
XIII. 24 septembre.	2.	Charles Péguy. Un nouveau théologien. M. Fernand Laudet.
XIII. 8 octobre.	3.	Les Milliet. IX. La guerre de France et le Premier Siège de Paris 1870-1871.
XIII. 22 octobre.	4.	Charles Péguy. II. Le Porche du Mystère de la Deuxième Vertu.
XIII. 5 novembre.	5.	Romain Rolland. Jean Christophe. *Le buisson ardent.* I.
XIII. 12 novembre.	6.	Romain Rolland. Jean Christophe. *Le buisson ardent.* II.
XIII. 26 novembre.	7.	Les Milliet. X. La Commune et le Second Siège de Paris. 1871.
XIII. 10 décembre.	8.	A. Suarès. Dostoievski.
XIII. 24 décembre.	9.	Les Milliet. XI. Un cas de conscience 1871-73.
XIII. 31 décembre.	10.	Joseph Mélon. L'ami désabusé. (Poèmes.)

1912.

XIII. janvier (?).	11.	Maxime Vuillaume. Mes cahiers rouges. VIII. *Deux drames.*
XIII. 24 mars.	12.	Charles Péguy. III. Le mystère des Saints Innocents.

QUATORZIEME SERIE.

XIV. 28 juillet.	1.	A. Suarès. De Napoléon.
XIV. 6 octobre.	2.	Romain Rolland. Jean Christophe. III. La fin du voyage. La Nouvelle Journée. I.

XIV.
20 octobre.

3. Romain Rolland. Jean Christophe. III. La fin du voyage. La Nouvelle Journée. II.

XIV.
novembre (?).

4. Julien Benda. *L'Ordination*. II. La Chute.

XIV.
1 décembre.

5. Charles Péguy. La tapisserie de Sainte Geneviève et de Jeanne d'Arc.

1913
XIV.
16 février.

6. Charles Péguy. *L'argent*. Langlois tel qu'on le parle.

XIV.
2 mars.

7. Th. Naudy. *Depuis 1880*. L'enseignement primaire et ce qu'il devrait être.

XIV.
16 mars.

8. René Salomé. *Les chants de l'âme réveillée.*

XIV.
27 avril.

9. Charles Péguy. L'argent. (Suite.)

XIV.
11 mai.
XIV.

10. Charles Péguy. *La tapisserie de Notre Dame.*

11. Maxime Vuillaume. Mes cahiers rouges. (Poèmes.) *Lettres et temoignages.*

QUINZIEME SERIE.

XV.
23 octobre.

1. Edmond Fleg. Ecoute, Israël. (Poèmes.)

XV.
23 novembre.

2. Julien Benda. Une philosophie pathétique.

XV.
14 décembre.

3. Joseph Reinach. La loi militaire. Fixité des effectifs.

XV.
28 décembre.

4. Charles Péguy. Eve. (Poème.)

1914.
XV.
25 janvier.

5. A. Suarès. François Villon.

XV.
22 février.

6. George Delahache. L'exode. (A description of the departure of French inhabitants from Alsace-Lorraine, 1871.)

XV.
24 mars.

7. René Salomé. Notre pays.

XV.
26 avril.

8.   Charles Péguy. Note sur M. Bergson et la philosophie bergsonienne.

XV.
14 juin.

9.   Maxime Vuillaume. Proscrits.

XV.
12 juillet.

10.   François Porché. Nous. Poèmes.

———

ŒUVRES. COMPLETES DE
CHARLES PEGUY.
1873-1914.

Œuvres de Prose
Introduction par Alexandre Millerand
Edition de la Nouvelle Revue Françoise
Tome I. 1917. Notre Jeunesse. Victor Marie, comte Hugo
Tome IV. Introduction par André Suarès.
Clio. Œuvre posthume.
Tome VIII.

These are the only volumes published up to date of going to press.

INDEX